Kent Mountain Adventure Center Inc.
P.O. Box 835
Estes Park, CO 80517 USA

The Great Outdoors

by David P. Barash

A Lyle Stuart Book
Published by Carol Communications

Library of Congress Cataloging-in-Publication Data

Barash, David P.
    The great outdoors / by David P. Barash.
      p.   cm.
    Includes bibliographical references.
    ISBN 0-8184-0496-5 : $17.95
    1. Outdoor recreation. 2. Outdoor recreation--United
States. I. Title.
GV191.6.B37   1989
796.5'0973--dc19   89-4387
                                     CIP

A Lyle Stuart Book
Published by Carol Communications

Editorial Offices
600 Madison Avenue
New York, NY 10022

Sales & Distribution Offices
120 Enterprise Avenue
Secaucus, NJ 07094

In Canada: Musson Book Company
A division of General Publishing Co. Limited
Don Mills, Ontario

Queries regarding rights and permissions
should be addressed to: Carol Communications,
600 Madison Avenue, New York, NY 10022

Manufactured in the United States of America
ISBN 0-8184-0496-5

Contents

Introduction

Outdoor Lovesongs to Serenade a Planet

This is a book of nonmusical lovesongs, rhapsodies to primitive pleasures of the Earth. Rather than a "how-to," it is instead a "what it's like" book. What it's like to experience the great outdoors in certain special ways. Or at least, what it has been like for me. It is a celebration of some of the ways in which modern Americans can transcend their Americanism, even their modernity, but not their humanity. In fact, I would like to think that it describes how to become more human. This book is a recognition that even in a hurry-up world of asphalt and automobiles, computers and nuclear weapons, active people can do things that reach back into the past, grasping as they do a piece of the Earth, and themselves.

We have books on the joy of sex, even the joy of cooking, excellent pastimes and admirable books, yet more concerned with technique than with joy. To be sure, technique—or, at least, a minimal competence—is helpful for most of the activities described in the pages to come, but as with sex or cooking, it is the joy that counts, that distinguishes a workmanlike performance from a gourmet feast. Just as there are sex manuals and cookbooks aplenty, there is no shortage of guides to backpacking, horseback riding, even bird watching. But there can never be too many lovesongs. Perhaps those who have sampled the pleasures described here will recognize them, even if they do not find themselves singing precisely

1

the same song. And perhaps those who haven't will feel that they better understand the actual experience.

When I told a friend about this book, he asked if I was going to write about finding joy in the mountains, at the seashore, in the canopy of stars, or astride a horse. I said no, that I wasn't sure I had ever found joy in any particular place or doing any particular thing; rather, joy has sometimes walked along with me for a while, in the mountains, at the seashore, during a starry night, or on a horse. But I have never caught it, held it fast in my hands like an insect pinned to a board, or a bird with salt on its tail. Joy, like the muse in creative life, comes when she will, and then goes. But just as we can establish situations—of quiet or, alternatively, of stimulation—when creativity is more likely, and just as we can increase the chances that a hummingbird will visit our garden by providing some nutritious red nectar, we can increase the chances that joy will visit us for a time. And a lovesong can help recall that joy to our minds; sometimes, even, it can coax it back for another fling.

Since I am a biologist, not only by training but also by belief, I see things in a biological way. Although *Homo sapiens* clearly had much to do with the current state of the planet Earth, the process has been reciprocal: our planetary home has also had its impact on us. It is in our blood, figuratively in the sense of our deepest yearnings, and literally, in that the saline makeup of our blood is remarkably close to that of our earlier liquid environment, seawater. It is also in our brains. Its impact can be seen in the shape of our hands and our feet, our eyes, our ears, our pain and our joys. Even our teeth. Try this: put a finger in your mouth (either upper or lower jaw), along the gums at the roots of your canines, the ones just on either side of the central incisors. That substantial bump, the "canine eminence," reflects our evolutionary heritage, a time when primitive primates had large, shearing canines—not unlike modern-day baboons—that required sturdy anchors in the jawbones.

Just as we change and shape this planet, sometimes for better and sometimes for worse, we have been changed and shaped by it as well. Just as the teeth of a baboon speak eloquently about life on the African savannah, and the wings of a bird are a dissertation on the physical properties of air, the human body—and more important, our mind—can tell us a great deal about the Earth. After all, we are literally the product of its oceans, mountains, rivers, forests,

and prairies. Striding across savannahs, crunching over Pleistocene snowdrifts, watching animals, and growing our own food, we
evolved, creatures of this planet.

What we did long ago of necessity—not for fun, but simply to
get food, avoid enemies, visit friends—many of us seek to recapture once more, calling it (accurately enough) re*creation*. In a
world grown ever more complex, confusing, technologic, and distant, many of these activities harken back to a simpler and more
primitive time, even though today they may involve an assist from
high-temperature alloys and space-age plastics.

The modern science of ecology has increasingly merged with
the ancient wisdom of the East, acknowledging that living things
(including *Homo sapiens*) are inseparable from their environment.
For a growing number of people, that environment is indoors, artificial, man- and woman-made. Yet, the environment in which we
evolved was not indoors but out, and not surprisingly, the outdoors
retains a powerful hold over many of us, if only via the imagination.
Maybe that is why the outdoors often seems so great.

Any doubters should consult those who really understand our
deeper yearnings, not psychologists, psychiatrists, or biologists,
but rather, the cream of the behavioral scientists: the advertising
executives. Modern advertising shows us how we would like to be,
if not how we really are: wandering in the mountains, riding
horses, playing in the surf, floating in small boats, climbing trees,
or sitting around a campfire. "It just doesn't get any better than
this," we are told. It is a self-image that may be especially strong
among Americans, imbued as we generally are with a pioneer, outdoors heritage. In any event, this widespread hankering for the
outside is not only a precious part of our collective mood, it is also
an important part of *ourselves* as biological creatures.

All of the activities discussed in the following pages take place
primarily or exclusively outdoors, and all of them are things I do or
have done often, although not necessarily very well. I don't love
them all equally, but love them all, I do. None of them require
extraordinary skills or expense, and all of them are further linked
by being noncompetitive, relatively solitary, environmentally sensitive, and ecologically appropriate. That is, they do not involve a
lot of noise or contribute significantly to pollution or to the abuse
of land or water. They are not directly powered by internal com-

bustion engines, and at some level, they arose in a distant time when things were not easier but at least simpler.

By and large, these songs are joyful, sometimes ecstatic. But they are also honest. Occasionally, therefore, the music is rather dissonant: it can be cold outside, and wet, and altogether miserable. Here and there, some of these lovesongs strike a minor key. But for better or worse, these activities connect us with our childhood as a species. Hence, they feel good—or at least, familiar—to a twentieth-century furless mammal that has gotten him and herself farther from the outdoors and into more trouble than is healthy or wise.

Why, then, in this time of troubles—political, economic, social, environmental—should we allow ourselves to acknowledge and sometimes even to feel rapturous about such private, even autistic, pleasures of the Earth? Why do people sing lovesongs? Because their hearts are full, and the sentiment overflows in music. And sometimes, they sing in the hope of softening another's heart. There is also gratification simply in the sharing of joy, in its communion. But most of all, we have the right—even the obligation— to celebrate these pleasures because the Earth is our home, and by touching Her, we invigorate ourselves, renewing our commitment to life: our private existence, as well as the larger life of this wonderful planet that is us.

"The end of all our exploring," wrote T. S. Eliot, "will be to arrive where we started, and know the place for the first time." And, he might have added, to know ourselves as well.

Gardening

Give Peas a Chance

Once there was a man who thirsted after knowledge. Well, not knowledge exactly, but rather wisdom and the inner serenity that comes with what the Buddhists call "enlightenment." In pursuit of his goal, this man—call him the Seeker—read lots of books and went to lots of schools and obtained lots of advanced degrees. But always the Seeker felt that something was missing, that the key to real wisdom was somehow denied him. Then he turned his attention to Eastern ways and apprenticed himself as disciple to the most renowned gurus, but again, his satisfaction was incomplete. Enlightenment remained elusive. Finally, the Seeker heard of the Master of all Masters, 150 years old, suffused with wisdom and peace, who resided alone at the top of a virtually inaccessible mountain. Moreover, in order to have any hope of success, the Seeker would first have to subject himself to painful mortification of the flesh, endure unspeakable torments and demonstrate—by many years of concentration and devotion—that he was earnest and worthy enough to be received by such a Master.

All these things he did. And so, it came to pass that finally the Seeker was permitted to climb the dizzying peak, where he found the Master of all Masters, seated cross-legged before a great fountain, his long white beard wrapped about his legs, and upon his face, a look of indescribable perfection.

5

What does all this have to do with gardening? Just this: When the Seeker approached, deferential and trembling with anticipation, he asked, "Tell me, Master, what is the meaning of life?" And the old man replied, calmly and with great dignity, "My son, life is like a garden."

Hearing this, the Seeker became enraged. Abandoning all self-control, the frustration of years and years of struggle and self-denial burst to the surface, in a torrent of bitterness and derision.

"What?" he screamed. "Do you mean to tell me that after I have absorbed the world's knowledge, obtained M.D., Ph.D., J.D., and a host of other degrees, and then after I have sacrificed most of the remaining years of my life to prepare my body, soul, and mind to meet you, after I have risked everything to climb up to this god-forsaken place, you have the nerve to tell me something so asinine as this?"

Whereupon, the Master's calm was shattered. His face changed completely. Quivering with doubt and despair, he croaked, "You mean, life *isn't* like a garden?"

Life is, in fact, quite a bit like a garden (more on this later). More to the point, however, a garden is like life. First, the ground must be prepared. Then, seeds are planted, small lives that—like a human embryo—are more potential than real. Eventually, sprouts appear, gaining in size and individuality, straining to complete themselves. And the gardener helps, removing unwanted competitors, providing necessary nutrients, watering the little darlings, it seems, with the very sweat of his or her brow.

The miracle continues, transforming air and water and carbon dioxide into unique and complex substances, capturing fundamental energy and making it into living stuff. And finally, after promise and effort, disappointment and fulfillment, the little drama runs its course and the microcosm swings round to a season of quiet, of restructuring, and often of death, until spring calls once again upon the land and the gardener alike. The rich, fertile soil gives birth to the youthful, optimistic shoots of early spring, which lead to the lush, powerful, green maturity of midsummer, and then, finally, to the yellow, dried-up, almost translucent rattling leaves of autumn, when the flesh has been harvested, and the sap and energy are gone.

"April is the cruelest month," wrote T. S. Eliot, because it is the season when gardens and gardeners begin to stir, when the soil is finally warmed again and life is once more awakened out of the dead land, when those who do not feel the strong pulse of spring within them (or who feel a memory of it, but with more pain than delight) are prone to resent the green, juicy throb of life renewing—in others—yet one more time.

So, a garden is most assuredly like life. Moreover, a garden *is* life, a miniature *tabula rasa* on which human beings—life-affirming creatures themselves—can work their will, but gently and with care. "Nature, to be commanded, must be obeyed," wrote Sir Francis Bacon, and this is one of the first things the gardener learns.

Human beings, we are told, were first created in a garden. Not a football stadium, or a safe deposit box, or a battlefield, or a factory, but in a garden. And of course, disobedience also began in that same garden, and as a result, we were cast out, forced to toil for our living. Many of us have been trying to recreate Edens ever since. It may well be that deep in our souls, we all recognize that a garden is not only like life, and a perfect metaphor *for* life, but also a necessity, if life is to continue. Paradise? Perhaps. But a very necessary paradise.

"I shall feed you," promises the garden. Such an offer is nearly irresistible.

After all, it is a truism—but one that is insufficiently appreciated—that all life depends on green plants. Only the special magic of chlorophyll can capture the sun's energy and render it material and usable by animals. The entire animal kingdom, ourselves included, stands ultimately atop a vast pyramid of green stuff and this means real, live, photosynthesizing plants, not astroturf.

According to the philosopher Martin Hidegger, "to dwell is to garden," meaning that to be alive is to act upon the world, to invest time and energy in one's survival and happiness. He was correct historically no less than existentially, since it was only with the discovery of agriculture that our ancestors were able to settle down and "dwell." Thousands of years ago, we learned animal and plant husbandry, the word "husband" meaning not only a married man but also a prudent manager, from the Icelandic *husbondi* ("hus" = "house" + "bondi" = "dwell"). And it was only with the taming of plants that we became capable of dwelling in one place, of husbanding the resources of the earth, and at last, becoming human.

My colleague at the University of Washington, ecologist Gordon Orians, has argued that human beings have a deep-seated fondness for parklike habitats—rolling lawns or meadows dotted with occasional trees—essentially as unconscious recapitulations of the African savannahs on which we evolved. Here's another possibility: maybe what we are really seeking when we foolishly insist on growing grass in southern California where cactus would be more appropriate, or when we demand golf courses in the Florida swamps, is a return to those good old days—many eons ago—when we tamed the land and built ourselves gardens to feed our bodies and nourish our spirits with the promise of plenty and the hope of peace.

One of the greatest advances in human cultural evolution took place when our ancestors discovered that plants could be induced to grow where (and to some extent, when) they were wanted, thereby making the transition from Paleolithic to Neolithic. Almost overnight, something new to the human experience was born: not only agriculture, but its payoff, surplus. People found themselves able to congregate in groups larger than hunter-gatherer bands, and in addition, some of us could specialize in doing things other than hunting or growing, since the hunters and the growers (especially the latter) were generally able to raise more food than their own mouths demanded. We developed artists, lawyers, doctors, carpenters, Indian chiefs.

So, the next time you go over to a neighbor (especially one who doesn't have a garden), bearing a few extra carrots and a ziplock bag full of green peas, remember to congratulate yourself. After all, you are recapitulating the origins of civilization.

It is easy—and all too often, appropriate—for people to develop a *mea culpa* attitude toward their own species. As we increasingly understand and decry the role of human beings in destroying the natural environment, we are in danger, perhaps, of forgetting that we have a constructive role as well. Carl Jung pointed out "man is indispensable for the completion of creation; that, in fact, he himself is the second creator of the world."[1] And this business of creating does not apply only to buildings, bridges, machines, and the apparatus of high-tech, nor just to art, music, poetry, and dance. We need, in addition to food for our souls, food for our bodies as well. After all, we have physical and biological needs; much as we protest the crimes of agribusiness, the pollution of the waters, and the rape of the land, we also have to eat. Hence, we have a creation to complete, daily. And agriculture, at least agriculture on a small and human scale, done with ecological sensitivity, is a way of producing (literally, making *produce*), of creating a sustainable and nonexploitative life for ourselves. From the destruction of tropical rain forests to nuclear weapons, from the greenhouse effect to the extinction of the Arctic auk, we have much to answer for. Gardening offers us the chance of some redemption.

Maybe this is why my own gardening inclines strongly toward practicality. As a child, I dutifully ate (as my parents exhorted) in order to grow. Now, an adult, I grow in order to eat. I grow what we can eat. True, Adam and Eve were punished for eating from the tree of knowledge, but that sin, at least, is behind us. Since we're stuck with the punishment, we might as well enjoy the fruits of the disobedience.

No disrespect to the fanciers of flowers, mind you, but even here, my preference runs toward the edible, such as my favorite, nasturtiums. (They not only offer a brilliant, long-lasting array of blossoms, adding bright colors to the various shades of veggie garden-green, but unknown to many people, the flowers themselves are delicious—rather peppery and surprisingly juicy as well.) Perhaps it takes a higher level of sophistication to justify time and effort creating a garden that serves no purpose other than aesthetics. And certainly, there is much to be said for pure aesthetics.

Moreover, even when the way to your hoe is through your stomach, it pays not to be too disdainful of appearances. Be an aesthete as well as an epicure. If a crop fails, for whatever reason (bugs, wrong variety, planted too late, or too soon, or in improper soil, or too much or too little sun, or water, or love), it is very useful to have reserved the right to admire the ensuing plants for their looks if not for their practicality. Indeed, it isn't sour grapes to admire

1. Carl G. Jung, *Memories, Dreams, Reflections* (New York: Vintage, 1965).

the lush foliage of a grape vine—whether or not it produces grapes[2]—or the graceful arching symmetry of an artichoke plant (with or without artichokes), or the lovely, leathery, leafy profusion of purply-veined kale and great, barbaric cabbages, or the tall, thin, aristocratic bearing of leeks, superbly green top, faultlessly white at the base. A seeming wall of snow peas with their delicate and vulnerable-green, like a newborn child, or a virtual cliff of pole beans, jungle dark and almost sinister in their intensity, a spiky gathering of onions looking like a miniature elephant trap, an expanse of squash, looking for all the world like small boulders strewn about the ground (a field sprouting rocks?), or the graceful profusion of fluffy, feathery, many-veined tops of carrots, silently witnessing their fleshy tubers underneath: it doesn't take an artist to see beauty when it presents itself right there in your backyard. And it doesn't take the promise of calories to make your mouth water.

If you have ever spent time smiling at the heaps of fruits and vegetables at a produce stand—a consumer's cornucopia—you may be even more inclined to appreciate the varieties of color and texture, shape and size offered by even a small vegetable garden. To Goethe, nature was "the living garment of God." To me—less divinely inspired and also much more atheistic—a garden is a living patchwork quilt, of nature if not god. The blue-greens here, the darker shades there, the blossoms showing in a bunch over in the corner, the tomatoes ripening on cue up in front—collections of useful, friendly, agreeable spirits, tasty to the eye as well as the palate, and relaxing to the mind . . . if not the back.

According to Francis Bacon, the first essayist in the English language, gardening is "the Purest of Humane pleasures. It is the Greatest Refreshment to the Spirits of Man; Without which, Buildings and Pallaces are but Grosse Handy-works: And a Man shall ever see that, when Ages grow to Civility and Elegancie, Men come to Build Stately sooner than to Garden Finely: As if Gardening were the Greater Perfection."

Several centuries later, Henry Ward Beecher, charismatic Congregationalist minister, sometime presidential aspirant and brother

2.   Nonetheless, if my vine keeps teasing us with leaves and no grapes one more
      year, it's into the compost pile with it!

of Harriet Beecher Stowe, extolled the moral benefits to be derived (by women, mind you) from gardening: "It would occupy the mind with pure thoughts, and inspire a sweet and gentle enthusiasm; maintain simplicity of taste; and in connection with personal instruction, unfold in the heart an enlarged, unstraitened, ardent piety."[3]

Whatever its effect on building moral fiber (and frankly, the Reverend Beecher may be a less-than-perfect guide in this respect[4]), gardening is also darn good fun. To begin with, the various seed catalogs are utterly irresistible. As winter melts away, it is time to pore over the glorious—albeit often misleading—full-color illustrations and breathlessly enthusiastic accounts of the latest new miracle varieties, imported from Thailand, or perhaps just developed by those magnificent French intensive-horticultural perfectionists. Adding to the seduction, seeds are wonderfully cheap.

There are more than a hundred varieties of tomatoes, dozens of different kinds of lettuce, scores of potatoes. Each has a special allure. Be the first on your block to collect the whole set.

The eventual reality, wonderful as it may be, rarely matches the catalog's promises, however. If you buy a toaster-oven, and the product inside doesn't match the picture on the box, you have legitimate cause for complaint. But if your beans don't measure up to the catalog's promise (if, as rarely happens, they're not worth a hill of beans), perhaps it is your fault: wrong soil, improper planting, not enough water, or too much, ditto for the sun, and so forth. Nonetheless, rather than cause for complaint, this variation and unpredictability is itself part of the appeal. You know generally what you're going to get: radishes, cucumbers or eggplant, but— especially if you're trying a new variety—not precisely what they will look like, where the fruits will set, exactly how large they will be or how they will taste. A crap shoot, but at least an organic one.

There is also the fascination of dirt, something that arises early in our lives, through the romance of mud pies, dirty fingernails, the love of digging to China, water, buried treasure. As very young children, we learn that we have to flush our feces away, but good

3. Henry Ward Beecher, *Plain and Pleasant Talk About Fruits, Flowers, and Farming* (1859).
4. His own piety was apparently insufficiently enlarged, since Beecher became enmeshed in a career-dimming scandal involving an extramarital affair.

old-fashioned dirt is right outside for the grabbing. And for adults, is there any better way—indeed, any *other* way—to justify going outside to play in the dirt than gardening?

And for children, is there anything else in which their effort can reap the same reward as a grown-up? My young daughter planted some peas; so did I. The seeds didn't know the difference and neither do the developing pods. But my daughter does. Her plants, the tangible rewards of her very own labor, are every bit as healthy and productive as mine. And you can bet she knows it.

Then there is the fun of trying new things, "putting in" sorghum one year, just to give the kids something delightfully sweet to chew on and turn them on to the whole enterprise. Or planting sunflowers a few weeks before the pole beans, so that the latter will cling to the former, thereby avoiding the use of artificial supports. Or maybe trying lima beans for a change, even though the experts claim it can't be done in your climate. (Perhaps you have an especially warm wall, one that catches and holds the long caresses of the late afternoon sun.) These are the voyages of a free-spirited gardening Enterprise: going bravely where no one has gone before, raising okra where, ostensibly, it is too cold, or broccoli where it is too hot. Planting squash among the corn, or a new, weird-looking variety of pepper, just for the hell of it.

There are also the pleasant surprises, such as the volunteer tomato, which somehow smuggled itself into the cucumbers, via the compost. Or the immense jungle of a pumpkin patch that grew from a few seeds sprinkled, and then forgotten, on our old manure pile. (There is a dark side, however—the only time my family was bodily threatened by our garden, this very pumpkin patch was responsible. It had grown so rapidly, producing such heavy, muscular stems that were so thick and spiny, and leaves of such alarming diameter, that it seemed prudent to keep our two-year-old beyond its grasp.)

In an age that seems divided between the extremes of immediate gratification on the one hand and seemingly interminable delays on the other, gardening offers a perfect compromise. It teaches patience and the value of reflection: gardening is slower than impulse buying or a snort of cocaine. But it also makes good on its promises, and within a reasonable time period: gardening is faster than working toward a Ph.D., planting an acorn, or working for disarmament. And when the rewards come—first visual as the plants grow, then tactile as they are harvested, then gustatory as they are eaten—there is nothing ethereal about them. Nothing is more earthy, for example, than grubbing up great handfuls of your very own home-grown potatoes: heavy, dirty, meaty, and thick, wonderfully satisfying and unquestionably real. Nothing symbolic or theoretical about them.

Expert gardener John Adams points to one of the charms of gardening when he notes that a freshly dug potato "suddenly has a flavor, a distinct, unique, and subtle earthiness, suggestive of native mushrooms or the mysterious wild."[5] And then he adds another, hitherto unappreciated dividend: "My wife says there is something erotic in their earthiness. I always grow lots of them."

For myself, I never knew that broccoli could be sweet, almost sugary. Or that tomatoes carried with them such a tart and tangy odor, coming from the leaves and vines, not to mention the remarkable crispness of the vegetable itself (or is it a fruit?). Sometimes I even take a certain perverse pleasure in the relative quickness with which my garden produce fades: commercial fruits and vegetables have been bred to store well, not to be the best possible representatives of their kind. My tomatoes aren't designed to be picked while still green, shipped a thousand miles, stored in fumigated vans, then sold two weeks later . . . and still look recognizably like tomatoes. Instead, they are indisputably tomatoes when picked, and lusciously so when eaten.

Between May and October, our vegetable needs—especially salads—are met just by stepping outside with a colander. Always fresh, never more than we need. And no dyes, no preservatives, no check-out lines. It's also easy to see why the early settlers planted two gardens, a small kitchen-garden nearby, featuring those things that might be used daily (lettuce, tomatoes, dill, etc.) and another one, designed for heavy-duty production, located at a site that may be less convenient but more suitable for successful crop growing in bulk.

On the other hand, perhaps the relationship of gardener to vegetable should be like that of fisher-person to fish: going fishing is one thing, catching fish is another. The means justify themselves,

5. John F. Adams, *The Epicurean Gardener* (New York: Knopf, 1988).

whatever the ends. It is nice to harvest a good crop from one's garden, just as it is nice to catch fish when you go fishing, but the pursuit of neither warrants going overboard. Sometimes, plucking the radish or clipping off the beans can be virtually an after-thought. The real satisfactions of gardening (at least for me) are in the doing of it. On the other hand, at least during the summer months, there is the righteous glow of walking right past the pro-duce counters at the Safeway or the A&P, with a self-congratula-tory, superior air, issuing faint contempt for those poor unfortu-nates reduced to battening off the yield of someone else's garden. Let it be noted, however, such feelings fade, and quickly, during the winter.

But, it must be admitted, gardening isn't always fun. Intended to be refuges from care and anxiety, the home garden all too often becomes a source of worry, a black hole sucking up any available time and energy, sprouting grief rather than greens, tumult more than tomatoes. It can be deeply saddening to watch a well-mean-ing plant—started too late, perhaps, or slowed by a sputtering summer—struggling in vain to ripen its fruit, which you know is doomed to lose the race. Pumpkins that get large and hearty . . . and irretrievably green. Corn that isn't as high as your own eye, never mind an elephant's. Sometimes, early in the morning and again in the evening, I come out and root, enthusiastically but without real hope, for the tomatoes: "OK, redden up, you guys. One, two, three, now, *RED.*"

I also stand accused by my oft-unweeded garden: "You are a lazy, good-for-nothing bastard." And convicted by my neighbors.

Competitive garden-gauging is the plague of the home horticul-turist. I can keep up with the Joneses just fine, but my corn, it seems, never will. Theirs is always eighteen inches taller, their to-matoes always ripen—and a full two weeks earlier, to boot—their cabbages never get wormy, and their strawberries, my lord, you should see their strawberries. Not to mention the engineering marvels they've built for their beans and the size of those grateful stalks. If Jack was nearby, he'd already be climbing . . . while mine are barely off the ground. The green of envy is tinged with chloro-phyll.

Even success can be disheartening. In the spring, the gardener's eyes can be larger than his or her stomach. And few things are more likely to buoy the spirits than the sight of the season's first lettuce (sown perhaps right on the melting snow of a tenacious winter) beginning to sprout. But then comes the fullness of summer, and with it the awful realization that something must be done with twenty-four eggplants, all ripening on the same day. A single five-pound rutabaga, all by itself, is enough to make strong men blanch. If the space is there, along with it is likely to come the powerful, unending temptation to make too big a garden, which leads inexorably to too much weeding and the extra work of too much harvesting. Just when the fruits (and vegetables) of all that labor are ready to be enjoyed, the gardener may be ready to burn out on the whole wretched business.

Even when you want and can use all that the garden produces, harvesting is a time of curious pressure, with the powerful productive mechanism of the living earth pushing stuff and more stuff out of the ground, swelling small bumps into edible fruits, and then more, and then yet more, a Sorcerer's Apprentice without a wise old sorcerer to come to the rescue. Just keeping the garden picked is taxing.

The profusion of lettuce leaves—sown with such innocent enthusiasm—can be truly alarming, especially since the forthcoming hot summer will cause it to "bolt," or go to seed, along with the spinach, long after our bellies are overwhelmed but equally long before we have even made a dent in the supply. The awful question arises: how can we retain a positive attitude toward brussels sprouts when confronted with them in industrial strength? Most of all, how to cope with the most dreaded of all gardening diseases: zucchini glut?

Whereas corn finds it difficult to get itself pollinated, zucchini finds it a snap, doing so without struggle and debate, no coaxing needed. If the fertilizing of corn is a difficult, often painful production, reminiscent of our own species giving birth, that of zucchini is like the breeding of rabbits. And their growth is like cancer.

Emerson once said that a weed was a plant for which we have not yet discovered a use. By the same token, zucchini is a weed for which we have. One such use, and probably the most popular, is to give it away. That's how you learn who your real friends are: someone who will accept your zucchini. As John Adams suggests, you can hide your zucchini at the bottom of a basket of giveaway garden produce, or perhaps you can work out a cooperative arrangement. The ultimate in "crop rotation" has nothing to do with growing different crops, successively, on the same plot; rather, it means taking turns growing zucchini, so that someone in your ken will always be available to relieve you of the burden of so large and prepossessing a vegetable.

Alternatively, there are other possible cures for zucchini glut. Try panhandling in front of your local unemployment office: "Please take my zucchini, I have three small children at home." Or insert them, late at night, into other people's gardens. Deposit them, perhaps, in mailboxes or sanitary landfills. The great American how-to book is yet unwritten: ninety-nine things to do with zucchini. Try zucchini soup, zucchini casseroles, fried zucchini, mashed zucchini, diced, sliced, boiled, and broiled zucchini. Zucchini bread, zucchini pudding, stuffed zucchini. Use them to ream out your chimney, as paperweights, shims for the garage, rent them out as day-care centers, or open a dildo shop featuring strictly organic products.

The truth is that even zucchinis aren't all that bad. They can be delicately flavored yet gratifying in their meatiness, and they stir-fry beautifully: tolerable if not admirable, so long as you don't have to deal with too many at once. Sort of like cousins.

Sometimes, overwhelmed by the possibilities, the work, the advice, the pests, the diligence of one's neighbors, the abundance (or shortage) of the harvest, the abundance (and never any shortage) of other things to do, more than one home gardener has been tempted to throw in the trowel. But in needn't be this way.

In fact, gardening needn't be any particular way at all, the various encyclopedias and gardening guides notwithstanding. It is sometimes useful to consult a good reference for information on when to plant rutabagas, or how deep to sow the seeds of a pole bean or the eyes of potatoes, but frankly, my heart just does not sing to such offerings as "Eight Ways to Better Broccoli," or "Soil Preparation: the key to straighter carrots." Even when it comes to questions of planting time, I far prefer such natural timetables as: put in broccoli when the pussy willows start to open (i.e., February), peas when the daffodils begin to bloom (late March), beets and parsley only after the apple trees have flowered (late May), and (my favorite) corn when the oak leaves are the size of squirrel's ears (early June).

It can be depressing to add up the costs of equipment, land, fertilizer, seed, and—most expensive of all, if you are inclined to calculate it—your own time, and then to contemplate a thirty-dollar bell pepper, a tomato that perversely refuses to ripen, or a glorious profusion of graceful foliage, in the center of which, proudly displayed, is a single, dismal, stunted artichoke. Not surprisingly, therefore, given the human yearning to grow things and the widespread fears of failure and of not getting one's money's worth, there are more "how-to" books about gardening than about anything else, more money spent than in any other outdoor hobby, more columnists, radio and TV advice-givers, and more experts and county, state, federal, and university extension specialists than in any comparable realm of human endeavor.

Keep the tilth, we are urged, and above all, don't neglect your sense of humus. And know thy plants: the leafy ones, we are told, do OK in the shade. Fruiting ones need more sun. Each vegetable is reputed to have a distinct personality, with preferences to match: one "likes" acid soil, another, alkaline. One cannot "tolerate" late afternoon sun, another thinks its just peachy. One is simply ga-ga over damp soils, another is appalled by the mere prospect of dampening its delicate little toes in the common muck.

I must confess to limited patience for such persnicketiness. I don't like my plants to be too fussy or finicky, and I have little sympathy with those that sulk if the weather is just a bit too hot, or too cold. It just isn't necessary to indulge a vegetable's every whim. After all, you don't do that for your loved ones, or yourself. Does your garden deserve more? Beans don't have to climb nine feet tall, cabbages don't really have to luxuriate in enough lebensraum to satisfy all the Junkers of East Prussia. There is much to be said for knowing the needs of your garden inhabitants, and adjusting your plans, or even your soil, to accommodate those that are reasonable: moist or dry, full sun or partial shade. Radishes and carrots can be tightly packed, whereas squash and brussels sprouts need a lot of room. Tomato plants are perfectly content to be all by themselves, but corn needs lots of company, since each individual kernel must be pollinated. Considerations of this sort are only common sense and worth keeping in mind when planting.

Melons prefer sunny, well-drained soil, cucumbers don't mind some shade. Tomatoes like acid soil, but squashes are partial to alkaline. So far, so good, but often it gets out of hand: some garden denizens, we are told, insist on a pH of 7.8 but not a decimal point higher, while others will positively mope if their precious little bit of ground isn't as acidic as 6.7 . . . but heaven forbid, no further than 6.5. And then, of course, there's the nitrogen balance, and the phosphorus, not to mention the various micronutrients, like selenium, zirconium and the other essential ingredients of a modern space shuttle or supercomputer.

I can respect essential needs; we all have them. And even quirks and preferences. But I just can't stand plants that insist on pressing the point or that pout when they don't get their way. Celery, for example, for all its abundance in the grocery store, is a problem plant. It needs cool, damp summers but is frost-sensitive. That's the celery's problem, not mine.

And speaking of fussbudget gardening, some people swear by what is called "companionate planting." Here, the idea is that certain veggies go well together—in the ground, that is, not necessarily on the plate—whereas others do not. Thus, tomatoes and asparagus are reputed to be good friends, but tomatoes and corn, by sad contrast, are mortal dangers to each other, since each attracts the same kind of pests. It is similarly adjudged a faux pas to introduce eggplants to potatoes, at least not without a good mixer, something with better social graces like parsley or dill, as a mediator.

The world, I am convinced, is much more straightforward than all this. My gardening philosophy is that the soil, rain, sun, and I are all on the same side. The plants especially. They want to grow every bit as much as I want them to; maybe even more, since sprouting, growing, and developing is their destiny, their *raison d'etre* . . . which is more (or is it less?) than I can say for myself.

In any event, nothing is more natural than a seed sprouting. Few things are more natural than trying to help, and enjoying the results. And nothing about gardening is as hard as the experts make it seem.

Starting a garden can be backbreaking. Only later is it heartbreaking.

I am thinking here of the unthinkable: pests and weeds. "What would become of the garden," wrote T. H. Huxley, "if the gardener treated all the weeds and slugs and birds and trespassers as he would like to be treated, if he were in their place?"[6] Huxley's point was that evolution involves the favoring of some forms over others. My point is that gardening involves exactly the same thing. To garden is to practice artificial selection. It's called thinning—although to me it feels more like genocide—removing the weak so that the strong can prosper.

After all, seeds are cheap; only the best deserve to survive. And otherwise, everyone gets stunted. (Still, pulling out some perfectly healthy carrots, just to make room for the others, seems like one of the more unpleasant tasks of omnipotence.) Moreover, our vegetables—and cultivated flowers, too—are domesticated species, whose ancestors were chosen by plant breeders because they provided something that was wanted: color, size, shape, taste, early fruiting, and so on. In the process, they have become pampered specialists, in most cases incapable of holding their own against their more rugged competitors, which are adapted to survive in the wide, wild world without benefit of *Homo sapiens*. To garden is thus to interfere with nature, to load the dice in favor of what we the people want, rather than the chickweed, the morning glory, or the crabgrass. Therefore, the Need To Weed.

Some of these wild species are chameleons, having evolved especially to be successful within a garden. I will swear, for example, that the weeds that most frequent my strawberry patch bear an uncommon resemblance to strawberries (although, not surprisingly, there is one thing that they do not bear: strawberries). No surprise here, either: those that are obviously different are readily weeded out, so what is left? Those that are more similar. And those weeds that successfully hide or mimic their way into freeloading in my garden have an additional, remarkable capacity: cunningly, they bide their time until the moment my back is turned, whereupon they suddenly make their move; i.e., they go to seed, trying in their sneaky way to make yet more little weedlings. Or is it weedlets?

A weedy garden is a silent rebuke. Up close, they fill your mind: great, huge, rank masses of weeds, threatening to take over the

6. T. H. Huxley, *Evolution and Ethics* (1893).

plump, delicate tomatoes, to ride roughshod over the carrots, to crowd out the spindly, innocent dill. So I march to the rescue, filling my wheelbarrows with the corpses of weeds laid low, showing no mercy, cutting like an avenging angel through the host of the wicked. But later, what gratification to look the garden over (preferably from a distance!) and see the tomatoes, carrots, onions, or parsley standing cleanly and righteously on their own, with scarcely a rude interloper.

Admittedly, however, weeding is not one of the finer pleasures of life. On the other hand, it can be oddly satisfying to pluck out the little offenders, one by one, especially when—like chickweed—they are easily grasped and pull readily and cleanly, roots and all. It is a perverse kind of joy, however, a bit like slapping a mosquito. On the other hand, unlike mosquitoes, whose maddening buzz can never be ignored for long, it is also possible to become temporarily oblivious to weeds, and then make it up to your long-suffering dill or your ravished radishes by some careful attention and perhaps a bit of extra watering as well. To paraphrase Mark Twain on smoking: it's easy to give up on weeding, I've done it lots of times.

If weeds are bad, however, animal pests are worse. Virtually nothing good can fairly be said about them, except to note that they are manifestations of biological diversity, and as such, understandable—indeed, interesting on occasion—if not laudable. "Is ditchwater dull?" asked G. K. Chesterton. "Naturalists with microscopes have told me that it teems with quiet fun."[7] Gardens, too. For example, not long ago, I was out for one of the finer although unremarked pleasures of life: taking a quiet, barefoot stroll through my garden in the sweet cool of the evening, filled with contentment at my modest but tangible accomplishments, feeling no malice, no agitation, no particular need to do anything other than drink in the quiet beauty of the place—so harmonious, docile, useful, and obedient. When I put my foot down on something slippery and slimy, something that writhed horribly, but in silence. A slug!

The world is full of remarkable and exotic places: the Himalayas, the Amazon, the Atacama Desert of Peru, the coral atolls of

7. G. K. Chesterton, *The Spice of Life* (1936).

the South Pacific. But of these, perhaps the most remarkable—on a par with ditchwater, perhaps—is your own garden. There, strange creatures lurk under the stalks of the brussels sprouts, enfolded in the heavy white corolla of the cauliflower or burrow unseen within the potatoes. And some, like slugs, have the temerity to ooze their way right across your path. The world of garden pests is awash not only with these shell-less escargots, but also with such elegant exotica as corn borers, tomato weevils, cankerworms, stem suckers, and root snippers. (Not to mention the various molds, mildews, rots, and bilious blemishes.)

Often, it is hard to identify the culprit, unless caught red-handed. One day the pea pod seems happy as can be; the next, wilted and thoroughly distraught. It's 2 A.M. Do you know what your cabbages are doing? Or rather, do you know who is doing what to them? Not many gardeners are willing to get up in the wee hours to see just what is transpiring underneath the cucumber's fuzzy leaves or deep in the innermost heart of the artichoke.

Certain veggies are especially attractive to certain insects. It appears that turnips, for example, are veritable Gardens of Eden for aphids, and perhaps the reason the cabbage family is so humorless is that they are so attractive to so many pests: cabbage fleas (especially in warmer climes), aphids inside the brussels sprouts (where they are particularly hard to eradicate, since they occupy the various tightly pressed layers of leaves). The dainty white and yellow butterflies that flit so charmingly about the heads of broccoli are seen in a new light, revealed to be the nefarious cabbage moths, purveyors of nasty little worms, whose color craftily matches the otherwise perfect blue-green head of a broccoli bud. (Often, they cannot be detected until the broccoli is boiled, whereupon the corpses float to the surface; in our family, we eat broccoli raw and try not to think too much about the occasional extra bits of protein.)

Organic gardeners such as myself see poisons and sprays as anathema. We'd rather put our faith in the precept that healthy plants will not attract many nuisance critters and will not be seriously injured by those that do come calling. Moreover, we have a special fondness for natural controls such as toads, ladybugs (by the cupful), praying mantises (by the egg case), trichogramma wasps (by the vial), and the delicate but voracious lacewings. We might be inclined to try certain natural pest-repellents, such as garlic, marigolds, mints, nasturtiums, etc. But nothing that stinks of a Superfund dumpsite.

The ancient Romans had a minor deity, Priapus by name, who was the god of gardens. Typically represented as a naked man with an uncommonly large, erect penis, statues of Priapus used to stand guard over Mediterranean gardens, threatening to rape anyone (woman or man) who stole from them: "Violate my garden," went the unspoken message, "and I'll violate you." Perhaps we might try conveying the same warning to modern-day slugs, insects and nematodes. If nothing else, it would give new meaning to the word buggery.

The most valuable piece of weaponry in the gardener's armamentarium, however, is not structural but mental, a kind of informed indifference. I do not elect to contest every head of lettuce, every pea pod, every radish. I am not inclined to work myself into a frenzy over the depredations of the bug-eyed broccoli borer, the granulated garlic gouger, or that ferocious fungus, the slimy spinach sucker. Maybe it bespeaks a lack of sensitivity, or inadequate personal hygiene, but frankly, I am not much bothered by occasional holes in my peppers, harmless black dots on my cauliflower, or even a snug slug, cozily situated underneath a cucumber leaf. Must we blanch at every bug, cringe at every caterpillar? Some battles are best left unwon . . . and better yet, unfought.

Why not share a little? If Ronald Reagan can shake hands with Mikhail Gorbachev, can't we allow a few cockaded cucumber clippers to clip themselves a tidy meal or two? There's plenty to go around.

Long ago, we used to sacrifice, willingly, for the success of our gardens and crops: a goat, a virgin or two, a bushel of ripe cantaloupes. Now that we're modern and scientific, and no longer go out of our way to propitiate the spirits, must we begrudge a fair tithe simply because the creatures who seek it are real?

But don't get the wrong impression. Tolerance has its limits; propitiation is one thing, craven capitulation is another. Gardening—even organic gardening—is several stages below sainthood. I at least am not above rage and fury, swearing vengeance and stomping about, ready to rend the villain who invaded my sweet peas. And as soon as it has been apprehended, I show no mercy, executing the offender on the spot, squashing slugs beneath my merciless boots, guillotining caterpillars and cutworms with my ferocious fingernails, rolling aphids to a miserable death betwixt thumb and index finger. I just believe in visiting my retribution directly on the culprit, rather than broadcasting death and destruction willy-nilly.

To some extent, gardeners cannot help joining our age-old competitive battle with pests and moochers. As a child, I rooted for Peter Rabbit, against nasty, dangerous, fat old Farmer McGregor. Now, I'm beginning to see the old guy's point. With age and the stoop labor of garden preparation and maintenance, comes proprietorship and a diminished ability to tolerate the little buggers that would freeload off my garden.

I do not use lethal sprays or powders and would sooner give up my garden altogether than build it on a rotten foundation of insecticides, herbicides, fungicides, or other poisons. Organic gardening is objective: I refuse to take sides. But I'll be damned if some dumb worm or wabbit is going to make a monkey—even a Neolithic monkey—out of me.

Weeds, pests, and all, a garden is indeed like life. There may even be some wisdom, if not ultimate enlightenment, in the misogynist Chinese proverb: "If you would be happy for a week, take a wife; if you would be happy for a month, kill a pig; but if you would be happy all your life, plant a garden." And if you would really and truly be happy, plant one without pests and without weeds.

Once, in the long-ago days when special permits were required for backpacking in designated Wilderness Areas, I had stopped at the U.S. Forest Service Ranger Station in the logging town of Darrington, Washington, seeking permission to spend a few days in the Glacier Peak region. As a secretary was doing the paperwork, I overhead a report, radioed in by a back-country ranger, "Dead elk by upper Agnes Creek decomposing nicely. Over."

If you have never been near a large putreifying animal, especially in the summer, you cannot fully appreciate the incongruity of that communication. Decomposing disgustingly, yes, also horribly, grotesquely, obnoxiously, odoriferously, or even loathsomely, but of all descriptive words, "nicely" seems one of the last that most people would have chosen. But if you have ever maintained a garden,

you can see the ranger's wisdom. Decomposition is the downside
of growth, the other side of the coin of life. And when it comes to
gardens, the naturalness, the organicness, the essentialness, the
downright niceness of decomposition becomes clear.

As plants grow, they take stuff from the soil. Eventually, if yields
are to be maintained, that stuff must be returned. Good gardeners
are, therefore, "into" compost, which decays—nicely—into humus and is then recycled back into the soil. As with gardening
itself, there is both an art and a science to composting, adjusting
the amounts of water, nitrogen fertilizer, the temperature, and so
forth. But as with gardening itself, composting is really doing what
comes naturally, or rather, letting the compost do so. Just like the
dead elk near upper Agnes Creek, leftover coffee grounds, corn-
stalks, blueberry pie, and English muffins are simply allowed to
return to a primordial undifferentiated state of organic slop-hood,
the end product of which is remarkably inoffensive and terribly
important to any sustainable living process. It is very, very nice.

It may seem that this aspect of gardening is not for the
squeamish, but if so, then the same thing applies to life itself. The
poet Richard Wilbur has written that

> We milk the cow of the world, and as we do
> We whisper in her ear, "You are not true."[8]

But, no matter what we whisper, somewhere deep inside we
know that the cow is true—that is, real—that nutrients cycle re-
morselessly from living things to dead, and back again, that milk
isn't manufactured in half-gallon cartons (skim, whole, chocolate,
and 2%), and that carrots don't grow in plastic bags. They come
out of the ground, covered with dirt.

Of course, it isn't all grubby and yucky. At its epicenter, the
sustaining life process is photosynthesis, the world's most wonderful alchemy, converting carbon dioxide, light, and water, with a
sprinkling of nutrients, into food. Above ground, at least, our pea
plants stand around, cleanly and neatly, pumping pea pods out of
the ground. (By the way, we never bother with the regular green
peas, those intended for shelling, since we can't develop the pa-

8. Richard Wilbur, quoted in *The Sun*, issue 152 (1988).

tience to wait for them to develop fully. Because we are forever
picking and eating the pods before they are ripe, it seems prudent
to plant only the Chinese or sugar pea varieties.) Alongside, the
carrots and parsnips are pumping carrot-stuff and parsnip-stuff
back into the ground, and the cauliflowers are hatching full heads
of cauliflower-stuff. Some, eggplants for their part, fairly astonish
with their determination, setting fruits that must weight three or
four times the plant's vegetative parts.

Bread may be the staff of life,[9] but the gardener learns that organic stuff—raw, dirty, sometimes gooey and smelly, the results as
well as the progenitors of an essential and altogether *nice* process
of decomposition—is the real staff on which all of us ultimately
lean.

But for most us, ultimately is a long way off.

In the short term, growing a garden is a way to learn about the
"cow of the world," not only its messier and more private details,
but even its basic anatomy. Until I had grown it and seen it first-
hand, I hadn't really understood what the edible part of a broccoli
plant really was, relative to the rest of the broccoli. (It is the early
stage of the growth that eventually becomes the flowers; yes, broccoli plants have flowers.) How many eaters of brussels sprouts can
describe how all those brussels actually sprout? (They cling to either side of the main stalk of a large, branching plant, tucked into
what seems like a small armpit under each leaf.)

Not knowing where to look, or exactly what to look for, the first-
time gardener can readily be deceived by plants whose fruits are
camouflaged, such as pea pods that perfectly match their surrounding leaves, or green beans that hang down, incongruously,
from skinny stalks hidden by wide leaves. (Turn the pea leaves
aside to reveal the pods, which may be nearly full-grown before it
is discovered that the parent pea is bearing any pods at all; sneak
up on the green beans from behind, and all shall be revealed.)
Tomatoes seem to be the epitome of home-garden fruit, perhaps
less for their good taste and wide use than for the fact that when
ripe, they are bright and brilliant red, clearly standing out from
their leaves and stalks. Only red peppers are comparably bold.

9. For people of European descent. For Asians, it is rice; for Latin Americans,
    potatoes and corn.

(Strawberries are no less red, but not nearly as eye-catching, since they crouch below a leafy roof.)

There are other private lives in the vegetable world, unseen by the oblivious produce-shopper. Only by growing my own, for example, did I discover the fine powdery film that develops on freshly growing blueberries, bringing back memories of the magical, light coating of bubble gum dust that used to bedeck the beloved baseball cards of my childhood. And consider the hidden secret of the asparagus: after its spearlike buds have been harvested, the underground asparagus root puts forth a tough, fernlike, above-ground plant, three feet high or more, golden brown by fall and covered with yellow and red berries. And there is more, such as the fact that certain vegetables—kale and carrots, for example—actually get sweeter if they are left untouched until the first frost; the low temperatures help convert some of the starch into sugar.

Then there is the question of when, exactly, is each vegetable ready for harvesting. Wandering along the produce aisles at a supermarket, we can squeeze, thump, shake, and scratch the piled produce, but we are limited in how well we can commune with their inner souls, since, of course, they have already been harvested, nearly always ahead of their time. Peas, beans, and summer squash, for example, are best picked while the blossom, attached nearby, is still withering. And watermelons are ripe when the tendril nearest the melon itself has just begun to turn brown. But when confronted with a pile of already-picked watermelons, no amount of fondling, carressing, or rapt examination of the light patch on the little darling's belly will reveal its true status.

Sometimes, the vegetable section of a grocery store is a sad place because you can see evidence that the fruit, like the infant Caesar, had been ripped untimely from its mother's womb: cantaloupes, for instance, with bits of stem still clinging desperately to the melon itself. Were they allowed to vine-ripen, the umbilical stem would have readily detached itself as soon as the plump child was ready to be born. Most gardeners have the option of more natural births.

Perhaps the greatest of gardening's unkept secrets, however, is that plants come from seeds, tiny things that usually belie what they will become. Lettuce and carrot seeds are remarkably tiny, too small, in fact. I like seeds you can wrap your hands around, like corn, peas, or shot puts. Fava beans are the most satisfying to plant, so large that a sowing feels more like a burial. Once we had to borrow a neighbor's tractor just to lower a few fava beans into the ground.

As we sow, goes the injunction, so shall we reap. But first, we have to wait . . . for warmth, water, sun, and the stirrings of inner life. Some things cannot be rushed.

Gardening, therefore, is not only a window into our organicness, our connectedness with peas and beans and decomposing elk, it is also a tonic for type-A folks like myself, people who can't wait to get something done, who want it finished yesterday ... if not sooner. The rhythms of plants are the rhythms of the seasons—spring, summer, fall—not exactly leisurely, but unpressured and unswerving, proceeding at their own pace. Till the soil, sow the seed, reap the harvest. What could be more steady, more regular, more imperturbable? It is also reassuring to know that something else is in control. Despite our best efforts, our most detailed plans and beneficent wishes, we do not grow tomatoes, or broccoli, or spinach. Rather, the tomatoes, the broccoli, and the spinach grow themselves ... although assuredly, they do it for us, by our leave, and with our help and our blessings.

There may be late frosts and unseasonably cold soil, which causes certain seeds (e.g., corn, beans) to rot rather than germinate. And there may be infestations of fungus or insects, or depredations from deer, woodchucks, or rabbits, but at least the gardener can be assured that—within reason—he will experience the wonder of biological continuity. As we learned from *The Fantasticks:*

"Plant a carrot, get a carrot, not a brussels sprout,
That's why I like vegetables, you know what you're about."

But as the song goes on to point out, parenting of our own species doesn't offer nearly the same constancy. You don't know what you've got until long after the seed is sown. We take it for granted that people will beget people-children; indeed, we'd be a bit surprised if women regularly, or even occasionally (the *National Enquirer* notwithstanding) gave birth to brussels sprouts. And so, all that we seem to see among our own children is their unpredictability and the individuality of our own species: her father's eyes, his mother's smile, grandpa's hair, etc. We hardly ever comment on how remarkable it is that nearly all of us are born with two eyes and one nose.

But gardens are reliable, and within the same variety, each plant is pretty much the same. You can count on carrot seeds begetting carrots and brussels sprouts, brussels sprouts. Period.

It is also reassuring for the impatient *doers* among us just to see that things which happen slowly, even so slowly that we cannot see them happening, nonetheless *do* take place. It calls to mind the old story of the farmer who picked up a newborn calf and did so every day, until eventually he was able to pick it up when it had become a two thousand-pound bull. If this sounds like a lot of bull to you, you're right. The moral of the Myth of the Farmer and the Bull Calf is that small changes are nonetheless real, and they add up. Similarly, the gradual, imperceptible changes in growth of a plant add up to a full, plentiful garden.

To my chagrin, however, I have never actually been able to see something grow, even bamboo, which reportedly can extend itself a foot or more per day, or pole beans, which greedily climb up a six-foot fence in two weeks. But changes can be seen: a whole new crop of parsley, obediently poking its hopeful little heads out of the ground one cool and misty morning, in near-perfect synchrony, giving structure and substance to a patch of ground from which nothing could be seen the night before. You might not believe that your crop of peas will require literally dozens of strings to hold itself upright, as well as a solid structure to bear a weight of perhaps ten pounds per square foot. But all I am saying is give peas a chance.[10]

In some cases, the speed of a growing garden can be astonishing. Asparagus spears are ready for harvesting, for example, just two days or so after first poking their pushy little phalluses above

10. Incidentally, the word "pea" is an American corruption of the original English word "pease," which was intended to be singular, as in "pease porridge hot . . . " It sounded plural to the Yankee ear, however, and so the artificial singularity "pea" was created.

ground.[11] And I will swear that once, in a large field in upstate New York, I actually heard the corn growing: a restless, rustling, sighing, and swishing sort of moaning and groaning sound, even though the stalks stood unmoving in the still wind under the withering, midsummer heat.

Similarly, there is reassurance in the fact of growth, especially when—unlike our own growth, for example—the changes are rapid enough that they can easily be perceived in a reasonable time span. The effect is more dramatic when growing crops from seed than when using starts. Starts are OK, mind you, but the result is largely more of the same—instant garden—whereas with seeds, the outcome is qualitatively different, something that is literally new under the sun. Lettuce leaves are nothing like lettuce seeds, nor are radishes like radish seeds . . . although admittedly corn kernels are very like corn seeds, peas like peas, and beans like beans. Even with such resemblances, it remains true that the enormity of a lush, green plant represents a dramatic transition from the dry and shriveled embryo, something akin to magic.

Equally magic, of course, is when garden life runs its course and the plant turns to its own reproduction. And how strange it is that we use disparaging words for the process: going to seed, looking a bit seedy, and so forth, because the ability to make seed is a sign of health, a time of fruition, of ripeness and fulfillment.

If seed-making is unfairly disparaged, the process of starting plants indoors may well be unduly prettified. There is something a bit comical in the procedures by which indoor seed sproutings are supposed to be introduced to the out-of-doors. Getting started inside, they are softies, so they must be "hardened," a bit like the city slicker going off to boot camp. First, you take them out for a brief walk, but not too long, of course. It might upset them. Then, the toughening continues as you leave them for a whole afternoon, all on their own. (It's all right to peek, but only through the window; if they know you're watching, it might make them nervous, poor dears, which, of course, would spoil everything.) Finally, the great

11. Unknown to many nongardeners, incidentally, the fat, juicy spears are preferable to the thin ones, which tend to be dry and stringy. The former have grown more quickly, and more happily, than the latter. Also, did you know that a healthy asparagus plant can live a century or more?

day arrives when the little darlings are ready to spend the whole night, by themselves!

Admittedly, plants lack something as companions, whether they started as starts or seeds, inside or out. They are not good conversationalists, although they are good listeners. But let's be honest: it would probably be difficult to work up a meaningful relationship with a broccoli stalk, even a loquacious one. In fact, as my favorite gardening authority concurs, the entire cabbage family is altogether humorless: "Try to work up a smile communing with a Danish ballhead cabbage, or a stalk of brussels sprouts. It's just not there. A tomato in a relaxed mood can crack you up, and even the stolid potatoes are fundamentally good-humored. By contrast, the inherently ridiculous kohlrabi is too earnest and takes itself too seriously ever to entertain comedy."[12] Then again, comedy isn't everything. What about empathy? And those old-fashioned virtues of perseverance, friendship, punctuality, and generosity.

Gardening not only provides us with the miracle of change and growth, as well as the sharing of private lives, it also gives roots, not only to the plants, but to the gardeners. It is *grounding*, in the literal sense of that overused and trendy word. A garden gets you in touch with what Robert Service called the "earth's clean dirt." (A green thumb is, in fact, a black thumb.) And it gives intimate acquaintance, in this time of mega-trends and supercomputers, with age-old basic peasant tools, unchanged by the centuries: shovel, hoe, rake, and, uh, well, Roto-tiller.

The gardener necessarily becomes oriented, and not only to the dirt and the sun, and has a unique compass-clarity. There is a basic directionality to life, which impresses itself upon the keeper of a garden: bright, southern exposures versus dark northern; whether your land catches the late afternoon sun via a slightly western slope as opposed to an eastern bias, which inclines toward the relatively cooler, morning sun; whether the land is tilted just a bit and drains, or is saucerlike, and marshy. There is little else in modern life that generates such a fundamental awareness of place. Do you park your car facing east or west? What about your mailbox? Does it face north? Does it matter? And is your kitchen stove oriented southwest to northeast, or northwest to southeast, or what? Does it

12. Adams, *Epicurean*

matter to your living-room sofa whether it points into the prevailing winds or nestles comfortably in their lee? Outside in the garden, by contrast, these are matters of consequence.

Finally, gardens are deeply reassuring, simply by virtue of their persistence and continuity. They tell us that there is pattern, predictable flow, reliability in life. Even Ecclesiastes, normally so cynical, takes comfort from the vegetables' time clock: "To everything there is a season and a time for every purpose under heaven . . . a time to plant, and a time to pluck up what is planted." Thereby, a certain tension is removed from the immediate present, making it all vanity, perhaps, but also diminishing the anxiety that maybe our lives are adrift after all, without a rudder, free-falling in a universe of uncharted particularities, demanding extraordinary and unimagined responses . . . of which we know ourselves to be incapable. Without a garden, many of us might be reduced to whooping and chanting, banging drums and making desperate sacrifices, lest winter threaten to last forever.

But I know better. I know that summer, for instance, will follow spring, because the seeds I have planted will yet sprout, grow, and make fruit. And I know that autumn will follow summer, because after my garden has produced (or failed*), I know that it will withe begin to rustle with the desiccation of old age. And I know that winter will follow autumn, because there is nothing more to be harvested and the land and its products are ready for sleep and for death. Most important of all, I know—deep in my bones I know—that winter at last will end and spring will come, because my garden is waiting.

Horseback Riding

In Search of Equine-imity

The experts seem to agree that the dog was our first domesticated animal. Maybe so, but the horse couldn't have been very far behind. We are also told that the dog is "man's best friend," and in fact, some of my best friends have been dogs. Certainly, most horses do not beg, roll over on command, or retrieve the morning paper, not to mention curl up on one's lap. But to some extent, friendship is as friendship does, and horses have almost certainly done more for people than any other animal.

Nothing in the twentieth century has approached the horse in undergoing so dramatic a transition from necessity to luxury. It is almost impossible for the modern American—whether equestrian or not—to appreciate the extent to which *Equus caballus* throughout history was entwined with *Homo sapiens*. Consider: not very long ago, the place now occupied by automobiles ("horseless carriages"), airplanes, tractors, railroads (the "iron horse"), jeeps, armored tanks, and diesel turbines was filled by horses. Even today, mobile army units are referred to as "cavalry," and the main transportation union is known as the "Teamsters," testimony to the days when teams of horses, not tractor-trailers, were driven. (The Teamsters union logo still prominently features two horses.)

Today, famous and successful racehorses are likely to be the only ones known individually to the public: Secretariat, Native Dancer,

Bold Ruler, Phar Lap. But not long ago, when horses were indispensable to getting around, they were closely associated with their
riders and almost as renowned. We are told that the great war-
horse, Bucephalus, could only be ridden by Alexander the Great.
And during the Civil War, General Grant's black charger, Cincin-
nati, was second in fame only to Robert E. Lee's grey gelding,
Traveler. The only survivor of Custer's last stand in 1876 was Co-
manche, a cavalry horse, whom nobody blamed for the defeat. As
recently as the Korean War, a small mare named Reckless carried
ammunition for a U.S. Marine platoon, earning a medal for bravery
under fire, as well as a battlefield promotion to sergeant. Perhaps
the most excessively praised and pampered horse, however, was
Incitatus, beloved of the depraved Roman emperor Caligula. Incitatus was made a priest and consul around 40 A.D., he drank wine
from a golden pail and was fed from an ivory manger.

In one of the more questionable suggestions in his otherwise
excellent book, *The Dragons of Eden,* Carl Sagan proposed that
perhaps the recurrent human ambivalence toward dragons—aver-
sion yet fascination—derives from a kind of dim, racial memory
that harkens back to a world made dangerous by dinosaurs. More
likely, if we carry any primitive, deep-seated animal image, it is an
appreciation of our relationship to, and dependence upon, the
horse.[1] Our bifurcated anatomy doubtless evolved as a means of
walking upright and freeing our hands for other, nonlocomotory
duties . . . and not all the better to bestride a horse. Similarly, the
long, broad back of the horse evolved for its own good reasons (to
keep the front and rear legs together?) and not to provide people
with a place to sit. And the toothless part of the horse's mouth
known as the diastema, that peculiar empty space between the
incisors up front and the molars in back, was not specifically designed to provide us with a place to put the bit (the part of the
horse's bridle that goes, conveniently, in its mouth). But for several
thousands of years, people have been chomping at the bit to be
closely associated with these animals. And the fit between horse

---

1. Some horse devotees—notably novelist Anne McCaffrey and my wife and
    daughters—see a similarity between horses and dragons, not only in their
    size and impressive temperament, but also in the bony ridges around the
    eyes. These days, most of us are unlikely to have a personal dragon; it is more
    feasible to have a horse.

and person, both physical and behavioral, is extraordinary.

If our racial memory of large reptiles is negative, our relationship with horses is positive in the extreme. The basic principle of evolution by natural selection tells us that, among all species, traits conferring success upon individuals have been more likely to be passed on to succeeding generations. Hence, we might expect evolution to have favored those among us who related well to our equine cousins, because for thousands of years, success has shined on whoever managed to forge good relationships with the horse. The horse has given us equine-imity.

Or, as an anonymous rhymester pointed out:

> Look over the struggle for freedom.
> Trace your present day strength to its source.
> You'll find that man's pathway to glory
> Is strewn with the bones of a horse.

In France today, this jingle has some truth: specialized butcher shops, called "Chevalines," sell horsemeat for human consumption. And in America, the bones of horses are still strewn about dog-food packing plants and glue factories. But for many of the rest of us, there remains something special about horses, both the image and the reality. Whether because horses pulled and carried us on our pathway to glory, or simply because of admiration for their grace, speed, strength, and nobility, or because of a deep-seated yearning to absorb some of the warmth and power of a large, strong, and benevolent fellow-mammal, horses exert a profound pull on the human psyche.

Whereas horses were at one time primarily creatures of utility, today—at least in the United States—they are kept overwhelmingly for pleasure. Of the eight top states in a recent horse census, California (number one in human population) is the leader, and populous New York and Illinois are numbers three and four. Only then is Texas (number two) joined by two more reliable cowboy states, Oklahoma and Montana. Then come Missouri and Kentucky, home of racehorses and immense breeding farms. Horses, in short, are found where there are people, and money, and not where there are horsey jobs to be done. (If the order of horse population by states is a bit surprising, that of nations is even more so: first Brazil, followed by the United States, and then, in turn, China, the USSR, Mexico, Argentina, Mongolia, Poland, Ethiopia, and Yugoslavia.)

Some people, to be sure, are afraid of horses. And that is appropriate, since one thousand pounds and more of muscle and bone, moving upwards of thirty mph and supercharged by wind and hormones, can be a potent force. Human beings are not the only creatures who sometimes feel their oats, and the speed and power of a horse is—to use that appropriate but recently overworked adjective—awesome. Judged by the number of fatalities per thousand participants, horse racing is the most dangerous human sport, exceeding parachute jumping or mountain climbing for this dubious distinction. And even if one isn't racing—and, in fact, very few people actually ride as jockeys—the potential for horse-caused injury is real. People can be kicked, or bitten, or crushed under a falling animal. More likely, they might fall off a horse (much easier than falling off a barstool, since the horse actually moves whereas to the drunk, the barstool only appears to do so), or be thrown off by an animal who bucks or rears up suddenly on its hind legs.

Despite these risks, however, there is a special joy to be found in a horse who is healthy and sturdy, eager to travel, oblivious to your weight. Aside from the historical tug of the man-horse connection, speed alone is a turn-on. So is the sense of animate strength, coiled and stored, ready to be expended at the rider's behest: flaring nostrils, a snort and a whinny, and rippling muscles ready to go. So, also, is the lordly position of height: a horse's back permits a better view, and a more dominant one, than a standing person. And moving through the world astride a horse is to experience a very special trip, not unlike a flying carpet or mobile throne. It was his horse, Al Borak, that according to Islamic legend carried Mohammed to the seventh heaven, and many people make a similar journey today.

There is more to it, though. The horse-rider relationship is intimate, not at all like that of vehicle-passenger, perhaps because it is a true *relationship*, with responses and sensitivities emanating from the horse no less than from the rider. Perhaps a better image is the centaur, the mythic creature of the ancient Greeks, with body of horse and torso of man (or woman). When things go right, the human brain is magically transplanted, onto a large, sleeker, and immensely more powerful quadruipedal body, in a partnership of tenuous domination and more-than-metaphoric extension of the self.

As Swinburne described it:

> The first good steed his knees bestrode
> The first wild sound of songs that flowed,
> Through ears that thrilled and heart that glowed,
> Fulfilled his day with joy.

* * *

People who do it don't call it horseback riding, rather, just "riding." The presumption is that equestrians are unlikely to go motorcycle riding, or riding the rails, for example. So from here on, riding it'll be.

But "riding" alone isn't sufficient. The Eskimos, for example, are said to have eleven distinct words for "snow," distinguishing between hard snow, dry and powdery snow, wet slushy snow, cornlike snow, sugary snow, etc. Similarly, the Bedouin have more than one hundred words for camel. People are splitters—using many different words to make fine verbal discriminations when it comes to anything that is particularly important to them—and lumpers, combining concepts into a relatively small number of terms, with things that they don't know very well or care very much about.

When it comes to riding, a similar pattern applies. To the unmounted, riding is riding: the crucial difference is between equestrian and pedestrian. But to the initiated, there are many different kinds of riding, each as different from the other as powder snow or slush to the Eskimo. In the United States, the most important distinction is between Western riding, as done by the traditional American cowboy, and English riding, associated (at least in the American mind) with the British tradition of horsemanship. In fact, so-called English riding has a long and substantial continental tradition, notably in central Europe where it includes the incongruously named Spanish Riding School of Vienna, with a history going back many hundreds of years. Both forms of riding derive from a practical, working tradition: Western, from cattle management, and English, from warhorses and the cavalry.

Western riding generally appears more relaxed. It is used for trail rides, working cattle in certain areas, and for shows, such as rodeos. English riding is preferred for jumping, for formal equestrian events such as the Olympics, and for the precise, gymnastic activity known as dressage.

It is easy to tell English from Western riders. First, the saddles: Western saddles tend to be large, heavy, often elaborately ornamented with leather carvings and sometimes jingling silver doodads. There is a handy structure in front, known as the pommel, or horn, originally intended for attaching a lasso, the other end of which is to have been circled around the neck of a cow. These days, the Western pommel comes in handy as a place to rest one's hands, as something to hang onto for dear life, and as something to jab you in the belly if you forget that Western saddles are not designed for jumping and attempt to take your steed over anything larger than a small log. All saddles are attached to the horse by a band that goes under it, just behind the front legs. In Western saddles, it is known as a "cinch" and is tied by maneuvering a leather strap in a manner vaguely resembling a necktie but much more practical. By contrast, the slim, trim English "girth" is fastened with a buckle not unlike a man's belt.

The English saddle is as light, spare, and sleek as the Western is heavy and gaudy. If the Western saddle seems to trace its ancestry back to an overstuffed sofa, the English saddle seems derived from a banana peel, designed to facilitate sliding the rider onto the ground. English riding uses a smaller, more gentle bit; Western, one that has more leverage and is more severe on the horse's mouth. English riding involves using two hands on the reins: pull lightly on the left one, and the horse goes left, and vice versa. The Western rider, by contrast, holds both reins in one hand, thereby (at least when the tradition developed) leaving the other one free to throw a lasso, smoke a cigarette, or—if a beginner— hang onto the horn. Western horses are trained to "neck rein," which means that they respond to the touch of the reins on the back of their neck. Holding the reins like an ice-cream cone, just above and in front of the horn, the Western rider turns his or her horse to the left by moving his hand to the left, as one might turn an airplane with a joy stick.

English and Western clothing differ as well. Formal English attire includes knee-high black leather boots, tight breeches, a riding coat that looks like a dark blazer, and—if jumping—a small, black, tight-fitting hard hat with a cute little brim. Blue jeans are de rigueur for the Western rider; also a set of "chaps," leather pant-legs worn over one's jeans and useful as protection against being rubbed by brush or cactus. English riders use, at most, small and rather inoffensive spurs; the Western rider, by contrast, may sport those spurs that jingle, jangle, jingle. And finally, the Western rider needs a bright-colored shirt, and of course, a cowboy hat. (Which, as you may have noticed from Western movies, never falls of.)

Ready to ride, your encounter with tradition begins immediately. A horse expects its rider to mount from its—the horse's—left side. (Some animals, notably those used for trail riding in the mountains, for whom mounting from either side may be a necessity, are trained to accept a rider from the right or the left; others may get very upset if approached on the "off" side.) Left-sided mounting apparently derives from military riding, since cavalry officers and medieval knights, being primarily right-handed, used to wear their swords on their left hip. It may be awkward at least, fatal at worst, to swing a leg-plus-sword up into the air and over a horse's back. Accordingly, horses were always mounted from the left, so the relatively unencumbered right leg did most of the moving.

So left foot in the stirrup, right leg up and over the horse. Then sit down and find the other stirrup. Next usually comes a pat on the neck, perhaps in gratitude for not running away, or just for holding up your weight and not collapsing underneath it. Horses have four natural ways of moving, or gaits: walk, trot, canter, and gallop. By judicious use of so-called natural "aids," consisting of voice, legs, seat, and hands, a moderately well-trained horse can be persuaded to move forward in one gait or another, and to change back and forth. The hands on the reins are used to slow the horse, and to indicate direction, and leg pressure also signals whether to go right or left: the horse moves away from pressure, going right in response to a left leg pressing its flank, and vice versa. Well-trained horses also respond very sensitively to the tension or relaxation in the rider's body and to extraordinarily small shifts of position. (There is also the issue of "bend." A horse is not like a hook-and-ladder truck; it should bend around curves, not tilt.)

Compare a horse and an automobile. Automobiles have differ-

ent gears, just as horses have different gaits. But there is no quali-
tative difference between, say, first and second gear; a car simply
goes faster, but in the same basic way, all four wheels rolling in the
same pattern. A horse's gaits, by contrast, are distinctly different
ways of moving, so that when a horse changes from one to the
other, it is really "shifting gears," qualitatively, as compared to the
pallid version found in your family car.

In walking, the slowest, each leg moves separately. The other
three legs remain on the ground, and so, the animal swings along
with an easy, 1-2-3-4 rhythm.

When trotting, diagonal opposites move simultaneously—right
front along with left rear, and vice versa—so that the rhythm is 1-2,
1-2. Trotting is faster than walking, and for the rider, considerably
more up-and-down. On a Western horse, the rider's job is simply
to sit in the large, soft, upholstered saddle. (Sitting tall is less useful
than sitting deep.) English riding, by contrast, employs a faster
(more "forward") trot, and whereas good riders are expected to be
proficient at doing a sitting trot, the classic way to ride a trot is to
"post"—about which, more later.

The canter is faster yet. First, a rear leg strikes the ground, then
the other rear plus the diagonal front leg at the same time, followed by the other front leg and a leap through empty space: a
rhythm of 1-2-3, followed by an airborne pause. Whenever a horse
canters, it takes either a left or right "lead," depending on which
front foot begins the sequence.

The classic riding music—at least for Americans who grew up
during the 1950s—is probably the *William Tell Overture*, better
known as the Lone Ranger's theme song: Ta-da-dum, ta-da-dum,
ta-da-dum, dum, dum, etc. A perfect, three-beat canter if ever
there was one. Beginners are inclined to think of a canter as intimidating, simply because it is generally faster than a trot, and because of the period of midair suspense. But in fact, most people are
nothing less than elated by their first canter, which is likely to feel
smooth and undulating, like floating on air.

Finally, there is the gallop, fastest of the four gaits. It is essentially an extended canter resulting in a four-beat rhythm, but different from the walk in that, like the canter, a galloping horse can
take left or right leads, and always has a period of complete suspension in the air. When galloping, the middle diagonal beat of a

canter is extended to two distinct beats because at high speed, the rear foot hits just a fraction of a second before the diagonal front foot.

Horses are immensely powerful creatures, and when cantering, this power surges up from the animal's muscular hind end, passing in a forceful wave through the seat of the rider. The trick, then, to cantering comfortably, is not to master that ripple of power but rather to *ride* it, like a surfer buoyed on the crest of a wave. But unlike the surfboard rider, who cannot change the wave on which he rides, the horse rider is not just on top of something, he or she is interacting with it. The rider's pelvis has to loosen up, so that the human bottom slides forward and back in the saddle, in rhythmic harmony with the movement of the horse. You can slow down a horse by leaning back and working into a more gradual rhythm or speed up by moving forward and becoming more urgent. Either way, the cantering rider squeezes force, power, and smoothness out of his horse, as though he or she was astride a giant four-footed tube of toothpaste.

As to galloping, few things match the sheer joy (and sometimes, terror) of abandoning oneself to an all-out burst of full speed ahead. Robert Browning wrote about it, in "How They Brought the Good News from Ghent to Aix," a poem that captures the sensation of galloping, not only through its words, but also its rhythm:

I sprang to the stirrup, and Joris, and he;
I galloped, Dirck galloped, we galloped all three;
"Good speed!" cried the watch, as the gate-bolts withdrew.
"Speed!" echoed the wall to us galloping through;
Behind shut the postern, The lights sank to rest,
And into the moonlight we galloped abreast

Walking is the other side of the coin, the original clippety-clop, clippety-clop. Ferdinand Grofe's musical "Grand Canyon Suite" probably captures the singsong, swinging gait of a walking horse better than words ever could. The gentle back-and-forth swaying is not unlike a person's walk, easy and relaxing. Maybe it is "vestibular stimulation," activating to the fluid-filled channels of the inner ear and much appreciated by infants, who for centuries have been rocked in their cradles or otherwise rhythmically jostled into complacency. Or maybe it is the grateful adult recognition that progress is being made (horse and rider are getting somewhere), but gently and safely. In any event, just as children are often soothed by regular swinging in cradle, teeter-totter, or swing, being astride a walking horse offers surcease to the adult psyche. "Nothing is so good for the inside of a person," goes the saying, "as the outside of a horse."

Or in Dryden's words:

> "Better to hunt in fields for health unbought
> Than fee the doctor for a nauseous draught."

* * *

On the other hand, the painful aspects of riding are legendary. The human leg is designed to proceed directly from the hip to the ground, not to curl around a horse's flanks. Even ten minutes on horseback can produce substantial pain—not so much immediately, as the next day (and sometimes for days after that)—as hip joints are stretched beyond their normal experience. And an hour or so: true agony. With time, however, the tendons and ligaments become stretched a bit and discomfort is gone. But for some, the stretching process is so miserable that riding careers are short-circuited without ever achieving the nirvana of being adequately "stretched out."

There is yet another source of pain, this time in the bottom rather than the hips. The classic, sore rear end of a beginning rider is typically caused by trotting, specifically the difficult experience of having one's bottom and the horse's back being out of synchrony—the horse going up when the rider comes down—so that the two slam into each other with a regularity that is depressing and painful for both. There are two solutions: learn to absorb the vertical movements in legs, ankles, and seat—that is to say, do a "sitting trot"—or raise your body in tune with the rising of the horse's back. This is done by standing up slightly in the stirrups, in regular rhythm, an activity known as "posting." While posting, a rider appears to be doing miniature deep knee bends. Although it is possible to post in a Western saddle, mobility is restricted by the horn as well as the width of the saddle, and in fact, Western horses are taught to do a very slow trot, known as a "jog," which generally makes posting unnecessary. They also typically learn a delightfully slow, rocking horse canter, known as a "lope." (You know you are loping, it is said, when horse and rider can circle round and round, all afternoon, never leaving the shade of the same oak tree.)

It may also seem that Western riding is inexorably slow and relaxed; this impression is vigorously disabused, however, at a Western show with barrel racing or other speed events, when horse and rider accelerate from a stop to forty miles per hour within a few seconds, in a phenomenal surge of muscle and nerve, leaving clouds of dust that could as well be smoke.

Even when just plain old riding along, across a meadow or following a trail, it is necessary to keep your wits about you, a need that can be deceptive. Thus, when a horse is walking quietly along a trail, the experience is a bit like an exaggerated form of "cruise control" in an automobile, with the addition that the animal—unlike the most modern car—has a self-steering mechanism. A relaxed rider moseying along on a relaxed horse can turn around, look this way or that, even throw a leg across the saddle.

But the deception lies in the fact that things can happen, and quickly, because a horse—unlike a car—interacts with its environment, sometimes in unpredictable ways. Horses are constantly sniffing, listening, and looking, whether standing still, walking, trotting, or cantering. The ears rotate almost completely around, like mobile radar installations, and the nostrils bring in great drafts of air, which are carefully screened for information-packed molecules. Sensing something new or frightening (the two are almost synonymous for animals that historically have been prey and not predator), horses are likely to respond to it, often in a flash . . . and they constantly seem to be sensing one thing or another. The eyes of a horse are larger than the eyes of any other terrestrial animal with the exception of the ostrich, and these eyes, located on each side of the head, move independently, like a chameleon. A horse's vision makes it appear to it that any objects moving from the side or back of the head are faster than they really are. As a result, horses may "shy" at the slightest movement—a butterfly, a falling leaf, the sudden darting of a squirrel or bird. With time and experience, a nervous, flighty animal will generally become less perturbable and more reliable, but unlike an automobile, which can be counted on to keep going in the direction it is pointed, a horse is a highly sensitive living creature, fine-tuned, and never entirely reliable or safe . . . or boring.

Horses can rear up, bite, or kick, and they are likely to do any of these when fighting with another horse. But for eons, they have had one consistent and overwhelming response to danger: running. They are superbly engineered for it, their legs having lost the capacity for lateral flexion, so that in today's model they bend only front and back. They have a unique structure, the so-called cannon bone just above the hoof, which absorbs the pressure of a landing, flexes, and then like a pogo stick, transmits the accumulated energy directly to the next stride.

Horses are so comfortable standing up that they often sleep this way and are also permanently "on their toes," standing like hyperextended ballet dancers on an elongated central digit. Hot-blooded, energetic horses are indeed the prima ballerinas of the animal world, and like their human equivalents, they can be high strung, demanding, and rather unpredictable. On occasion, they can "run away" with a beginner or even an experienced rider.

To some extent, this can occur simply because horses like to run and will do so if given half an opportunity. In addition, if frightened or otherwise excited, and then not adequately restrained by a competent rider, they can give themselves up to their fundamental escape response, the same behavior that has repeatedly saved hundreds of thousands of their ancestors, living freely in the plains and prairies of the Old and New Worlds. Many people, unfortunately, have their sole riding experience on a broken-down, tired nag, who is reluctant to exert him or herself for an inexperienced dude and who wants only to get back for the next feeding. (Toward the end of the ride, returning to the barn, the most decrepit and low-energy horse may take off like a racing thoroughbred.) Or alternatively, they may find themselves astride an equine tornado, raring to go and likely to do so. Matching the horse's temperament to the rider's capacity is no less important than matching the right key to a lock.

Although many riders may yearn for a "push-button" horse, dependable and reliable, the truth is that part of the mystique of horsemanship derives from the fact that each animal brings a different temperament to a ride, and the chemistry of rider and horse is crucial to success. It is well known that horses can detect the mood and level of confidence (no less than the competence) of a rider. Accordingly, conventional wisdom is right: it is important to let the animal know who is in charge.

It is also important to send the right "vibes" of encouragement. Nowhere is this more true than in jumping. Not all horses are jumpers. Some excel in "flat work" only and wouldn't consider leaving the ground in a serious way. Others simply love to leap over obstacles. For the rider, the sensation is almost indescribable, a bit like straddling a short-range rocket ship. But once again, communication between horse and rider is absolutely crucial. Even a seemingly "push-button" horse will not follow instructions unless these are given clearly and unambiguously, especially in the case of jumping. For a twelve-hundred-pound animal to launch itself several feet above the ground, carrying an adult human being on its back, there must be no doubts, hesitations, or failures of coordination and communication. Successful jumping involves more than pointing your horse toward an obstacle and then holding on, hoping for the best; it is necessary to maintain a mental image of success and then to act on it. The rider must be totally committed to what is about to happen, and some of the oldest advice to would-be jumpers remains valid today: "Throw your heart over the jump first." Point your horse in the right direction, make it clear that this is what you have in mind, stand up slightly in the stirrups, bend a bit at the hip toward the horse's neck, and let the force of the horse be with you.

There is a paradox here. To help the horse over the jump, a rider must move forward, in a sense transferring his weight in the direction the horse is expected to go. At the same time, by leaning forward, one is terribly vulnerable to Newton's First Law of Motion: once moving, thing tend to keep going that way. If the horse stops short ("refuses") or turns aside at the last moment ("runs out"), the body of the forward-leaning rider is likely to follow his or her heart and go flying obediently over the jump, while leaving the horse behind. To lean back is to make success unlikely; to lean forward is to make failure dangerous. True, the animal does most of the actual physical work, but the rider, interacting intimately with the horse and often staking his or her safety on the coordination of person and beast, is indispensable; indeed, the two are inseparable.

In most sports, the more you learn, the more you can do. A downhill skier begins perhaps with a snowplow turn, then progresses through simple stem turns to parallel turns, whereupon he or she can eventually master steep runs, carve impressive patterns in deep powder snow, and so forth. The same is true, to some extent, in riding: experienced, athletic riders can gallop without anxiety, trot for hours without the slightest soreness, direct their horses over jumps, or put on an elaborate dressage exhibition. But of course the rider is doing plenty. In fact, the less he or she appears to be doing, the more is actually being done. Just as the expert skier seems to move effortlessly, the expert rider helps his or her horse to move in any number of ways, without seeming to do anything at all.

The general rule holds for most types of riding: the less movement by the rider, the better. This is particularly true for dressage. To the uninitiated, watching an expert ride a dressage "test" is about as exciting as watching your faucet drip. To the cognoscenti, however, it is more like witnessing a ballet performance or tai chi: horse and rider go through a demanding and rigidly preset routine of movements, which look effortless in proportion as years of time, effort, and skill are in fact invested. It takes ten or more years of daily, diligent work to train a dressage horse-and-rider team, and even then, most who try will never achieve real distinction.

The well-trained dressage horse also has gone through a body-building course. Normally, about two-thirds of a horse's power comes from its front legs. The dressage horse, by contrast, has developed enormous strength and power in its rear, which frees the front end for a wide range of precise and delicate movements. And when the animal is "on the bit," responding precisely and smoothly, keenly sensitive to the rider's every movement, a centaur has been born.

Anyone who has admired horses can relate to Shakespeare's suggestion, in *Henry V*, "Think, when we talk of horses, that you see them printing their proud hoofs in the receiving earth." But anyone who has ridden them understands that a horse in a pasture or moving over the "receiving earth," beautiful as it may be, is only half of the equation.

Riding is a sensory extravaganza. There is the sensation of movement, from the swinging pace of a walk to the sharp, staccato
bounce of a trot, to the rocking horse float of a canter. There is the
compelling invasion of sound, from the wild, blood-tingling neigh
of one great animal calling another, the warming and cheery deep-
throated burble when they ask to be fed, the viscerally pleasing
rhythm of the walk, or the airy spring of the canter as the hooves of
the horses tattoo the ground in their ancient drumbeat pattern.
Riders add to the sound, loudly kissing the air to encourage speed,
speaking softly to reassure a nervous mount, or lightly trotting the
tongue in suction against the roof of the mouth.

But most of all, riding has its smells. Of all senses, smell is our
oldest the most primitive gateway into our brains. Although human olfaction is relatively feeble compared to that of our mammalian cousins, odors may well provide the most direct entry into our
unthinking minds. The smells of riding are abundant, rich, "funky,"
and oh so organic, from the leather of saddle, bridle, and boots, to
the clean aroma of alfalfa or even (more intense yet) timothy or
grass hay, to the nutty flavor of oats and the richness of "sweet
feed," a mixture of seeds and corn, bound together with molasses.

The horses themselves are also aromatic. In addition to periodically opening the sluiceways and releasing veritable Niagaras of
pungent urine, horses are manure factories, making about thirty
pounds of it every day. To be around horses is to be around horse
manure; you can't have one without the other . . . lots of the other.
Because of something extraordinary in their neurological and muscular wiring systems, horses are able to defecate while walking,
trotting, or cantering, with complete indifference and without bat-
ting an eye or missing a stride. So the south end of a horse heading
north is likely to introduce a rider to the seamier side of life's meta-
bolic processes.

Fortunately, however, horse manure is about as innocuous as
such a substance can be; some of us even think it smells good, a bit
like lapsang souchong tea. (Although unfortunately, not at all like
jasmine or orange pekoe.) In this respect, vegetarian animals have
it all over their carnivorous cousins. It would be very difficult, by
contrast, to be nearly as sanguine about the by-products of one-
thousand-pound dogs, or cats, or people. On the other hand, when
automobiles were first introduced just after the turn of the century,

they were heartily supported by the environmentalists of the day, who rejoiced in the fact that horseless carriages would eliminate that disgraceful pollution problem: hundreds of tons of horse manure on city streets.

Finally, there is sweat. Unlike dogs, which do not perspire through their skin, but rather regulate their body temperature by dripping liquid from their drooling mouths and lolling tongues, horses—like people—are abundantly equipped with sweat glands throughout their bodies. When a horse has been running hard and long, it gets wet, often so wet that its perspiration actually appears to foam along its chest and flanks. We say that it has become "lathered." And in the process, horse and rider have come to share the warmth and the odor of exertion and of life itself.

But contact with reality isn't all that *Equus caballus* provides. Horses are also meant for fantasies. The unicorn has long been emblematic of that which is mysterious, exquisitely beautiful, long sought-after, yet too perfect and hence, impossible. The flying horse, Pegasus, symbolized a special kind of unattainable speed and grace, and the centaur has long represented strength and virility, unmatched by anything in this all-too-real, all-too-imperfect world. But in their mixture of ethereal beauty and earthy body, real live horses go a long way toward making certain fantasies come alive.

I confess to a bias in favor of natural scenes, those in which the obvious presence of human beings is minimized, or better yet, absent altogether. Yet there are a limited number of cases in which even the most pastoral, unspoiled landscape is aesthetically enhanced by a human touch: One is a sailboat cutting across a lake or inlet pulled along by white sail and gaily colored spinnaker; another is a horse and rider moving through a rolling, grassy meadow. At such times, fantasy and reality become one.

There are more than a hundred different breeds of horses, some of them dramatically different from each other. Small, bonsai breeds stand a mere two feet high at the shoulder and weigh only eighty pounds or so, whereas some of the massive draft horses—the Belgians, Percherons, Clydesdales and Shire horses—can be more than six feet at the shoulder, weighing twenty-five-hundred pounds. There is a curious symmetry in measuring the height of people and horses. In both cases, the human body has served as the historical referent: people are measured by feet (of which they have only two), and horses, by hands (of which they have none). A foot (twelve inches) was originally the length of a king's foot; and hand (four inches), derived from the width of someone's hand.

Generally, if the animal measures more than 14.2 hands (that is, 14 hands and two inches, or fifty eight inches) at the shoulder, it is considered a horse; less than that, a pony. Tall, massively muscled and heavily boned animals are generally preferred for competitive jumping and dressage. But size can easily be overvalued. Often, a small well-muscled horse is preferred by people who have to rely on them for a full day's work. The traditional "cow pony," for example, is often a pony indeed. And perhaps the highest compliment is for such a pony to be "handy," that is, small, smart, and agile. The quarterhorse, an American breed, is the classic cowboy's horse, bred for rapid acceleration—ostensibly running a quarter mile race even faster than a thoroughbred—and the instant maneuverability needed to cut out a single cow from a milling herd.

Another nice term, this time for jumpers, is "scopey." A horse is scopey if it is flexible, not just physically but conceptually as well, able to handle almost any kind of jump. How? In stride, of course.

The spotted Appaloosa is another traditional American breed, descended from animals introduced into the New World by the early Spanish explorers. Legend has it that they trace their ancestry from escapees among those horses that first accompanied the conquistadors. The truth, however, is a bit more pedestrian: Spanish missionaries, moving into today's Texas and California in the sixteenth century, brought horses with them, some of which escaped and prospered in the arid Southwest. The Plains Indians quickly became extraordinary horsemen and the association between people and horses prospered as well.

Early on, horses and people trod different paths. The forerunner of today's Kentucky Derby winner or great Clydesdale was a tiny creature known as Eohippus,[2] about the size of a small cat and with many toes on its splayed feet. It inhabited moist terrain, swamps, and marshes, and ate leaves and perhaps fruit. Then as its environ-

2. The modern, technical term has been changed, for some reason, to Hyracotherium, but I like Eohippus—literally, "drawn horse"—better.

ment dried up, certain descendants of little Eohippus were larger
in stature, better able to prosper on solid, desiccated prairies,
standing on a single massive toe, eating grass, and able to run like
hell.

The Arabs say that horses were God's gift to man. If so, that gift
may have been first accepted in the New World, although with a
grisly kind of gratitude. Thus, some anthropologists and paleontol-
ogists speculate that horses and certain other large hoofed mammals (like the rhinoceroslike titanotheres and elephantlike masto-
dons) were eventually hunted to extinction by the Stone Age
human inhabitants of North and South America. However, just as
primitive people used the Bering land bridge to migrate to the
Americas from Asia perhaps twenty thousand years ago, it appears
that horses had the good sense to go the other way and establish
themselves in sparsely populated Mongolia and Siberia, from
whence they ultimately gave rise to the modern animal, as well as a
living equine fossil, the unpronounceable Przewalski's horse
(*Equus przewalskii*), several species of African zebra (*Equus grevyi,
E. burchelli,* and *E. zebra*), various donkeys and asses (*Equus
asinus*), and the kiang or onager, also known—so help me—as the
half-ass, *Equus hemionus.*

In any event, we can safely assume that when horses were rein-
troduced into the New World by the Spanish explorers, the human
inhabitants had long forgotten God's gift. Perhaps this is why the
Incas are said to have feared and worshipped the conquistadors as
gods or, more accurately, centaurs.

Horse breeding has a long history, and—given the many different horse breeds now in existence—substantial success to its
credit. The renowned thoroughbreds are all descended from three
Arabian stallions (Darley Arabian, Godolphin Arabian, and Byerly
Turk by name) who were bred to local, European mares. Although
most of the time and money is directed toward breeding animals
for the racetrack, specialized stock have proliferated for pulling
wagons, rounding up cattle, and more recently, pleasure horses
including those for the show-ring. Welsh ponies were developed
for work in the cramped confines of Welsh mines. (Note: ponies
are not simply young horses; rather, they are distinct breeds, that
remain small. A young horse is a foal. If a male, it is a colt; if a
female, a filly.)

Different horses and, to some extent, different breeds, most assuredly have different personalities: quarter horses and Morgans
(another American breed, derived from a single stallion, owned by
one Justin Morgan) are relatively placid and reliable; thoroughbreds are high strung and especially unpredictable, etc.

It is all too easy to be misled by a horse's appearance. If you
can't tell a book by its cover, it is even more true that you cannot
tell a horse by its looks. There are specific traits considered desirable for different breeds: a small head and dished muzzle for Arabs, long Roman nose for American Saddlebreds, etc. Beyond this,
nearly every horse lover has a favorite color combination and others that seem perfectly despicable: chestnuts (all brown) versus
blacks, or whites, or grays, or strawberry roans, or bays (brown
with black mane and tail), or splotchy pintos, spotted Appaloosas
or golden Palominos with silver-white mane and tail. In fact, it is
easy to register a horse's appearance and, thus, easy to be misled.
It is much more difficult, and yet infinitely more important, to
assess its behavior. To my knowledge, there is no reliable correlation between color pattern and behavior in horses . . . no more
than among human beings.

Pick a car, any car. It doesn't require a degree in automotive
mechanics to predict quite well how it is likely to function: the
displacement of its engine—four, six, or eight cylinders—will suggest its power, top speed, and gas consumption; the condition of
the shock absorbers, plus overall weight and size will indicate
quite accurately whether the ride will be comfortable, and so
forth. On the other hand, pick a horse and you are far more likely
to be wrong. To some extent, to be sure, there is a correlation
between how a horse looks and what it is capable of doing: a broken-down old nag is unlikely to compare with a well-muscled thoroughbred in speed or endurance. But when it comes to horses,
looks can be mightily deceiving.

My current horse is rather small, about 14.2 hands, and thus, a
pony by some definitions. (I've always admired tall, graceful
steeds—16 hands and up.) He's more than a little swaybacked and
is blind in one eye. (Frankly, I prefer my mounts to have a
straighter back and the full complement of eyes.) He is stocky, with
heavy bones and thick legs. (I like the graceful, gracile shape of
Arabians.) And he is an Appaloosa, covered with spots. (I hate

spots.) But he goes when I want to go, jumps over anything I point him at, stops when I want to stop, doesn't buck or rear when a car honks or a dog comes running up barking or a snake crosses the trail, comes readily to be saddled, stands patiently when patience is called for, doesn't kick or bite—either other horses or me—and I wouldn't trade him for the Black Stallion himself.[3]

I learned to ride on an old white mare named Zip who had huge ears like a mule, a peculiarly twisted front foot, and two extraordinarily ugly pink eyes. I thought twice about riding her the first time, just because she looked so bizarre that I was sure everyone would laugh. But she was obedient yet eager, her trot was as smooth as her walk, and her canter was like riding on a cloud.

There may well be a special human talent that can identify a good horse from a bad, irrespective of aesthetic prejudice, but to my mind, real horse sense—in people—is the knowledge that among our equine cousins, beauty is as beauty does. Anything else is a horse of a different color.

The key to why riding feels so good to those who do it may also be the key to riding well: interaction. Even if they couldn't be ridden, horses would probably be admired just because they so beautifully embody strength and speed, on a scale to which humans can relate. After all, a whale is remarkably powerful and so—for its size—is an ant. But these aren't person-sized, and so, their accomplishments feel foreign and distant. Moreover, we can't directly experience their feats. But the extraordinary, astounding fact is that people can actually travel on the very backs of horses, somehow partaking of that embodiment of strength and speed, making it their own through the magical addition of obedience. This makes the prospect, and the creature, all the more compelling.

Clearly, this precious interaction is made easier if you have a "good" horse, but just as clearly, any horse—no matter how good—can be bad news for a bad rider and can even be made "bad" (or "sour") by prolonged bad riding. (Or sometimes, just by too much riding, even if it is adroitly done.) A horse is a distinct creature, separate from its human rider, and yet it is by transcending

3.   Shortly after writing this, my old friend went totally blind and has since been (literally) put out to pasture as a companion to racehorses.

that separateness and achieving a oneness of purpose that good riding is achieved as well as a feeling of unity with horse and with life more generally. Riding, then, is a process of exchange, an uneven exchange to be sure, since the horse is ultimately induced to reflect the rider's will and not vice versa. But once this is achieved, the rider also experiences the feeling—not entirely an illusion, either—that the horse *wants* to do precisely the same thing that the rider has in mind.

Like two lovers who are particularly warmed by the sense that the other knows his or her desires without their being spoken, it is uniquely gratifying to think "canter" or "trot" or "turn left here" and have the horse respond as though the animal was body to the rider's brain. At such times, riding can offer much the same gratification that comes from making love: the special excitement of feeling unity combined with differentness, of appreciating—even revelling—in the distinctness of another being while simultaneously feeling the boundaries of bodily isolation melting away.

But unlike human lovers, for whom ideally the building of love as well as the act of love itself is two-sided and entirely reciprocal, horse lovers have the opportunity and, indeed, the responsibility to guide and direct the interaction. Horses are relatively smart, as animals go, but the truth is that compared to people, they are woefully dumb. It is the trainer's job to bend that dumbness to human ways, and the rider's job to reinforce the animal's willing acquiescence. Writing about 400 B.C., the Greek soldier, historian, and essayist Xenophon gave us his "Treatise on Horsemanship," no less cogent now than two millennia ago. Xenophon very sensibly urged the rider to exert authority over the horse, but to make it a kind of gentle partnership, in which the sensibilities of the animal are respected and encouraged to grow in a direction compatible with the rider's desires:

> The hand must neither be held so strict as to confine and make the horse uneasy, nor so loosely as not to let him feel it. The moment he obeys and answers it, yield the bridle to him; this will take off the stress and relieve his mouth, and is in conformity with that maxim, which should never be forgot, which is to caress and reward him for whatever he does well. The moment that the rider perceives that the horse begins to place his head, to go lightly in the hand, and with ease and pleasure to himself, he should do nothing that is dis-

agreeable, but flatter and coax, suffer him to rest a while, and do all
he can to keep him in this happy temper. This will encourage and
prepare him for greater undertakings.

The rider, then, is asked to walk a delicate line in pursuit of the
ideal interaction with a horse. On the one hand, be The Boss, get
Your Way, and don't brook any revolution or independence of
spirit; after all, the horse may easily outweigh the rider by ten to
one and in strength by about the same ratio. But on the other hand,
effective interaction requires "flattery and coaxing," as Xenophon
put it, and also, a respect for the animal as the separate being that
it is.

It quickly becomes apparent to anyone who works with horses
that these are highly social creatures. Left to themselves, like the
wild mustangs of the American West, horses aggregate into herds,
typically groupings of mares associated with a single stallion. Even
after they are domesticated and saddle broken, today's horses still
feel a yearning for safety in numbers. They simply love to follow
one another, sometimes in a single file with the nose of each cozily
tucked into the butt of the next one in line. And other horses,
moving rapidly in any direction at all, are almost irresistible. Leave
several horses together for a few weeks or so, and they are likely to
become "herd-bound," after which they will cheerfully go anywhere so long as they are in each other's company. Should I pre-
sume to ride my horse and leave the others (my wife's mare and
my daughter's pony) behind, all hell is liable to break loose. The
mare gallops back and forth in her pasture, stopping only to paw
the ground or kick the fence; the pony neighs loudly and indig-
nantly; even my trusty steed, normally so dependable, is likely to
balk and toss his head as though to ask, "Do you really expect me
to go without my friends?"

Horses say a great deal with their faces, especially their ears,
and whenever the rider seeks to get a horse to do something
against his or her nature—like leaving a herd or walking through a
seemingly bottomless puddle—those ears are likely to speak eloquently. Ears back means the animal in unhappy, and flat against
the head means that something seriously nasty is being contem-
plated. Ears forward, on the other hand, says "All is well," and/or
"I am interested in what is going on." (I confess that I have been

tempted to short-circuit the animal's own likes and dislikes by modifying its expression of discontent rather than its cause; in short, I've tried pushing a recalcitrant horse's ears forward, in the hopes of putting it into a more receptive attitude. Nothing doing. If you want a happy horse, you have to interact with it—ask it to do something different or teach it to like what you ask—and not commandeer its body.)

People, of course, are creatures of habit. Only we rarely notice our own habitual tendencies, since these we take for granted. Riders, by contrast, cannot help noting the repetition-compulsion of their horses. It doesn't take more than three or four episodes of turning right at a particular intersection for most horses to insist on turning right at that point whenever given the opportunity. And if you find it irresistible to canter up a particularly inviting stretch of rolling meadow (cantering up a gentle incline is, in fact, especially pleasant because in such cases the horse tends to develop most of its propulsion from its hind legs, which imparts a particularly smooth and soft ride), the animal will almost certainly break into a canter whenever that meadow is encountered. The question then arises: who is more the slave of habit, the horse or the rider? For the former to break out, the latter must do so first and be strong willed about it. Turn left sometimes at the intersection; walk or trot up the meadow, whatever your preference, just don't canter all the time, or your horse will insist on doing the same.

And finally, no discussion—however brief—of horse behavior can be complete without at least mentioning the role of hormones, which, drop by drop, exercise such subtle influence on attitudes and inclinations. They are not overbearing tyrants, those extraordinarily potent yet unseen and often unappreciated squirts of chemical message; rather, they work behind the scenes, setting the stage, influencing overall tendencies and dispositions. A horse's hormones do not dictate its precise behavior, specifying "Do this" or "Don't do that," but an animal's hormonal state is nonetheless crucial in influencing its way of meeting the universe.

Anyone who doubts the effectiveness of hormones should meet, in turn, a stallion and then a gelding. The former is almost invariably feisty, hot tempered, high strung, and nearly uncontrollable when around a mare in heat. The latter is almost invariably laid back, easygoing, and little more interested in mares than in other geldings. Stallions are in fact prohibited from many horse shows and even from certain residential communities where mares and geldings are most welcome. To tell the truth, I have never met a stallion that I really liked.

If a young stallion is not gelded early enough in life, or if the job is done incompletely (a situation known, with more than a touch of testicular bias, as a "proud cut"), then even a gelding can be downright obnoxious. As to mares, they admittedly have a tendency—not surprisingly—to be a bit "mareish," which is to say, a bit headstrong or grumpy. And when in heat, they are particularly apt to be jumpy and unpredictable.

No surprise there either. If you had reason to think that fifteen hundred pounds of stallion might be lurking somewhere, huffing and puffing, and with his bulging, bloodshot, salacious eyes on you, you'd probably be kind of "mareish," too.

If wishes were horses, we are told, then beggars would ride. Joining them would be lots of other people, notably, preadolescent girls. At literally thousands of horse stables throughout the nation, young girls descend in droves every afternoon when school lets out. And for every child who actually gets to ride regularly—whether her own horse or someone else's—there are hundreds begging for the opportunity. Books about horses, from the near-infinite *Black Stallion* series to *National Velvet* and *Black Beauty*, experience even more popularity than cat books. Once again, girls make up a disproportionate share of the audience.

It is not intuitively obvious why this should be. After all, it was not very long ago when the cultural stereotype of American he-manhood and heroism was the cow*boy*, always closely associated with *his* horse: Roy Rogers on Trigger, the Long Ranger on Silver. And there was a whole slew of horsey male heroes: Wild Bill Hickock, Buffalo Bill, Hopalong Cassidy, Zorro, the Cisco Kid, etc. Only Annie Oakley cantered along on the distaff side.

To be sure, there are many little boys (and grown men, like myself) who retain a love for and fascination with horses and riding. But the extraordinary appeal of *Equus caballus* to young girls (and many grown women) requires a special explanation, particularly since, if anything, it goes against the predominantly male-biased, sexist stereotypes of American culture.

One interpretation holds that women find riding sexually stimulating, simply because of the contact of saddle with crotch. Indeed, more than one woman (adult as well as child) finds the image of Lady Godiva, riding through town naked on her white horse, to be viscerally compelling. But as a general explanation for female-biased "equiphilia," the role of direct physical stimulation is a crude and inaccurate caricature and downright wrong. Most women report that in fact the opposite is nearer the truth: riding can be somewhat unpleasant and uncomfortable on the female (and male!) bottom, more likely to be bruising than sexually titillating.

On the other hand, there may well be some truth in the general notion that love of horses and of riding derives from erotic motivations, but on a more subtle level than the gross misperception of direct physical stimulation. Thus, to ride a horse is to have something powerful under one's bottom and between one's legs (which in this respect is not dramatically different from the predominantly male-based identification with motorcycles). More important yet, it is to have achieved a close—often emotionally intimate—identification with the perfect mate: a large, potentially dangerous, but fundamentally benevolent fellow mammal who offers the exciting combination of strength, energy, and competence . . . under careful restraint. And moreover, to ride is to maintain a primary position of control and authority—hence, not deeply threatening to selfhood and autonomy—while constantly feeling the Other's power and, indeed, surrendering one's self occasionally during flights of fancy, rapid accelerations of speed, or real flights as when galloping or (literally) when jumping.

Finally, there is probably no better assertiveness training than for a small girl, weighing perhaps fifty to one hundred pounds, to be the unquestioned boss of an animal weighing perhaps five hundred pounds (if a pony) to fifteen hundred pounds (if a full-sized horse). We bestowed a tiny 9.2-hand pony, aptly named "Peanut," on our youngest child when she was two-and-a-half years old. Within a few days of her third birthday, Nellie suddenly figured out how to steer, stop, walk, and trot. Her grin could be seen several miles away. Our ten year old—riding since she was four—can do just about anything on a horse, with a quiet, flowing grace that makes the most difficult maneuver seem easy.

Closely related to the allure of riding itself is the varied panorama of horse maintenance. Indeed, horse*keeping* doubtless exceeds horse *riding* in its requirements of time, money, and devotion. The harried parent, seeking to gratify a child's (or a spouse's) horse habit may quickly conclude that the sport itself is physically less demanding than the daily requirements of horsetending. Horses eat and must be fed. In the wild, they graze almost constantly. Unlike a dog, however, which will thrive on one large meal per day or a pet snake which may eat only once a week, horses must have a relatively large number of meals: at least two per day and, better yet, three or four. Even if kept in a large pasture, the natural grass alone may well not suffice and must often be supplemented with grain and/or vitamins. And if there is enough grass, then it is likely that in the spring, there will be too much: like goldfish, horses can overeat, especially on very rich, high-protein forage and get so sick they might even die.

Near urban areas, most horses are kept in stalls, with either dry straw or wood shavings on the floor. The soiled material must be removed daily and replaced with fresh supplies, along with prodigious quantities of water and regular exercise. Horsekeeping, no less than horse riding, teaches some basic virtues, notably responsibility and consistency, because these things must be done every day, winter and summer, rain or shine, and whether or not you have ridden on a given day. In our family, "first aid" is taken literally: the horses must be fed and watered *first*, before we provide ourselves with any aid, such as breakfast.

Horsekeeping is a metaphor for much else in life, particularly having a family. There is an other-centeredness about riding, as well as an opportunity—indeed, a necessity—for the development and expression of competence. From picking a pony's feet and attending to scrapes, to putting on a saddle and inserting the bit into that rather formidable mouth, much is demanded and much returned. Moreover, the large, fundamentally compliant and helpless animal is a perfect foil for childhood dreams, a mirror of expanding accomplishments.

In addition to grooming and feeding, horses or ponies also need a lot of plain, old-fashioned love and caring. And herein, for many, lies a large part of their charm. Beyond the excitement and satisfaction of riding, horses demand to be nurtured; fortunately, it seems that preadolescent girls often have an equally compelling inclination to give. A horse or pony is as needy as a baby, more interactive than a Barbie doll, less troublesome and more age-appropriate than a boyfriend. Horses and ponies need to be brushed and groomed, their manes can be braided, unbraided, then rebraided once again, special haircuts and clippings undertaken, and so on *ad infinitum.*

My wife the psychiatrist maintains that a close association with horses is the best—and perhaps even the cheapest—possible insurance against some of the more unpleasant excesses of adolescence. Horses are cheaper than psychiatry or pregnancy. On the other hand, even the most horse-bestowed teenager may at some point display a tendency—understandable, though regrettable—for interest in two-legged rather than four-legged creatures and of the opposite sex, yet. Excesses of this sort must be rooted out immediately, whenever they appear.

Of course, horsekeeping brings other delights, such as the innumerable vet bills, for worming, inoculations, and the extraordinary range of illnesses—notably afflictions of the bone, muscle, and ligaments, as well as that equine bugaboo, "colic," with its potentially lethal upset of the digestive system—to which horseflesh is heir. If a horse eats too much good food, it might "founder." If it strays out too long in the rain, it might develop "bumps." And because the hooves keep growing, they must be trimmed regularly, and the horseshoes replaced by a professional farrier (in earlier times, a blacksmith) every six weeks or so.[4]

In short, if you are ever offered a gift horse, you should very definitely look in its mouth (and also, in your checkbook), because whereas there may in fact be some free lunches in this world, there most assuredly is no such thing as a free horse. When it comes to care and maintenance, every equine is a Trojan horse.

Even after the feeding, the care, and the loving, there remains a relatively lengthy ritual to be enacted before actually getting in the saddle: the hooves must be checked for stones, the region of girth and saddle carefully brushed, the saddle put on, along with bridle and bit. Then, after riding, all these things should be done again in reverse order. In addition, if the animal has gotten very warm and sweaty, it must first be "cooled off" by being walked for upwards of

4. Our family spends far more on horseshoes than on human shoes.

fifteen minutes before you are finally free to deal with other matters . . . such as the titanic struggle to take off your boots.

The saddle is hung up and your legs feel oddly empty between
the knees. Even stranger: in order to move from here to there, you
must balance on your own two tenuous pillars rather than sit on
top of four. Meanwhile, the horse grazes calmly in the meadow, a
wisp of steam still rising from its back. Its great head, so easily held
high, now with comparable facility swings down to caress the
grass. You have, for a time, been blessed, made part of something
much bigger, much faster, much stronger, and, in a way, much
more perfect than yourself. There *it* is, a creature of simple, loving
grace, and here *you* are, lord of all creation, yet grateful to have
been allowed, if only for a time, to be its partner.

Beachcombing

Periwinkles, Pebbles and Pieces of Eight

A beach is neither here nor there. Liquid on one side, solid on the other, it is impermanent and shifting, but it is neither shapeless nor without substance. It is a place between, a transition, not only in space, but also in time. It is an arena of conflict and compromise, where life first clambered out of the sea, and where it continues to do so today as it did several hundred million years ago. It is also the place where ocean storms most dramatically vent their fury, because the sea's real violence is actually felt not on the open ocean, but where water meets land. After all, waves at sea—even big ones—really just go up and down, oscillating around the same point; it is only when they reach the shore that they come crashing down in fury and ruin. Out in the open water, it makes little difference when the tides rise or fall. What does it matter if the top of the sea interposes itself against a few feet more or less of air? But against a sloping or even a rocky shoreline, those same few feet of vertical height can mean hundreds of yards of horizontal length, uncovering myriads of worlds.

And the beach, finally, is where things from the land, having ventured presumptuously onto the vastness of the oceans, get tossed back, almost with disdain.

Like a line in geometry, having length but no width, beaches

61

occasionally seem to be not things themselves so much as demarcations, boundaries between things. For thousands of miles, beaches snake along the continents, on one side the land, on the other, the sea. Sometimes, beaches are ramparts—defenders of the land—as along the rocky shores of northern New England or the high bluffs of northern California. In other places, beaches are more gentle integrators of land and water, as when dry land slopes down, almost imperceptibly into sand and then sea. But most of us know that beaches—whether rocky or sandy, cobbly or muddy— are also more than a vigorous confrontation between opposites or a gentle merging of solid and liquid. They are places in their own right, and places of contradiction, at that: delicate and fragile but enduring, ancient but ever-renewed, useless but infinitely precious, seemingly monotonous yet endlessly fascinating, sometimes frightening and at other times profoundly reassuring, barren and forbidding wastelands of extraordinary diversity and richness, war and peace, change and continuity.

Beaches are transition points, and ecologists know that such regions (termed "ecotones") are better supplied with life than their homogeneous counterparts. Thus, there is much more diversity of plants and animals at the edge of a forest than within the deep woods or out on the open prairie. In the same way, the seashore is richer than the open ocean or a Kansas wheatfield. It is a kind of cutting edge.

The first life may have developed at the interface of water and land. And then, perhaps 400 million years ago, some of the earliest animals pulled themselves heavily from water to land (probably first in freshwater ponds, where they sought to drag themselves from a desiccating pond to another where they could survive). Ever since, beaches have been places of change and of exploration: even in the Space Age, we think of "landings"—on the Moon, Venus, Mars—and in an earlier age, on new islands or even on the coasts of new continents right here on Earth.

The North American continent is perhaps four thousand miles across, edged east and west with beaches that are rarely more than 1/10 miles wide. That means that any line drawn east and west will intersect approximately 2/10 miles of beach and four thousand miles of land, for a ratio of about 1 : 20,000. There can be no doubt that our shorelines are disproportionately important and intriguing; certainly, they occupy more than 1/20,000 of our time and attention.

And well they should.

The edge of the sea—like the surface of the Earth—is only a very thin film, a paper-thin interface, but (like the precious outer layer of living stuff on our planet) it is worth far more than its actual mass, or volume, or area, or its land value as measured by the purveyors of real estate. "The health of the eye," Ralph Waldo Emerson pointed out, "demands a horizon." And with the sprouting of power lines, highways, and highrises, the seashore is one of the few places where horizons can still be found . . . out toward the ocean, at least, even if the seashore itself is getting "built up."

The value of seashores cannot be estimated, even going beyond their worth as irreplaceable ecological habitats or sites of natural pollution abatement. One hundred fifty years ago, Henry David Thoreau prowled the beaches of Massachusetts and Connecticut, extolling the virtues of "simply seeing." There have long been mariners, fishermen (sometimes, women), nautical adventurers and traders, and, of course, human beings can be pretty good swimmers as well. But fundamentally we are terrestrial, air-breathing creatures, and the easiest, surest, and safest way for us to return to our maritime roots and make contact with a large body of water is to linger along its periphery, by the edge of the sea. It is a kind of going home. After all, we evolved from the oceans, and even now, our most intimate fluid—our lifeblood—contains a concentration of salt that mimics the makeup of seawater, bathing our cellular innards in a substitute for the early ocean's salty touch.

On the northern New England coast, there are three species of small snails known as periwinkles. Two of these, the smooth periwinkle and the common periwinkle, can easily be seen on almost any rocky shore, moving about on the rocks, making a living by scraping algae off the hard surfaces. Although both the smooth and common periwinkles are well adapted to life out of the water, both are nonetheless still held fast by the sea since they can only reproduce by shedding their eggs directly into the ocean. By contrast, a third species—the rough periwinkle—gives "birth" to live young, which emerge from a kind of cocoon that develops within the mother's body. Like another species, *Homo sapiens*, the rough periwinkle is freed from its dependence on the ocean . . . at least in its anatomy and physiology. But even the seemingly emancipated rough periwinkle reveals itself to be ocean bound at heart: kept in a laboratory or a home aquarium, out of reach of the changing tides, it continues to respond with a built-in biological "memory," since it is most active every two weeks, precisely when high tides would normally be covering it.

Maybe human beings also feel a faint stirring of biological memory when it comes to the ocean. Maybe our well-documented behavioral weirdness during full moons isn't simple *lunacy* but rather a consequence of those tidal rhythms which, in turn, are cued by the moon. And maybe when we go down to the seashore, we're not really looking so much for a suntan, or a swim, or driftwood, or anything else that we can identify, but rather, maybe we are seeking to recapture in the smell and the sound and the taste and the look and the feel of the ocean something that we—like our long—lost cousin the rough periwinkle—appear to have outgrown, but actually have not. And probably never will.

Why do so many people find peace at the seashore? After all, it is actually a place of ceaseless conflict: the ocean constantly assaulting the land, now with more force, now with less, but never giving up, never walking away from the contest. Sometimes, to be sure, there is a change of technique or a new, temporary tactic, but the bottom line remains as always. Perhaps that is part of it: at the seashore, we can witness conflict and struggle as land and sea engage in an unending, primal push and pull. But at a fundamental level, the conflict is not destructive. As land is washed away or as rock is battered to pebbles and the pebbles ultimately ground to sand, there will be more land, more rock, more pebbles, more sand to come. And even as the sea retreats, maybe because land is uplifted through geological processes or because water is captured in the ice caps, there will ever be more ocean water to assail the land. Even when the seacoast is violent and scary—and especially during a winter storm, it can be downright terrifying—we can witness the sea with some complacency. We know that the ebb and flow, the give and take of land and water has been going on for a long time, and we can rest assured that the struggle—fundamentally benign despite the superficial violence—will go on.

Like gazing at a fire, so hypnotic with its constant yet minutely irregular movement—like life itself—to watch the ocean gnawing on the shore is to witness a kaleidoscope of movement, a whole universe of ever-changing patterns, all of which are variations on the same theme. The steady buildup, the expectant rush and then the culminating crash—repeated again and again, endlessly rocking—can be profoundly soothing. Often, in the biological world, internal body rhythms get "entrained" by external events: alternating cycles of shortening days and lengthening nights can persuade certain animals to hibernate (entrainment by light cycles), and young women can experience a kind of communal entrainment of their menstrual cycles when housed together, as in a college dormitory or sorority (entrainment by each other's body cycles, presumably via chemical signals). The measured, pulsing rush of the waves, throbbing in a regular pattern, may yet be found to entrain some of our deeper internal rhythms. Thus, the Vietnamese Zen master Thich Nhat Hanh has emphasized the importance of breathing correctly: mindfully and in peace. The rhythm of the waves is rarely faster than every five seconds, and rarely slower than every twelve or thirteen. Usually, in fact, it sucks itself in and then tumbles out at just the pace of a relaxed human being, inhaling and exhaling.

Once I sat by the ocean determined to make my breathing coincide exactly with the rhythm of the waves. After about ten minutes, I was neither hyperventilating nor short of breath; but I never found out if I could have kept it up longer. Because I fell asleep.

The seashore is also the landshore. Just as it is the edge of the sea, where the water gets progressively more and more shallow and where free-swimming creatures give way to those that burrow into sand or hold fast to rock, surviving periodic exposure to air, so it is the outermost margin of land, where things become progressively wetter and more salty, where plants and animals, adapted to the land, must cope with the world of water and spray, wave and sand. And so it for us: going to that shore is also pushing the known, extending the boundaries of our terrestrial home, to its very edge. It is literally as far as you can go and still be standing on your own two feet. And then, wonder of wonders, delight of delights, how sweet is is to find that after all that pushing of limits, with all that constant movement and violence, and conflict and wearing down and building up, to find that the place is, in fact, downright convivial!

(Much of the time, anyhow.)

From the picturesque and gnarled seaside trees, a bit poignant in their desperate beauty, through the intervening beaches of sand or rock, to the restless water itself, the edges of the sea call to us, and in nearly all cases—at some time or another—we cannot help but answer. Something inevitably compels our attention: maybe it is a caucus of gulls, gossiping together on wooden pilings, or the waves themselves, like a living fire of sapphire blue and emerald green, with glimpses of orange and ruby, gold and yellow, topped with a fluffy white lace. Or perhaps it is a crop of sea gooseberries[1] littering the sands with little oval balls of clear jelly about the size of marbles that pop underfoot. Or the close, immediate, undeniable, and yet not unpleasant evidence of death: where else but a beach (littered with the remains of dead clams, dead snails, dead crabs, dead seaweed, dead starfish, dead urchins) can we be surrounded by death but not find it offensive or scary? Or the smells: the pungent, oddly pervasive aroma of creatures exposed at low tide. Or maybe just the wild disorder of flotsam and jetsam, tossed up willy-nilly by the restless sea and enjoying a kind of temporary peace in the bosom of terra firma. Beaches are for lying on, for resting after a swim, for picnicking, and for intercepting photons. Better yet, they are also for prowling, for discovering the life that is there, that was there, and for contemplating what will be. They are places for kicking at the sand, turning things over and finding little furtive beings, for admiring the crashing surf and the stinging spray and for hearing the wild sea-noises.

There is also a particular joy in accepting the offerings of the ocean, with, as T.S. Eliot put it:

Its hints of earlier and other creation:
The starfish, the hermit crab, the whale's backbone;
The pools where it offers to our curiosity
The more delicate algae and the sea anemone.
It tosses up our losses, the torn seine,

1. Not quite a jellyfish but rather a comb jelly, member of the class ctenophora.

The shattered lobsterpot, the broken oar
And the gear of foreign dead men. The sea has many voices,
Many gods and many voices . . .[2]

* * *

Beachcombing has not always been seen as a wholly honorable occupation. My dictionary defines beachcomber as a "vagrant who lives on the seashore, and who makes a living by gathering items tossed up on the beach." In Mexico, a beachcomber is a "vagabando del mar," vagabond of the sea. And northwest beachcomber/author Amos Wood quotes an earlier description of the town of Port Townsend, Washington, as "a notorious resort of beachcombers and outlaws of every description."[3] But now that relatively few people count on beachcombing for their survival, it may start coming back into respectability, more savory as an avocation than as a livelihood.

The beachcomber's prize is the ocean's vomitus, spewn on the sands by high tides and strong winds. Rachel Carson described it as a many-stranded, multihued fabric, of strange makeup,

> woven with tireless energy by wind and wave and tide. The supply of materials is endless. Caught in the strands of dried beach grass and seaweeds, there are crab claws and bits of sponge, scarred and broken mollusk shells, old spars crusted with sea growths, the bones of fishes, the feathers of birds. The weavers use the materials at hand, and the design of the net changes from north to south. It reflects the kind of bottom offshore—whether rolling sand hills or rocky reefs; it subtly hints of the nearness of a warm, tropical current, or tells of the intrusion of cold water from the north. In the litter and debris of the beach there may be few living creatures, but there is the suggestion, the intimation of a million, million lives, lived in the sands nearby or brought to this place from far sea distances.[4]

To the seasoned beachcomber, the smallest item may be treasured: a chip of wood, sandblasted by salt and sun, a smoothly

2. T. S. Eliot. "The Dry Salvages," *Collected Poems, 1909-1962* (New York: Harcourt, Brace and World, 1963).
3. Amos Wood, *Beachcombing the Pacific* (West Chester, Pa: Schiffer Publishing, 1987).
4. Rachel Carson, *The Edge of the Sea* (Boston: Houghton Mifflin, 1955).

polished agate, a chip of broken coral that must have travelled several thousands of miles from the nearest coral reef. For many, there is special delight in the detritus of our own species, things thrown overboard from ships at sea or washed by accident into the open ocean, and also (more often than one might think) the remains of shipwrecks or even airplane crashes.

For beachcombing of this sort, the West Coast offers better pickings than does the East. Although the occasional easterly storm may bring goodies to the Atlantic Coast, the predominant East Coast ocean current is the Gulf Stream, which flows south to north, depositing coastal water farther up along the coastline: Florida's artifacts are stranded in Georgia, North Carolina's in New Jersey, etc. By contrast, the West Coast receives broadside the direct, perpendicular flow of the Japanese Current, sweeping across several thousand miles of Pacific Ocean, from Vladivostok, the Philippines, and Japan, straight to the shores of California, Oregon, Washington, British Columbia, and Alaska.

The beachcomber is part treasure hunter, part prowler (in the sense of meaningful sauntering, looking for something . . . almost anything): bits of dimension lumber lost from a cargo ship, broken fishing gear or oceanographic equipment, bottles of all shapes and sizes, the especially prized ones heavily encrusted with many generations of seafaring gooseneck barnacles. Some West Coast beachcombers have become experts in the medical problems of Japanese fishermen, deduced from the diversity of pill bottles washed up on the Pacific shore. Others—especially along the Northwest shoreline—specialize in brown- or amber-colored glass fishing floats, used by the Japanese longline tuna fishing fleets to support their nets. Torn free by winter storms (the Pacific can be decidedly un-pacific), at this very moment literally hundreds of thousands, maybe millions, of these floats are riding the waves just waiting for the Japanese Current to convey them to some delighted beach walker who happens to stroll the seashore after a period of sustained onshore winds or an especially productive midwinter blow. (Regrettably, the Russians use ugly steel floats, and the American salmon gill-netters are partial to crummy white plastic; the Japanese glass balls are definitely the cream of a surprisingly abundant crop.)

The beachcomber's world is ever renewing. The West Coast in

particular reaps a never-ending harvest from the Japanese Current, also known as the Kuroshio, the "Black Stream." But west or east, the wind and tide daily bring new goodies, an erratic stream of oceangoing stuff. Look out to the horizon. You can be sure that there is a floating garden lingering out there, with the fruits of the sea bobbing along barely out of view, just waiting to be plucked tomorrow from a pile of driftwood logs or scooped out of the blowing sands where an unusually high tide will drop them off during an eventful night. If you don't harvest them, someone else will.

To go beachcombing is to be on the lookout, attuned for something out of context. Some objects are unlikely to survive the tumultuous passage through the surf, region of crashing and breaking waves, to the relative serenity of the shore. To go beachcombing is to discover that ketchup bottles, for example, seem to be remarkably well designed to make just this journey, intact. Some objects—like hundred-pound flour sacks from an ill-fated ship's galley—might at first blush appear to be ruined by several months' immersion in the sea. To go beachcombing, however, is to find an unexpected resilience in such things: the outermost inch or so hardens into a tough crust, leaving the inner substance perfectly preserved and ready to become several years' supply of pancakes.

One of the beachcomber's best friends is a small relative of the jellyfish, technically known as Velella, more poetically as the by-the-wind sailor. About two inches long, blue, with a triangular white sail, Velella (like the better-known but probably less-abundant Portuguese man-of-war) is actually a colony, many individuals, each specializing in a different task, such as reproducing, catching food, digesting it, or catching the wind. Velella can be beached in enormous numbers, quickly losing their delicate beauty as they die, and making the littered shore downright slippery to walk upon. But when Velella is blown to shore, you can be sure that other oceangoing things will shortly follow, also sailing by the wind, although less efficiently and, hence, less quickly than the by-the-wind sailors themselves.

As Velella comes, so do the glass floats. Birds along the beach are another good sign because they are typically attracted by something to eat, so the chances are that some offshore goodies have just "blown in." For the same reason, freshly deposited kelp also gladdens the beachcomber's heart, as does a goodly helping of sea-foam; just as the beer drinker admires a head of suds in the glass, the beachcomber admires a healthy deposit of foam along the seashore, for this means that the winds are blowing from sea to shore. And the beachcomber's brew is by far the more intoxicating.

Probably the same thing that draws people to Zen gardens or bonsai trees also makes driftwood so popular. With its irregular, almost random shape, it introduces a wonderful unpredictability into appearances, and with its history of being tossed about, colonized by barnacles and shipworms, marinated by the ocean water, blasted by sand, pickled by salt and fried by the sun, it is the embodiment of persistence and toughness, a kind of triumphant old age, like Gandalf the wizard or some sort of arboresque Methuselah.

Most driftwood originates as trees growing inland, along rivers; they fall into the water, are carried seaward, and then eventually are tossed back on land. More surprising, perhaps, is the large amount of driftwood that originates from ships at sea, either having been washed overboard or the aftermath of wrecks. Yet perhaps we shouldn't be surprised at all, since the accumulation of several million square miles of ocean is regularly strained and pressed against a narrow line at high tide. Driftwood also makes marvelous fires: its accumulation of salts and oceanic fellow-travelers conjure up flickering tongues of scarlet, green, gray, and purple, technicolor contrast to the gray sameness of the weather-beaten wood itself.

The remains of old wooden boats—perhaps wrecked on a nearby shoal, cast up on the beach and then buried in the sands— can be uncovered again by a strong, steady wind or turbulent offshore waters. Stark, dry, and barren, they perch like the skeletons of some prehistoric mammal or maybe a great beach-roaming dinosaur. As with vertebrate fossils, the soft parts rot away or are gnawed by sand and spray and scavenging animals (and people), leaving only the hardest, heaviest, and most insoluble remains. Left are the vacant spars, barely hinting at an earlier volume; we even call them "ribs," those curved reinforcements that guard not a thorax but a man-made hull. Ironically, the modern boats—of aluminum, steel, or fiberglass—are like fossils of an earlier time: if wooden ships leave remains like ancient vertebrates, these newer creations of the shipwright's art conjure up images of the earliest large denizens of the sea, trilobites, eurypterids, and the other huge invertebrates with massive exoskeletons but no ribs at all.

Of course, real vertebrates regularly beach themselves as well, complete with skin and flesh as well as bones. Sometimes they are still alive, like the dolphins and pilot whales that inexplicably insist on stranding themselves. Sadder yet, however, are the dead ones, especially the large whales that with growing frequency, it seems, are washed up on New Jersey shores: lacerated along the head or back, they are the oceangoing equivalent of road kills, victims of the huge high-speed propellers of modern freighters and ocean liners.

Beaches are places of throbbing, twitching, crawling, hopping life, but they are also, ironically, great natural morgues, sort of a modern-day LaBrea tar pit. They are repositories of dead bodies of all sorts, strewn about with the fierce casualness of the sea. While walking the beaches of Cape Cod, Thoreau encountered some of the most gruesome of vertebrate remains, the bodies of some ship-wrecked Atlantic sailors and was moved to write that "The car-casses of men and beasts together lie stately up upon its shelf, rotting and bleaching in the sun and waves, and each tide turns them in their beds, and tucks fresh sand under them. There is naked Nature—inhumanly sincere, wasting no thought on man, nibbling at the cliffy shore where gulls wheel amid the spray."[5]

Most East Coast beachcomers are unlikely to find human corpses; similarly, they cannot look forward to the regular, cheerful appearance of glass floats, like their West Coast counterparts. They can lay claim, however, to something even more exciting, if more rare as well: genuine buried treasure. Spanish doubloons and pieces of eight have been retrieved from the sands off Cape Canaveral, Florida, and remains of Blackbeard's treasure have been found in the beachside strips of Beaufort County, North Car-olina. The infamous Jean Lafitte is said to have deposited some of his spoils along the shores of Delaware Bay, and Captain Kidd os-tensibly buried treasure on Block Island or Gardiners Island, off New York's Long Island.

But for the vast majority of us, "treasures" are what we make of

5.   H. D. Thoreau, *Cape Cod* (New York: T. Y. Crowell, 1961).

them. Usually, "trophies" are more to the point: an old crab or lobster pot, broken from its moorings long ago, a stretch of fishing net destined now to serve as a backdrop for other precious discoveries such as a pocket-sized piece of dunnage[6] complete with Chinese, Filipino, or Malay inscriptions. Finders keepers, even though in most cases the losers are likely to have remained dry-eyed. Each one has a story, such as the time you dislodged an avalanche of loose logs trying to get at that ancient bottle now peacefully displayed on the mantle, or the day you seized this broken oar and then forgot that because of the rising tide, clambering over the rocky headland—so easy two hours ago—would mean wading through angry knee-high swirling foam on the return trip.

And like their soul mates, the fishermen, ardent beachcombers have their supply of "big ones that got away" stories. The serious beachcomber is invariably haunted, for the remainder of his or her days, by what had to be left behind: because it was too big, or too heavy, or too securely wedged behind a malevolent rock.

How to qualify as a beachcomber? That's easy, just prowl the shorelines, whether east or west, particularly after winter storms, and especially along the high-tide line where almost anything that floats is apt to *a*light on the beach, thence to *de*light the finder. Good pickings to you.

In James Joyce's *Ulysses*, young Stephen Dedalus walks along the sea wrack of the Irish coast at low tide, closing his eyes "to hear his boots crush crackling wrack and shells," and ruminating about the undeniable reality of the world of forms and substances:

> Listen: a fourworded wavespeech: seesoo, hrss, rsseeiss, oos. Vehement breath of waters amid seasnakes, rearing horses, rocks. In cups of rocks it stops: flop, slop, slap: bounded in barrels. And, spent, its speech ceases. It flows purling, widely flowing floating foampool, flower unfurling.

And as Dedalus watched, the narrator tells us that

Under the upswelling tide he saw the writhing weeds lift languidly

---

6.   Wood used to maintain space between cargoes or for tie-downs, as shims, etc., on oceangoing freighters.

and sway reluctant arms, hissing up their petticoats, in whispering
water swaying and upturning coy silver fronds.

You don't have to be a collector of words (like Joyce) or of
things, or even be a rough periwinkle, to feel the pull of the waves
on shore. An old Welsh legend has it that waves are the white
manes of great galloping sea horses. Certainly, in those pounding
waves, there is a kind of thunder of hooves. And in the supple bend
of a breaker, when the waves come in majestic, huge and green,
they raise a curved transluscent neck, firm with a well-muscled
tautness just for an instant before crashing in upon themselves,
only to rise again and again. Majestic, blue and poised to deliver,
they become a marbled white: vertical power transformed into su-
pine foam.

The bigger they are, the farther out they fall. Only the smaller
ones break close to the land, tripped up by the sand underneath.
Dedalus was right: there is an undeniable "suchness" about the
meeting of water and land, and that is putting it mildly.

T. S. Eliot captured the ambivalence of liquid toward solid
when he recognized "the menace and caress of waves." For caresses, go to the edge of the sea in summer; for menace, try winter.
Too many of us only know the beaches of summer, when they are
calm, caressing . . . and often crowded as well. The tides then are
gentle, the storms almost nonexistent. The smells of seawrack, the
sounds of gull or snapper shrimp—almost, the song of the surf
itself—all are drowned out by the odor of suntan lotion and the
noise of beachfront enterprises, lifeguard whistles, or screeching
bathers. The tangiest smells at Coney Island are the condiments
on the hot dogs.

Whitman called it the "slappy shore," that carefree place of easy
motion that he knew along the summer shores of Long Island.
When the days are bright and long, the waves lick gently along the
sandy margin, talking in low whispers. To be sure, the summer
waters rise to their high tides, but only halfheartedly. Waves, such
as they are, slither obediently over the sand, then retreat eagerly to
the ocean's bosom, passing in a thin sheet of liquid glass. There is a
Maoist guerrilla movement in Peru known as the "Sentero
Luminoso," or Shining Path. Hearing that phrase, however, I think
less of violent revolution than of the moon on the peaceful sum-

mertime ocean, unfurling a liquescent shining path from itself to me.

But even when the sea is calm and in the gentlest of seasons, there is apparent a suppleness of movement, a subsurface restiveness, a quiet flexing of enormous sinews, hinting at the immense power just barely held in check. And sure enough, by autumn the tone changes. An ominous, foreboding hint is added, as winds perk up and the sun and moon join forces to make for the highest of tides. The waters become strangely dull in their mounting anger, downright sullen in contrast to their summertime openness, keeping it in like a psychotic waiting to explode. These are the times, more than any other, when you can feel, as by some ancient sense, the passing of vast schools of great fish, just beneath the surface. And as the wind picks up, it does just that, picking up, quite literally, sea-foam, loose leaves, and sand, whose thin hiss contrasts markedly with the deep thunder of the crashing waves, which have begun flinging their spray in mounting challenge to the land.

And by winter, all hell breaks loose: the waves may roar in fury and rage, harsh green and menacing (the "snot-green sea," snorted Dedalus' friend, Buck Mulligan), or pewter-gray and filled with intimations of violence. When resisted by rock or cliff—as compared with the recumbent and accepting sandy beach—then explosions of water may leap straight up like geysers, raging against the sky itself in their indignation at being thwarted. Immense energy, built up over thousands of miles of unobstructed ocean, crashes full force against anything with the temerity to stand against it. At such times, there can be no doubt: it is the ocean assaulting the land, not the other way around.

A wave is, as Jack London put it, a "communicated agitation," one that can also communicate considerable agitation to human bystanders: "When the top of the wave keeps on going, while the bottom of it lags behind, something is bound to happen. The bottom of the wave drops out from under, and the top of the wave falls over, forward, and down, curling, and cresting and roaring as it does so."[7] The result is pressure that can exceed that produced by a mid-sized nuclear explosion.

Even when the sea is calm, and the shore is a smooth and gently

7. Quoted in Seon and Robert Manley, *Beaches* (Philadelphia: Chilton, 1968).

inclined beach, you can watch the contortions of water on sand, as
the battle is joined. In this corner, the force of gravity, drawing all
things back together, calling the liquid tentacles back to the ocean.
And in the other corner, the ocean's expansiveness, pushing its
pseudopods up the beach, over obstacles toward the land and the
faraway moon and sun. (The land is at best a passive participant.)
The water forms thin sheets as it does the ocean's bidding, pros-
trating itself as far as it possibly can—and then, just a little bit
farther—before it slides back, twisting and writhing, complaining
as it retreats, only to be pulled yet farther along if by this time of
day the moon and sun are collaborating in their landward use of
gravity.

It is surprising that there isn't more drama announcing the turn
of the tides, since it is such a primal, cosmic event. Instead, there is
just a gradual, almost imperceptible shift, the progressive appearance of wet rocks where—if the tide is coming in—shortly before
they were submerged. Or alternatively, the progressive moistening
of ramparts that previously had been high and dry. The very sand is
uplifted, or so it appears, as by some vast geological process, and
rocks emerge that just minutes ago had been deep within the skirts
of the sea. Maybe, on the other hand, if the twice-daily changes
were heralded by lightning and thunder, or great celestial pag-
eantry, they would seem more out-of-place and thus, more suscep-
tible of interruption or modification. As it is, "time and tides wait
for no man," and in the smoothness of their transitions, we can
sense how inexorable they are.

The waves have called forth joy and elation, or sadness and despair. Wordsworth yearned to

> Have sight of Proteus rising from the sea;
> Or hear old Triton blow his wreathed horn.

Yet Matthew Arnold heard only an "eternal note of sadness" in
the ceaseless flinging of ocean pebbles onto Dover Beach. In the
waves, he felt the "turbid ebb and flow of human misery," and as
the tide withdrew, he thought of the universal withdrawal of human faith.

Even so enthusiastic an observer as Henry Beston was occasionally moved to glumness at the stolid, even terrible, repetition of

the waves. Commenting on a winter's storm off Cape Cod, when
the fog lay so thickly that everything seemed to vanish in a "universal dark," Beston noted how

> great breakers born of fog swell and the wind rolled up the sands
> with the slow, mournful pace of stately victims destined to immola-
> tion, and toppled over, each one, in a heavy, awesome roar that
> faded to silence before a fellow victim followed on out of the dark-
> ness on the sea.[8]

But of course, there is nothing fundamentally contradictory
about the sea having many moods. Its "monotony" is short-lived.
As Beston well knew, it speaks with many voices:

> hollow boomings and heavy roarings, great watery tumblings and
> tramplings, long hissing seethes, sharp, rifle-shot reports, splashes,
> whispers, the grinding undertone of stones, and sometimes vocal
> sounds that might be the half-heard talk of people in the sea . . . It is
> also constantly changing its tempo, its pitch, its accent, and its
> rhythm, being now loud and thundering, now almost placid, now
> furious, now grave and solomn-slow, now a simple measure, now a
> rhythm monstrous with a sense of purpose and elemental will.[9]

Listen to it yourself. Listen to the sea as the tide climbs the
beach, as it laps and slaps, swirls and swishes against the rim of the
land. Listen to the sea as it roars and whispers, crashes, thunders,
purrs, and hisses. Listen to the sea as it beats like your heart, pulsing with an essential, salty life: rhythmic, constant, patient, yet
ever so insistent. Listen. Is it speaking to you? Or is it you, speaking through it. Listen.

The ocean is vast, a synonym for enormity. And yet, to appreciate life at its margins, you must get small and focus on the details:
the tiny lives being led among the holdfasts of rockweed, the bizarre little parchment worms inhabiting their narrow, U-shaped
tubes, the clinging Irish moss with its covering of bryozoans, tiny
slithery brittle stars and limpets no bigger than a fingernail. Often,

8. Henry Beston, *The Outermost House* (New York: Holt, Rinehart & Winston,
    1949).
9. Beston, *Outermost.*

life is implied rather than spelled out: dimples in the sand where a cockle sticks up its syphon; a dried-out "mermaid's purse," a tough, flat, black rectangle with diabolical looking prongs at each end that is actually the empty egg case of a skate.[10]

At the sea's edge, life is everywhere: drilling into rocks, cemented onto kelp, clinging to crevices, burrowing beneath the sand. And for the beachcomber interested in discovering the living nonhuman world as well as the artifacts of our own species, there is no better place to be.

The pulsations of the tides create distinct patterns of zonations, most visible on rocky shores: highest is the "black zone," named for its dark green lichens, also boasting a few snails and periwinkles and marine isopods (the so-called "sea cockroach"). The sea itself doesn't reach into the black zone, although it sends plenty of salt spray when the tide is up. Next comes the barnacle zone, eerie profusion of tiny white volcanoes that appear devoid of life so long as the tide is low. Also found here: great masses of dark blue-black mussels (oysters, south of New York) and the short, stubby, leathery rockweed, as well as limpets that clasp the rock in defense against the pounding surf, small curlicue white and pink nematode worms, and amphipods like tiny shrimp. Farthest toward the sea is the region accessible to the beachcomber only when the tides are low, the richest habitat of all: home of sea cucumbers, starfish, sea anemones, urchins . . . a whole universe of strange and wonderful creatures exposed all too briefly.

The beachcomber looking for human artifacts will concentrate on the high-tide line, as far up-beach as practical; for glimpses into the animate world, on the other hand, Shangri-la is the down-beach, low-tide line. People have long been fascinated by high tides, writing songs and poems about the majesty and force of the sea, the grandeur and persistence of its crashing waves. But what about low tide, when the beach lies exposed, dripping, and forlorn, water drained out and puddled up like the aftermath of a half-hearted attempt at defrosting a recalcitrant refrigerator? We need a laureate of low tide, place of funny smells and peculiar creatures. This is where (or "when") the vast mud and sand-flats stretch out to the clam digger, where the enterprising explorer can gently lift

10.   Flat-bodied relative of the sharks.

the limp wet cape of rockweed whose heavy dank hair falls over a boulder, sheltering a myriad of creatures, where the profuse disorder of tide pools lie ready for our examination, giving us a glimpse into a world as strange as that of any extra-terrestrials.

Low tide is not majestic in any traditional sense; its grandeur is that of diversity, novelty, miniaturized perfection, the temporary exposure of mysteries normally submerged, revealed in a snapshot of helter-skelter profusion. Kick over some seaweed, high on a beach, and millions of beach-hoppers (tiny amphipods) explode in every direction, peppering your legs. Lower on the beach, when the tide has withdrawn, the same seaweed will likely reveal an array of slower-moving but more exotic creatures, more adapted to the water than the air: skittery crabs, ponderous starfish, pincushion urchins, all hoping to wait out the onslaught of air.

This is where it pays to move slowly and look carefully. Rocky shores are more difficult to explore than their sandy counterparts, but much more rewarding, since their collateral lives are found *on* rock, as opposed to *under* the sand. Also, the solid substrate offers places of attachment, as well as crevices where water remains even after the main body has withdrawn. For the low-tide beachcomber, it pays to develop a taste for the nondescript. It also helps to have a child along, because children, it seems, have eyes that focus best at about two feet away; they may not notice the gorgeous sunset or give two hoots about the subtle colors, melding delicately from shoreline to horizon, but you can be assured they won't overlook the tiniest mud shrimp or a miniature sculpin, no bigger than your fingernail, darting between the tines of a sea urchin.

Life abounds here in the tide pools, only don't expect it to roar down upon you like a herd of buffalo. Let your eyes linger over a cranny, get in tune with the pulsations of a dimple in the sand that may be a mollusk's siphon or the tube home of a small, ornately carved pink worm. On a flat, sandy beach with few obstructions, where the water at low tide spreads out like a thinly stretched mirror, watch the seemingly barren sand, as whole regiments of tiny mole crabs emerge from their burrows, all decamping at the same moment, eerily advancing up the beach like surfers on an advancing wave. (Later, they will retreat the same way, hitching rides back down with the withdrawing surf.)

Tiny coquina clams also violate our stereotype of molluscs as lazy and sedentary; they seem to be constantly on the move, advancing up the beach, digging themselves in, then dying in appalling numbers and leaving their delicate remains as memories of coquina outposts now abandoned. It is said the first colonists in Florida waded ashore through literally knee-high piles of seashells, and even today the beaches of west Florida offer some of the best shell-prospecting in the world. Serious collectors, however, disdain the usually broken specimens found on beaches, preferring to dig or dive for live ones, unscathed.

For air-breathing, walking-about creatures such as ourselves, low tide is a time when we can explore the life of the shore. And yet, low tide is also when things seem the most lifeless. Take barnacles, for instance. Few panoramas seem as altogether dead as the barren, mineral-looking, white volcanic landscape of barnacle-encrusted rocks. The sea squirts, starfish, urchins, and anemones may be discomforted by low tide, exposed and even mortally endangered, but at least we can see them and admire their diversity and aliveness. Barnacles, by contrast, which are in fact perfectly adapted to air and not threatened by it at all, nonetheless appear utterly lifeless. Nobody home. But let them be covered with just a few inches of water, and lacelike shadows flicker everywhere, so fine that you almost wonder if you have really seen them at all, as feathery plumed arms reach out to strain the invisible plankton from the surrounding, nourishing sea.

Best of all, however, are the tide pools themselves. Walk down the beach, toward the ocean when the tide is out, and there, revealed for only a short time, are small limpid worlds, peopled with their own dragons and fairy princesses, worlds of beauty and danger, ferocity and calm. There is a special place on the Maine coast, a reflecting pool perhaps four feet across, that exists only during the lowest of low tides, hidden within a jumble of car-sized boulders. Nearby, stolid barnacles patiently await the tide's return, and sea anemones exposed to the air shrink down into the innermost core of their salty, animal selves, meeting your eye as nothing more than thick, leathery globs; a hapless starfish bakes and desiccates in the sun; and there sits a small, inscrutable crab. Abandoned by their mother-ocean, they wait to be reclaimed once again; in the meanwhile, you get to examine the temporary orphans.

But the real show is within the pool itself, perhaps eighteen inches deep. The same anemones that appeared so formless and unappealing in air are spread out like the most delicate flowers, swaying gently. There is a small brittle star, body perhaps one inch across and bristly legs four inches long, moving sinuously and surprisingly fast, whipping a leg quickly out of reach. Sea cucumbers, which out of water collapse to shrunken raisins perhaps one half inch long, expand in their liquid home to six inches of soft, fleshy substance, waving brown and green tentacles from a dark purple tube. A couple of sponges add colorful stage props: a medium-sized crumb-of-bread sponge, green-rimmed from algae, and a striking yellow sulfur sponge. Where they are exposed to heavy surf, these sponges grow thin and crusty; protected, as in this pool, they put out marvels of elaborate and branching complexity.

A magnifying glass can be useful in examining—no, entering into—a tide pool. If you like small worlds, try the microcosm in a shallow basin of seawater. Some of the most rewarding are Thumbelina sized: lay down, put your face right up to the edge, and let yourself wander amid the enormous green trees, the mountainous clump of dark blue mussels, the sudden appearance and retreat of a hurrying, scurrying bristle worm, busily about its predatory mission. Alice's adventures down the rabbit hole are tame compared with the goings-on within such a place.

There are elaborate and precise scientific taxonomies for such creatures, of course, but the nonspecialist tide-pool explorer will agree that for practical purposes there are four kinds of tide-pool life: those that are immobile (barnacles, bryozoans, mussels); the creepers and crawlers, easily overtaken (starfish, snails, chitons); the fast walkers, about as quick afoot as a person is quick of hand (brittle stars, scallops, crabs, annelid and nereid worms); and the zoomers, residents more of the water than of rock or sand, which just happened to be temporarily marooned at low tide (eels, fish, octopus, shrimp).

There are also the smells of low tide: the soft, lingering odor, not strong but oddly persistent, of crabs and sandhoppers, decaying seaweed and worms and jellyfish and mussels; the curious garlic odor of a heavy, webbed Leather Starfish; the sulfurous emanations of sponges or the iodine-laden air above a boulder festooned with rockweed and its wildly diverse menagerie of miniature creatures underneath.

Low tides at night are especially strange. A rocky shore, illuminated only by the moon, when the ghost crabs are no longer cow-
ering from their arch enemies, the gulls, is transformed into an
unforgettable and goblin place. And the sounds of hundreds of fid-
dler crabs, scuttering about on tiny starched feet, is like the unexpected crackling of old parchment amid the newness of a wave-
washed beach.

Storms bring surprises and treasures for the tide-pool beachcomber, just as they do for the birder seeking exotics for a "life
list." The remnants of deep-sea creatures may be deposited on the
shore, like the delicate ram's horn shell, Spirula, found within a
squidlike creature normally living in the darkness of one thousand
feet under water. Or on-shore winds may sweep in creatures of the
open-ocean surface, like Portuguese men-of-war or those living
sails, the Siphonophores. In the immediate aftermath of a persistent southerly gale, strange, bright-colored, and dainty tropical
beasts, with ornate shells and unique colors, may appear as far
north as Long Island. Churning submarine waves can rip bottom
dwellers like sea squirts and sponges from their moorings, thrust-
ing them into the merciless air where they lie prostrate and helpless. Later, with the immigrants dry and expiring on the sand, the
beach has become a killing field, and the smell of death floats overhead. The sounds of flies buzzing in culinary excitement and the
hordes of skittering ghost crabs underfoot tell the beachcomber
that it is already too late.

On the one hand, the sea makes everything afresh, washing
away the tracks of yesterday's midday sanderling hustle or the fur-
rows of last night's reproductive orgy by the sea urchins. Each day
begins anew, with fresh arrivals, new deaths, new lives, new patterns on the sand, new encrustations on the rock. But the seashore
is also a kind of contact with time and slowness, an unchanging,
reliable renovation that smacks of eons, if not eternity. Looking
wizened and world weary, even when young, most of these creatures were already old when the the very first vertebrates dragged
themselves onto land. They are old salts, indeed. On shores
throughout the East Coast, you can watch horseshoe crabs bull-
dozing their way up and down the beach, mating, depositing their
eggs, and returning home. They seem helpless, slow, and vulnerable; you can easily pick them up by their tails and deposit them

where you will. (Tons of horseshoe crabs have been harvested to be ground up for fertilizer.)

I once saw a single horseshoe crab, alone on a beach, making its way doggedly back into the water. My heart went out to it, so pitifully small it was against the vast, uncaring anonymous immensity of sand and sea. And yet, horseshoe crabs have been around— essentially unchanged—for about 500 million years. They don't need anything from us, and maybe we can learn a few things from them, like persistence and maybe even hope as well.

Walking just before sunrise by the edge of the sea, at least one early morning beachcomber has also seen the rose-red promise of dawn reflected upon the white breast of a soaring gull, heralding yet another day.

Sand. Sand in your trousers, sand in your hair. Sand in your ears, the sand-which is there. Sand between your toes, sand in your socks. Sandy shoes, sandy food, sandy shells, sandy rocks. Sand that is dry and blowing and fine. A long sandy strand, in a smooth, curvy line. Sand that is wet and heavy and hard; sand like the snow, piled in drifts, by the yard. As Margaret Wise Brown[11] might have concluded, "I like sand."

Others have liked it too. William Blake saw whole worlds in a grain of sand. Anaxagoras drew his designs of the universe in the sand. Jesus and his disciples walked along the beaches of Galilee. Robert Louis Stevenson, Rupert Brooke, Paul Gauguin, Thoreau, and Nathaniel Hawthorne all wrote of sandy beaches, as did Keats, Shelley, and Byron.

Sand deserves contemplation, probably even more than it receives. The sands of human time, passing through the narrow neck of an hourglass, are as nothing compared with the sands of geological time, passing through their incarnation as granite rock into smaller and smaller pieces of quartz and feldspar under the patient prodding of wind and wave. It is not rock that is durable, but rather, sand. A piece of the rock isn't nearly the passport to permanence offered by a handful of sand. And not surprisingly, sandy beaches are gentler, less ill-tempered, than rocky coasts: the sandy beach is an older environment, whose components have mellowed

11. My favorite children's book writer.

over time, maybe even learning a bit of humility through their lengthy encounter with the sea.

There are other kinds of sand: the coral sands of southern Florida, made of pulverized and weathered coral skeletons; the black and red sand beaches of Hawaii, composed of ground up lava of various colors. But any way you pile it, sand is gritty, homogeneous, and relatively fine, just fine.

Sand is also synonymous with unaccountable abundance: it could have been one of the labors of Hercules to number the grains of sand on an Aegean beach. It is also the epitome of teeny-tininess: physicists can keep their quarks, muons, gluons, and hadons, everyone knows that the littlest, most elementary particle is a grain of sand. It is the standard of human experience against which claims of smallness are measured.

Sand is also the best of all things for digging, for making holes down "to water" if not to China. It is infinitely malleable, becoming almost instantly a dam, a mountain, a canal, or a pie. It can be sculpted or thrown, heaped or smoothed, and washed off your hands in the water. (But not your feet, at least not for long.) It fills small pails like nothing else and is utterly scrumptious for covering up legs and feet, even your belly and chest, then making little tell-tale cracks when you breathe. And, if it is fine enough, sand is the only substance in the world that will do for that ultimate of all childhood creations, the drip castle, with elaborate gothic spires, towers, and minarets that can put the Kremlin to shame.

Sand, more than anything else, brings out the difference between children and adults: children seek it—in sandboxes or on the beach—while adults, pretending to like it, in fact avoid it as a gritty annoyance. Adults somehow manage to keep their food from getting sandy; likewise, their wet swimsuits. They stand or (more rarely) squat or (most often) sit primly on blankets, towels, or elevated beach chairs. Children, on the other hand, know what's good for them: they have no compunction about applying a wet derriere to the caress of the clingy stuff, even to the point of rolling around, breading themselves as though to be deep-fried.

Sand lasts for ever, it seems; like matter and energy, it can neither be created nor destroyed, only piled about in different ways. A grain of sand in a child's seaside castle tumbles down to become part of a brown, wet, featureless plain, to be rolled up the beach

and dried out to join the snowy white soft drift covering an old
weather-worn log, to blow back toward the water and help sand-
blast a fragment of a glass bottle, leaving it frosted and smooth, and
then to slip inside an unwary oyster, tickling its innards and wind-
ing up inside a pearl, to adorn the ear of the wife of a furniture
dealer from Bismarck, North Dakota. All this movement amid constancy is also appropriate, because the sands of time are also notoriously shifty: leave your footprints in the sand, and they will be
gone with the next tide, perhaps the next wave. Like their more
ephemeral cousins, the snowflakes, sand grains easily receive the
impression of what passes upon them, but despite its promises,
these images don't last. The tracks of a striped skunk, digging for
worms at the shore, are erased by the next tide, along with the
marks of a starfish's struggle to open a stray mussel, or whole keels
of ships. Sand even covered the mighty works of Ozymandias, King
of Kings, so that "boundless and bare the lone and level sands
stretch far away."

Actually, sands are not really as barren as many people think.
"Bearing on its surface only the wave-carved ripple marks, the fine
traceries of sand grains dropped at last by the spent waves, and the
scattered shells of long-dead mollusks, the beach has a lifeless
look," writes Rachel Carson,

> as though not only uninhabited but indeed uninhabitable. In the
> sands almost all is hidden. The only clues to the inhabitants of most
> beaches are found in winding tracks, in slight movements disturb-
> ing the upper layers, or in barely protruding tubes and all but con-
> cealed openings leading down to hidden burrows.[12]

A hungry moon snail may lurk beneath, betrayed only by a miniature molehill of moving sand. Follow that flat track to a sand
dollar, or look beneath those tiny black cones to find a lugworm,
doing for the beach what the earthworm does for the garden.

By all means, walk on the beach, digging your toes into the sand,
but keep in mind—as Rachel Carson did— that you are treading
on the thin rooftops of an underground city:

> Of the inhabitants themselves little or nothing was visible. There

12. Rachel Carson, *Edge*.

were the chimneys and stacks and ventilating pipes of underground dwellings, and various passages and runways leading down into darkness. There were little heaps of refuse that had been brought up to the surface as though in an attempt at some sort of civic sanitation. But the inhabitants remained hidden, dwelling silently in their dark, incomprehensible world.[13]

But sometimes, we invade that dark and incomprehensible world, armed especially with that redoubtable narrow shovel known as a "clam gun." For sand is where—and of course, low tides are when—claims are dug. Fast-moving razor clams, great stout horse clams (almost invariably with a pair of tiny pea crabs cozily ensconced in each), softshell clams originally from the East Coast that seem nearly to have dispensed with their shelly armor altogether, or Pacific Northwest geoducks,[14] with their enormous, oversized "feet."

Few things match this shock, even when you are expecting it: suddenly to encounter a geoduck siphon, while prostrate on the beach, up to your armpit in two and a half feet of wet, cold sand. For a split second, there is the horrible certainty that you have discovered a dead body, by grabbing hold of its huge, flaccid penis ... the closest some of will ever get to a homoerotic experience. (Unless maybe you count eating the thing.) But the geoduck is anything but dead. Instantly, it somehow manages two contradictory actions: it springs erect but at the same time, it pulls back powerfully to itself, so you hold on for all you're worth. All the while scrabbling to dig the monster out with the other hand.

On the northern coast of the Olympic Pennisula, in Washington, experienced clam diggers are connoisseurs, not only of the bivalves but also of location. They know just where to dig for what they prize most: for butter clams, the eastern edge of Dungeness Spit, for steamers, Dungeness Bay, for horse clams or geoducks, the eastern edge of Cline Spit, and for softshells, Sequim Bay. All within ten miles of shoreline. Some of us, however, are so gluttonous and indiscriminating as to eat whatever we find, even the cockles, heavy bodied, heavy shelled, and chewy. Razor clams must be

13. Rachel Carson, *Edge*.
14. Pronounced "gooey-duck" and nominated by some to be the Washington state bird.

pursued, sometimes with a posse of two, one to dig vertically and another to tunnel sideways, terrierlike. And geoducks, as we have seen, require a viselike grip and no sense of shame. But I am partial to easier prey, the lazy person's clam digging: turning over the oozy-rich, sandy mud of a special place, uncovering, with each spadeful, perhaps three or four steamers and a cockle, each the size of a small golf ball, and maybe even a butter clam or two, no smaller than your fist.

"There's one." "Here's another." "Look at the size of that one." Perhaps the biggest problem is greed, the insatiable desire to turn over yet another cubic foot of sand, to poke gently with your shovel and see what is revealed, to gather in just a few more nuggets of mollusk treasure. Sure, eating them is wonderful, but the real treat comes first, as you harvest the beach.

"So long," we might say in jest, "it's been—real." And nothing is more real than the salt and the smells and the sounds and the life at the edge of the sea, with its scuttling crabs, crawly worms, crusty barnacles, leathery starfish, needly urchins, hammy seapork, clammy siphons like penises, and oysters inside all slimy and vulva-esque. No surprise, therefore, that when T. S. Eliot's Prufrock, hesitant, middle aged and fearful, decided to brave the world, he vowed not only to eat a peach, but also to walk upon the beach (perhaps even to do so barefoot), where he has "heard the mermaids singing, each to each." Yet, he confides, "I do not think that they will sing to me."

They will sing, however, of that we can be sure. The question is, will we be listening?

Sand between your toes is the best walking of all, but a boardwalk is better than no walk. One problem with boardwalks, however, is that you almost have to wear shoes. (Otherwise, slivers in your feet.) Another is that they attract people, and with them, arcades, cotton candy, noise, pollution, and the obliteration of nearly everything that otherwise constitutes a living beach.

Most of us only visit the beach during the summer, and then, only at recognized bathing places. Part of the drift of this chapter is that beaches offer a whole lot more, for anyone willing to go beyond Coney Island or Malibu. On the other hand, there can be something compelling and downright erotic about bathing beaches: the oily, sensuous, perfumed aroma of suntan lotion, the high-pitched murmur of so many people aggregated for nothing but hedonism, the carnal allure of wide expanses of skin and the press of mostly naked bodies. Let's face it: beaches are very sexy places.

Why is it that novels and movies of first love and of adolescence-coming-to-age are so often set on a beach? It must be more than summer time-out-of-mind. Maybe we are aroused by an unconscious knowledge of the billions of animal gametes shed voluptuously and profligately into the waters of every living beach: conches spewing forth ribbons of egg capsules looking like miniature folded-accordions, purple sea hares extruding thin green strings with millions of eggs coated in jelly, sea urchins pouring out bright red ova and the males, gallons of milky white sperm, funky smells and salty embraces, from grunion beach parties on the California coast to the palolo worms of the tropical Pacific, roaring waves and pounding surf, the languorous sweep of warm horizons, the urgency and consummation of breakers . . . all conspire in the erotic nature of warm waters.

I grew up in Far Rockaway, New York, ostensibly part of New York City, but in fact—before the subway was extended, above-ground, to its nether regions—more like a small, beachside town. The population more than tripled every summer, as refugees from the steamy city crowded into the tenamentlike beachside "bungalows" along the Rockaway Peninsula. My own recollections of Far Rockaway are of boardwalks smelling of creosote, of secret places that we, the natives, knew and where the tourists never went, where the horseshoe crabs and mud worms spawned, and where I desperately wanted to spawn, too.

"Under the boardwalk, down by the sea.
On a blanket with my baby, that's where I'll be."

Or so I hoped.

"Making out," we called it, and maybe they still do. There was one renowned spot, relatively private as such places go, a popular make-out site, where the boardwalk overhead was relatively low, screened on the side by protecting sand-dunes, and especially favored by young Puerto Rican couples. I sometimes lay nearby, mostly buried in the sand, secretly listening to the fevered goings-on in this place of deep breathing, a hideaway which, had I been able to look twenty-seven years into the future, I might have called "Manila manor." Because more than once I heard a memorable, urgent refrain, as a young, nubile Hispanic voice whispered something that I later learned to translate into English as "Darling, not here." In Spanish, it went: "Corazon, aqui no."

Most of all, I remember my own beach-blanket adventures. It seemed "only natural" then, but in fact it is nothing less than extraordinary that—like virtually every other form of life on the edge of the sea—my entire attention could be riveted on the body of another *Homo sapiens*, not coincidentally, one of my own species and the opposite sex, lying next to me. I can think of no stronger testimony to the power of biology and the strength of matter over mind. Thousands of miles of ocean rippling against millions of grains of sand and surrounded by hundreds of other creatures of all sorts, yet I was almost oblivious to everything but a particular bellybutton, accented by the most delectable hint of soft blonde hairs. Amid the wonders of nature, by far the greatest wonder stood about five foot three, with thin bands of metal struggling to tame a few errantly angled teeth. The susurrus of lazy waves, the scream of gulls quarelling over someone's leftover popsicle stick. Transfixed by two magical mystery mounds, softly rising and falling, and at the top of each, just the faintest outline of a perfect nipple. Convinced, absolutely convinced, that no one and nothing else on that beach—indeed, no one else in the world—was a virgin. Oh God, why only me? Lying on my belly so the excitement wouldn't show. (A Chinese finger puzzle, this, since the firm sand perversely evoked yet more.) Wondering how to get into the water, or anywhere for that matter, without everyone seeing and laughing.

There are times when male horseshoe crabs have eyes only for lady horseshoe crabs (and vice versa), when sandworms think only of other sandworms, and there still remains, indelibly fixed in my memory, a slender foot, delicately poised in the soft, warm sand. I would have given anything, anything, to run my fingers over the graceful curve of her arch, to suck ardently, precisely and appreciatively on those curving, little pink toes, each delicious, one at a time. But that is an outdoor lovesong of another sort.

Stargazing

A *Peeping Tom in the Sultan's Harem*

Scott Simon, thoughtful host of National Public Radio's "Weekend Edition," was interviewing two young adventurers who had sailed a small boat from the North Pole to the South Pole. Their journey had taken them past tropical isles, through fierce storms, alongside great groaning glaciers crashing ("calving" is the proper term) enormous icebergs the size of the Houston Astrodome into the sea. Mr. Simon was especially interested in the contrast between the world's immensity as seen and felt by the two seafarers, and the small, close, familiar confines of their little boat; the vast world out *there* as opposed to the much more limited world, the *here*, in which the travelers lived and on which they depended.

It is a contrast that should be familiar to all of us, because, of course, we are all seafarers, traveling in a very small craft. To see the vastness of the ocean in which we float, we need only raise our eyes to the night sky.

The unquenchable human spirit has long been a favorite topic of writers, poets, philosophers, and often political activists, as well: that our bodies can be imprisoned, but not our minds or our thoughts, or our souls. If one is in the market for such contrasts, there is no more dramatic image than the fact that our human flesh, although Earthbound—with all that this implies—is nonetheless sensitive to signals that are literally extra-terrestrial: the light of distant worlds, the emanations of stars.

A cat may look at a king, according to the saying, but what is more remarkable by far is that a person—any person—may look at a star. The gulf between cat and king is nothing compared to that between Earthling and even the closest star, Proxima Centaurus. How far, then, can a person see with the unaided eye? Here on Earth, a mile, ten miles, maybe seventy miles on a clear day with a mountain or cloud bank to light upon in the distance. But in fact on a clear *night*, you can see almost literally forever, more than two million light years.[1]

It is something precious, to be cherished, savored, and altogether appreciated, this ability of ours to eavesdrop on other worlds, to register in our transient, quivering little cell membranes the titanic convulsions and interstellar effusions of raw energy, unimaginable mass and unfathomable distances. And it's ours for the looking, so long as the sun is down (so sunshine doesn't overpower the more delicate starshine), our vision is average, and the night isn't foggy or overcast. The sun is remarkable enough, providing all our energy including almost all our light. Even the shimmering, surreal Northern Lights, the magical light of the moon, and the pinpoint light by which the planets glow, are all nothing but sunshine on the rebound. But starlight is truly different, not of our world, or even our solar system.

We are creatures of the day, not of the night. Our ancestors feared the night, probably because of the creatures it harbored: large, fierce cats with sharp teeth and merciless claws, strange insects and maybe poisonous snakes, inactive during the heat of the day but slithering about in the cool of dusk. Even now, with nothing to fear (take that literally: no *thing*), we still fear night in general and keep it at bay with artificial lights, incandescent and fluorescent, and with almost frantic excess of noise.

And yet, night offers something—a quiet, a peace, a smoothing and softening of hard edges and reflective glare. It also offers not only starlight but an opening outward into immensity. During the day, our lives go on, focused almost always on the here and now, typically on what can be grasped by the human hand. But at night,

1. One light year is more than five trillion miles.

and especially if artificial lights are extinguished, there is nowhere to look but out, not a few feet out or a few hundred yards, but really *out*, millions of miles.

The next day, immensity collapses once again upon itself and the world at hand is, as it should be, the one that counts . . . but the memory lingers of how night makes our bodies small and our spirits large.

There are few things that remain more or less fixed and reliable, whatever our personal experiences and pretty much wherever we go. But unless we travel far north or south, the stars and planets can be counted on, even if they can hardly be counted; they are there, come what may. And they are the same, for farmer or factory worker, bus driver or surgeon, mariner or mortgage broker.

I would have liked to say that the heavens—so far from Earth as to be indifferent to our discrepancies and unfairnesses—are equally accessible to all of us, regardless of geography or sociology. It would have been nice to rhapsodize over the availability of stargazing to everyone, including the residents of our urban ghettos; but sadly, even the sky is increasingly blighted for these folk. Along with the other, better known forms of pollution, those who would lift their eyes unto the heavens now must confront *light* pollution, the photonic barrage (from streetlights, automobile headlights, advertising lights, etc.) that makes it more and more difficult for the city dweller to appreciate or even to see the stars. Even the pie in the sky is getting dim. Soon, the only way to see stars will be to get hit on the head.

Actually, there can be a silver lining in the cloud of light pollution. Since the fainter stars are essentially obliterated, the neophyte urban stargazer is less likely to be confused by hundreds of lesser lights. The bright ones such as Arcturus, Castor and Pollux, Sirius, Procyon—the important "land" marks of the sky—can therefore be recognized all the more readily.

But anyone looking to be knocked out by the full-fledged spectacle of the skies can only mourn the dimming of the heavens. Professional astronomers have been similarly deprived: only when Los Angeles was blacked out because of fear of Japanese attack, in 1942, were the experts at Mount Palomar Observatory able to get a good enough look at the Andromeda Galaxy—the farthest stars to be seen with the naked eye—to evaluate its size, and also, its distance from us.

It is my favorite place to gaze. This vague, rather *nebulous* smear of light in the constellation Andromeda was long known as the Andromeda Nebula (from the Latin, meaning vapor or cloud). As star-stuff goes, it appears unremarkable: a dimly glowing disc about one-half the size of a full moon overhead. For hundreds of years, experts assumed that it was produced by glowing interstellar gas. Only in this century have astronomers determined that the Andromeda Nebula is nothing less than an entire galaxy in itself, fully twice as big as our own Milky Way, and composed of perhaps 200 billion stars: not just a world of its own, but a peephole into an entire galaxy of worlds. Before this, the Andromeda Nebula was thought to be within the Milky Way, just as the Milky Way was thought to be the entire universe. The Andromeda Galaxy is in fact the only galaxy that can be seen from the Northern Hemisphere without aid of telescope; there are two such galaxies, the Greater and Lesser Magellanic "Clouds," visible in the Southern Hemisphere.[2]

Looking up at the nighttime sky, all the other stars that we see are within our own galactic home, the Milky Way. (A galaxy is a major collection of stars and associated celestial stuff. The word derives from the Greek *galacto*, meaning milk: according to myth, the stars of the Milky Way are the unhomogenized overflow from Hera's breasts. With the help of telescopes, many additional galaxies can be seen, and it is currently estimated that there are literally millions of them.) In any event, as vast as the Milky Way is, a star traveler heading from it to the Andromeda Galaxy would see that inconspicuous, homogeneous little smear of starlight expand until it seemed to swallow all existence. It would be like falling through Alice's rabbit hole, into a new world—or rather, a new collection of worlds—from which the complexity of the Milky Way might appear to be no more than a speck in the sky, if indeed it was visible at all.

We have now learned that there are many extragalactic nebulae (a very pleasing mouthful, that), and that many of them are galaxies

2. This chapter will be concerned only with stargazing as it can be done with the naked, unaided eye; that is, as it has been done for thousands of years.

in their own right, such as the renowned Crab Nebula, in the constellation Taurus, the Bull. Some—like our own Milky Way—are arranged with vast spiral arms, like an immense pinwheel, sixty thousand light-years across. Others are more conservatively disclike. We have also heard that the heavenly bodies travel in predictable patterns, readily calculated by the use of known physical laws. In addition, we have learned that the visible stars are not really numberless: the unaided human eye can make out about two thousand stars in the Milky Way from one horizon to another (and people in the Southern Hemisphere see approximately another two thousand). But this is less than a fraction of a thousandth of those present in our galaxy alone, and the universe is now thought to consist of about 200 billion billion stars, many of which presumably have planets, moons, and the associated paraphernalia that we take so for granted here on Earth. But most important, we have learned a bit of humility. For the more we are privileged to witness the celestial pageant and to admire the various dramas being played out all around us, the more we must admit that the universe is really very, very large, and far away, and we are very small indeed.

Some of those tiny stars—the same pinpricks that seem like they might be the smallest things imaginable—are so huge that if one was substituted for the sun, it would fill most of the volume of the Solar System with star stuff. The Earth would be entirely within the gross body of such a star: Antares in the constellation Scorpio, for example, has a radius of 150 million miles, while the distance from the Earth to the sun is "only" 93 million miles. And others are larger yet, the biggest having a radius of one-half billion miles, one thousand times larger than our sun. These so-called Red Giants are actually somewhat cool by celestial standards, but they make up for their low temperature with immense size.

The preceding doesn't mean, however, that we are insignificant. But it does mean that a little humility should go a long way ... light-years, for example. And such humility should include not only recognizing our diminutive size and out-of-the-way location, but also our likely inability even to perceive this universe, never mind to comprehend it. Paleontologist George Gaylord Simpson said this about the pomposity of experts: "The most the biggest of them know is that what little they do know mostly isn't true and what is true isn't very important, at least not in comparison with what isn't known and isn't knowable."[3] There is something about the stars that helps us see things this way, like sailors in a small boat, strangers in a huge, strange land of space and stars.

As a young child, I can remember looking with amazement at the streams of traffic driving along a busy highway at night. Each car, complete with its own private set of headlights to light its own private path, contained someone, hurrying along to something, without any concern for me; indeed, not even knowing that I existed. This was unacceptable, and so I imagined instead that the cars were great double-eyed fireflies, and I made out patterns in their movement, patterns that were, of course, directed in some mysterious way toward myself.

Most likely stars are like those automobiles, self-contained, complete, oblivious to us . . . whether we like it or not. Historically, however, people have thought otherwise. They have personalized the stars. More than four thousand years ago, the ancient Babylonians and Egyptians were acutely aware of the positions of the stars and planets, convinced that they were omens directed to us on Earth. Thus, astronomy had its origins in astrology, with its certainty that events on Earth are influenced by those up above. For some reason, as star-study progressed, people became not less self-centered in their celestial imaginings, but more so. By around 500 B.C., astrologers turned from general predictions about the future to the casting of individual horoscopes. Even though during the past four hundred years astronomy has outgrown its natal association with astrology—just as chemistry has outgrown its birth as alchemy—people still look for significance, which for most of us means human meaning, in the night sky.

Hollywood boasts many stars, as does television. Star quality is cherished, although it will not do to be starry-eyed, or star struck. The Stars and Stripes—and for some, the Star of David—commands devotion. And of course, there was that Star of Bethlehem, which ostensibly rose in the East two thousand years ago. It seems

3. George Gaylord Simpson, *Simple Curiosity* (Berkeley: University of California Press, 1988).

that we human beings have long been on a star-vation diet, for good or ill.

Comets, for example, have long been seen as presaging disaster. A fearful, even panic-stricken, public awaited Halley's comet when it visited the Earth in 1910, and although nothing untoward took place, believers could point to the death of Mark Twain that year, the sinking of the Titanic two years later, and two years after that, World War I. Sometimes, however, comets really are disasters, to themselves if nothing else: Biela's comet, first identified by the German astronomer Wilhelm Biela in 1771, returned for a time about every six-and-one-half years. By 1846, it was seen to have split in two. By its next appearance, in 1852, the halves were even further apart, and Biela's comet was never seem again. Apparently it had self-destructed. Several cycles later, when another visit would have been anticipated, there was instead a meteor shower, coming from precisely where the comet's head should have been. (It is at least possible that meteors are the ghosts of comets past.)

Comet Kahoutek, which arrived in 1973 to much anticipation, was a disaster in itself, simply because it didn't live up to its advance billing, and the same must be admitted about Halley's comet on its most recent return trip in 1986. We know that comets are little more than dirty snowballs, and that the moon is made of rock, not green cheese. The stars are mainly hydrogen, with some helium thrown in for good measure; they aren't made of fairy dust or the sparkling eyes of great beasts, sent by the gods for no other purpose than to warn, punish, guide, or delight the inhabitants of the third planet from a nondescript star toward the edge of a so-so galaxy. Comet Tago-Sato-Kosaka was last seen in 1969; it is scheduled to come around again in four hundred and twenty thousand years . . . a periodicity that would seem to minimize its significance for us, or ours for it. The astronomer Fred Hoyle is duly skeptical about the portentous qualities of celestial events. "Perhaps the most majestic feature of our whole existence," he writes, "is that while our intelligences are powerful enough to penetrate deeply into this quite incredible Universe, we still have not the smallest clue to our own fate."[4] As Shakespeare's Julius Caesar put it, the

4. Fred Hoyle, *The Nature of the Universe* (New York: Harper & Bros., 1950).

fault is "not in our stars, but in ourselves." And that's also where the future is to be found.

But there is something about those things up there, comets, stars, planets—shining *at us*, or so it seems—that simply demands that they must be speaking *to us*, as well:

> Star light, star bright, first star I see tonight,
> I wish I may, I wish I might
> Have this wish I wish tonight.

* * *

For millennia, people have been bestowing their wishes upon the stars. Wishing on a star—especially a falling star (that is, a meteor)—involves putting our hopes for the future onto something else, apart from us, something that is not only distant but likely to stay that way. In the process, we keep ourselves safe from judgment or response. Nothing more is required, because the covenant is secret, private, unenforceable, and also unimpeachable. Like throwing coins in a fountain, we cast something from us, into a void, a note in a bottle, a whisper upon the wind. Like some great psychoanalyst in the sky, the stars sit there imperturbable, taking anything and everything we throw at them, looking back at us unfazed and unimpressed. If nothing else, they offer a marvelous projective test, a Rorschach image as wide as the horizons. And like the Bible, people can see whatever they want in the stars.

The constellations are the most dramatic example. In some cases, the patterns and associations are not entirely fanciful. For example, the ancient Babylonians noticed that the rainy season occurred when the sun was in a certain group of stars, so they named that group Aquarius, the water-bringer. And the Greeks perceived that since spring was a time of energy, and also a time when the ancient world went to war (because summer crops in the fields would provide provisions for a campaigning army), they named a prominent springtime constellation after Aries, the energetic god of war.

In mid- to late-summer, we have the "dog days," which were not named for the lazy behvaior of overheated canines, but rather because—as first noted by the ancient Greeks—the Dog Star, Sirius, rose with the sun during times of hot sticky weather, in July and August. Sirius is part of the constellation Canis Major, the Great

Dog, companion of Orion the Hunter. (To find it, follow the three bright stars making up Orion's belt and confirm that it is also the brightest star in the sky.) There is debate over Sirius: some claim that it is a jewel hanging from Fido's collar, while others swear that it is nothing less than his fierce and glaring eye.

As a child, I thought the constellations were downright dumb. They didn't look a bit like a lion, hunter, whale, etc., not to mention anything as sappy as a virgin.[5] So, I made up my own: tyrannosaurus, Willie Mays making his unique basket catch, a mushroom cloud. These constructions said more about a ten year old, and the events of his day, than about the stars. Whereas the same can be said for the Greeks' imaginings, as well, we must admit that theirs have stood the test of time. (It is also interesting to consider the effect on human civilization if the stars had in fact been organized into distinct, recognizable patterns: what if when we looked up, for example, there was a genuine, perfectly sketched image of a great hunter holding a dead animal or a huge dragon?)

The stars themselves have stood that test as well and when we admire the Great Square of Pegasus, or the densely packed little W of Cassiopeia, we can bet the Greeks admired them too. They also recognized the connection between the heavens and that most shared of experiences, the passage of time. The spinning Earth defines a day; the rotating Moon, a month; the rotating Earth about the sun, a year. All over our planet, people have used the changing patterns of stars to tell them of the passing of seasons: when to plant and when to harvest.

Stargazing, then, is a way of achieving connection with the past and also with others currently alive on Earth . . . or at least, in the same hemisphere. It can be delightful to meet someone who grew up in your old neighborhood, or who went to your school, even if you didn't know each other at the time. Or to discover that you share a major work of fiction, like *Lord of the Rings*, perhaps, or maybe *Gravity's Rainbow*. The particular appeal comes from landmarks held in common: "You're from Topeka? Do you know . . . ?" When you look into the western sky shortly after sunset during late winter and see Jupiter or Venus (or, if you're lucky, Jupiter *and*

5. The sole exception was Scorpius, who really did—and still does—look like a scorpion.

Venus), two "evening stars," each of them brighter than any real
star in the sky, you can be assured that other people on Earth are
looking, too, and probably feeling much the same mixture of wonderment and appreciation.

The Arabs used the following as a quickie eye-exam, and you
can too: can you distinguish the two stars Mizar and Alcor, in the
handle of the Big Dipper? It's a long way from you to Jupiter, or to
the Big Dipper (and even farther to the Andromeda Galaxy, for
that matter), and longer yet all the way back again to another point
on Earth where someone else stands still, receiving photos from
the same source out there in space. And it is a long way back in
time to the Babylonians, ancient Greeks, or the Arab star-fanciers.
But by such a triangulation, stargazers do something peculiarly
important to their species: they make *contact*.

Give me a lever long enough, and a place to stand, said Archi-
medes, and I can move the world. The stars are a fulcrum of this
sort, not for moving the world, but for holding it still, for keeping it
intact and solid. They are something shared, and as such they provide an area of common ground, a matrix for relationships among
people, even people who never meet in any other way. "Oh, you're
from the planet Earth, do you know Pisces?"

Most primates don't see the stars. Our close relatives are overwhelmingly diurnal: when it gets dark, they go to sleep. And they
wake up at dawn, rarely before it. Although there are a few exceptions, such as the aptly named night monkey and some of the weird
little prosimians, including the galagos, tarsiers, and lemurs of
Madagascar, stargazing is a uniquely human activity. (Even on clear
nights, it is difficult to see the heavens from within a heavily leafed
tree; maybe our emancipation from the trees gave us the opportunity to appreciate the stars.)

The best place to see stars is on a ship at sea, or on top of a high
mountain, or failing that, in a wide open prairie, as far as possible
from competing lights and the haze of polluted air. Montana adver-
tises itself as the Big Sky Country, but in fact, the Montana sky is
only big in the eastern part of that state; in the west, big mountains
make for smaller skies. In a pinch, however, any place will do, and
many a stargazer has plied his or her trade from an apartment
house roof or even a nocturnal window. Clouds are the stargazer's

bête noire, and accordingly, the arid Southwest is the happiest of celestial hunting grounds, not only for amateurs but professional astronomers as well. In Palm Springs, or Tucson, or Phoenix, with summer temperatures around one hundred degrees or higher, night is the best time of "day" anyhow, with the sky show an added bonus. Or for anyone, anywhere, who would like to shuck off the day's cares and crowds and be alone—just yourself and hundreds of millions of other worlds!—there is no better place to relax.

The horizon grows steadily darker, especially in the east, as the Earth's shadow rises while the sun goes down. Soon, the horizon is blacker than the sky above. This is the only time, incidentally, when this happens; normally, the horizon has a faint glow (light reflected from the sun on the other side of the Earth) and is brighter than the sky above. During winter, Sirius the Dog Star may be the first to appear, sparkling blue-white in the south, or perhaps Capella, brightest star in Auriga the Charioteer, glowing yellow high in the northwest. During spring and summer, it may be orange Arcturus, the Guardian of the Bear, which, later in the evening, can be found by following the curve of the handle of the Big Dipper. In the spring, look for Arcturus in the eastern sky; in later summer, look west. And don't ignore the western horizon, because even before the sun sets, the "evening stars," Venus and/or Jupiter, may well appear. Even though Jupiter's light is entirely reflected sunlight, when it is visible it will outshine anything in the night-time sky, except for the moon.

Stars are generally predictable, reliable landmarks. In a world of chaos and change, there is something comforting in their rhythmic predictability. Planets, by contrast, are quixotic wanderers. Therefore, they are not incorporated into any constellations. When they are inconspicuous, like Uranus—which can barely be seen by the most sharp-eyed gazer—their wanderings make them especially likely to be overlooked. Venus and Mercury, whose orbits are between the Earth and the Sun, will inevitably be seen near the sun, if they can be seen at all. Hence, they are especially good candidates for "evening stars" and "morning stars," visible just before sunrise or after sunset. They are to be found high in the sky during winter, and low during summer. Mercury is easily overlooked, both because of its dull, leaden color and its location as well: it is never more than two hand-widths or so from the sun. On the other hand,

Mercury has the distinction of being the only planet that twinkles.[6]

The extraordinarily bright surface of Venus is enhanced by its atmosphere of dense silvery clouds, a beautiful sight indeed, although a disappointment to anyone seeking a magnified view: because of those clouds, a telescope or binoculars reveal no more detail than does the naked eye. Every nineteen months, Venus appears highest in the evening sky; then it fades—victim of the setting sun's glare—and is invisible for nearly a month, after which it tries again, this time in the morning sky. Once more, it rises higher every day until again it is swallowed up, this time in the brightness of the rising sun, whereupon it modestly hides its face for two months, only to reappear once more in the evening sky, starting the coy cycle all over again.

Since the orbit of Mars, like that of the other planets, is outside the Earth's, it can sometimes be seen near the sun (like Mercury and Venus) and sometimes away from it. The "red planet" really does appear red and more than a little menacing, as befits the god of war. Mars is also paradoxical: its unblinking stare suggests regularity, yet its motion, if followed for a few weeks at a time, is erratic.[7] Every two years, Mars rises with the setting sun, and remains in the sky all night long; two months earlier, it rose at midnight and could have been seen in the southeast for several hours before dawn; and for two more months to come, it will rise in the early evening and set by midnight. Both Jupiter (which appears white) and Saturn (yellow) can be seen in the morning sky and evening sky for roughly five months of each year, with Jupiter taking twelve of our years to make a complete orbit around the sun. It spends a year in each of the twelve major constellations that astrologers call the zodiac. Saturn, which takes thirty years to make its orbit, is a more leisurely visitor in each constellation, loitering for nearly three years at a time. Sadly, neither the rings of Saturn nor the great red spot of Jupiter can be seen with the naked eye.

It can be almost overpowering to encounter, suddenly, the full-blown majesty of a starry night, with the heavens blazing in sharp

6. But when they are directly overhead, stars don't twinkle very much, either.
7. Of course, the motion of Mars isn't really erratic at all; rather, it appears erratic because of the way its orbit interacts with the movement and rotation of the Earth.

points of light. It is also magic, but of another sort, to watch the buildup, the gentle transition to evening, as the stars begin peeking through the rapidly fraying daylight curtain. First there are no stars at all and then perhaps one in a whole vast quadrant of sky. Then another. And then yet another. Now, stare at any part of the sky and watch carefully, for you are at a crucial, delicate balance point in the relation between cosmos and consciousness: like fish jumping and breaking the surface of a glassy lake, new stars will pop suddenly into view—all the more remarkable because of their silence—first slowly and then building speed until they are bursting forth faster than you can count, each one responding to the flick of a celestial switch. With a delicacy and precision that must be seen to be believed and a cosmic chuckle that can almost be heard, the stars are turning themselves on.

Better than artificial fireworks, this show is free and it runs every night. It can't really be appreciated, however, standing bolt upright with head tipped uncomfortably so that the back of the neck is bunched in a tight little knot. In the interest of appreciative relaxation, and if only out of respect for the vast distances and the magnitude of the drama about to unfold, stargazing is best done lying flat on one's back, possibly in a sleeping bag, under a blanket, or maybe just enveloped in the warm summer air. Stretch out luxuriously on the ground and be grateful that it is solid, comfortable, and relatively cool, not—like the stars—seething with hundreds of thousands of thermonuclear degrees. If you like to identify what you see, a portable star map might be helpful, as well as a small flashlight for reading it. The only other thing needed is a little bit of patience.

The night sky, you will notice, isn't black, but rather deep gray, or blue, or even a dark maroon. What is really black is the setting in the foreground, whether trees, mountains, telephone poles, or buildings. Depending on where you are gazing, these props will, of course, vary, but not the stars of the show, the stars themselves.

Although at first glance, all stars are white or diamond-sparkly, a closer look shows variations on the theme: Rigel appears blue, Vega is white, Sirius is blue-white, and huge, oversized Betelgeuse is red. The daytime sky is, of course, quite changeable: sunny, perhaps some rain, varying pattern of clouds and light. By contrast, the night stars are reliable. They can be counted on, even if they can hardly be counted. They seem to remain pretty much fixed, at least from one twenty-four hours to the next. But if you are lying near a tree, fix the location of a few of the most conspicuous stars relative to the branches just above you; after a few minutes, you will see that the stars appear to have moved, from east to west just like the sun.

You have just entered into one of the great double truths of stargazing: the stars are simultaneously fixed yet changing. They seem to move during a single night, just as the sun appears to move during the day, and for the same reason: the spinning of the Earth. Of course, the stars aren't really moving, we are. Similarly, they seem to move as the seasons change, so that the night sky in summer is quite different from that of winter. In fact, a careful observer would notice that the night sky at, say, 9:00 P.M. on January 2 is just a bit different from what could be seen exactly twenty-four hours earlier on New Year's Day. The dome of heavens has come to rest with a slight displacement to the east. In fact, the displacement is just about 1/365th of the whole, so that after a year, we are back where we started from. In the Northern Hemisphere, this massive wheel of fortune seems to revolve around Polaris, the North Star, which rises more or less directly above the North Pole. At any time of year, we can judge latitude by the height of the North Star above the horizon: nearly straight overhead if you are standing at the North Pole, almost invisible at the horizon if you are on the equator. While the heavens spin slowly, north is always north.

Imagine that the sky is a gigantic umbrella, whose central supporting shaft runs from the Earth, through the North Pole, to Polaris. As the Earth spins slowly around its northern pole, it therefore appears to us that the heavens above are rotating in the opposite direction, with only Polaris—directly at the apex, above the Pole—remaining fixed.[8] As a result, although the other constellations come and go with the seasons, on any starry night in the Northern Hemisphere, the Big Dipper (pointing to the North Star) and the Little Dipper (home of the North Star) can always be found.

For millennia, people have been aware of the apparent move-

---

8.   Unfortunately for navigators south of the equator or for southern people
     simply wanting a bit of stability in their lives, there is no comparable Pole
     Star in the Southern Hemisphere.

ment of the stars, during any given night, combined with their eventual return—365 days later—to where they had been. Maybe the recurrent, wheel-like rotation of the stars is connected to the Hindu conception of the great wheel of death and rebirth; but celestial recurrence needn't only be seen in such a pessimistic light, something to be escaped. The apparent year-to-year constancy of the heavens also carries within itself a positive message, a guarantee of seasonal renewal. As the Earth begins to swing into position such that the days in the Northern Hemisphere are going to become longer and warmer, we begin to see constellations that we couldn't see before, harbingers of growth and reawakening. Indeed, the springtime constellations such as Virgo, Libra, and Scorpius were there all along, right up in the sky where they belong; they just couldn't be seen because they were shining merrily in the *daytime* sky and were therefore invisible to us.

Similarly, winter constellations cannot be seen during the summer because they are in the daytime sky, and similarly for spring and fall. At any given time of year, the sun is between the Earth and about one-half the stars. The other half can be seen when the Earth spins on its axis so that night falls—in other words, when we face them rather than the sun and see at last what has always been there.

Probably the strangest of all stargazing opportunities happens during that quintessentially strange event, an eclipse of the sun. For a short period of time, as the moon passes between the sun and the Earth, the world is suddenly out of whack, and you listen for the grinding of great gears. Someone, it seems, has thrown a monkey wrench into the cogs of the universe. The sun in eclipse becomes a kind of black hole, a blank spot gouged painfully and precisely out of the sky. Dogs bark, or howl, the horizon burns red and orange and gold, and an owl awakens drowsily, thinking it is prematurely evening. Unfortunately, during such an eclipse, nearly everyone wastes time looking in the wrong place—carefully inspecting the sun through mylar sheets, smoked glass, and whatnot, under the well-meaning advice of countless experts—while ignoring the best show of all. Because during a solar eclipse, the stars are suddenly revealed, and in midday yet, obediently responding to the summons of darkness, reluctantly surrendering their accustomed daytime privacy. And moreover, there in the daytime the appreciative gazer can see a delicious, seductive array of stars normally visible only under the blanket of night, maybe six months later. It is as though we are granted a sudden, surprise glimpse of the naked beauties in some exotic harem . . . while most of us waste the delicious opportunity by staring at the overwrought sultan.

It is sometimes claimed that the Earth is remarkably—indeed, miraculously—fitted for us. Thus, if it was a bit hotter, or colder, or wetter, or drier, or darker, or lighter, or endowed with more oxygen, or less, etc., it would not support *Homo sapiens*, and indeed, maybe not life at all. This argument is not terribly compelling, however, since if the Earth wasn't as it is, and indeed, we weren't here, then either we would not exist at all, or intelligent life, existing somewhere else, would be congratulating itself (or its favorite deities) in the same way, on another planet.

As cosmologist Stephen Hawking puts it,

> The conditions necessary for the development of intelligent life will be met only in certain regions that are limited in space and time. The intelligent beings in these regions should therefore not be surprised if they observe that their locality in the universe satisfies the conditions that are necessary for their existence. It is a bit like a rich person living in a wealthy neighborhood not seeing any poverty.[9]

But here is something that is remarkable, and perhaps miraculous, although rarely identified as such: the fact that the moon circles the Earth at precisely the correct height so that it casts its shadow just right and occasionally produces a total eclipse of the sun. This wonderful machination has proved useful for novels in need of a deus ex machina, such as *Dr. Doolittle*, *King Solomon's Mines*, and *A Connecticut Yankee in King Arthur's Court*. It also provides stargazers with reassuring proof that even when we can't see them, the stars are still there, just biding their time until they can appear to us under what is for us—if not for them—more normal, nocturnal circumstances.

To the Greeks, Polaris was known as Kynosoura, and although the name has changed, the concept has become enthroned in our

9.   Stephen Hawking, *A Brief History of Time* (New York: Bantam, 1988).

vocabulary: a "cynosure" is a center of attention. To find the North Star, our celestial cynosure, first locate the best known of all star formations, the Big Dipper (actually part of the constellation Ursa Major, the Great Bear). Then follow the "pointer" stars that make up the end of the dipper's scoop. The North Star itself is the final star in the handle of the Little Dipper (in the constellation Ursa Minor, the Little Bear). Because of its seemingly fixed position in a constantly rotating sea of stars—not to mention the intolerable perversity of the planets—the North Star has long been the most important orientation point in the heavens. Even as the world turns and the Big Dipper spins along, the pointer stars continue to show the way to Polaris: in winter, the Big Dipper is east of the Little Dipper, and it points west to Polaris. In summer, the Big Dipper is displaced to the west, and so, its pointers aim obediently east. Escaped slaves used the Big Dipper to keep heading north, toward freedom; there is even a folk song based on this astronomical wisdom, "Follow the drinking gourd."

The ancients were long aware of celestial movement. Around 150 A.D. in Egypt, Ptolemy cataloged more than one thousand different stars and their wanderings. And more than two hundred years earlier, Hipparchus, a Greek, drew up the first known star charts. Nonetheless, people still cherished the belief that whereas the stars move about en masse, as individual entities they were unchanging. The stars were made of eternal, supernatural stuff, ideal Platonic embodiments of a perfection unattainable in the secular hurly-burly of Earth. The stars were equated with the heavens—a word, interestingly, that we still use today—and their reliability and permanence was also indicated by another, more arcane usage, the "firmament."

Then, in 1572, the Danish astronomer Tycho Brahe put a crack in the firmness of the firmament by showing that a star had exploded (become a supernova). The stars, evidently, were not incorruptible or infinitely serene. In 1718, Edmund Halley found something much more important than his famous comet: he discovered that the stars had actually moved—not just in their daily or seasonal patterns, but in their orientation relative to each other—since the recordings of Hipparchus.

In fact, we now realize that the stars are moving away from us, in all directions, and moreover, the farther away they are, the faster

they are traveling. It is also generally agreed that this heavenly
diaspora provides the answer to one of astronomy's most puzzling
riddles, known as Olbers' Paradox. It may also "explain" why we
have not been burned to a crisp long ago.

Olbers' Paradox is embedded in the question, why is the night
sky dark? Given that the universe is for our purposes infinite, with
unending layers upon layers of stars, there should in fact be no
dark spaces between the points of light we call stars. The heavens
should be a great blinding blaze of light, so much light that the
accumulated radiant energy would make life on Earth—or anywhere else—impossible. But clearly, there is a flaw in Olbers' Paradox, and here it is: the universe is expanding outward and rapidly
(presumably, as a result of the primordial Big Bang). And as a
source of light moves away from us, its energy undergoes a transition known as the "red shift," which causes it to be distorted toward the red end of the spectrum, thereby losing energy at the
same time. So, the sky is dark and our planet is cool enough to
support the kind of molecular stability we call life . . . all because
the stars are not really perfect and imperturbable after all. For
that, we can all give thanks.

Not only have the stars moved, but so has the position of the
Earth. An interesting result of the Earth's movement in space is
that the signs of the Zodiac, so beloved of astrologers, no longer
correspond to the constellations for which they were originally
named. But astrologers don't seem especially troubled by this . . .
or by the fact that the geocentric universe has been overthrown.

More changes. Two thousand years ago, the Earth's Pole Star
was not Polaris but rather Alpha Cepheus.[10] (Also within the constellation Cepheus is Delta Cepheus, the brightest of the so-called
"pulsating stars"—of these, more in a few pages.) Polaris cannot
rest on its laurels, for in another twelve hundred years, it will be

10. By astronomical tradition, in addition to a possible unique name—e.g., Po-
     laris, Vega—stars are named with a Greek letter followed by the constella-
     tion in which they are found. The brightest member of the constellation is
     designated alpha, the next is beta, etc. Thus, Alpha Cepheus is the brightest
     star in the constellation Cepheus. (Cepheus, by the way, was the husband of
     Cassiopeia and father of Andromeda.)

replaced in turn by Vega, which currently is sometimes known by the lovely phrase "arc light of the sky." Vega is the brightest star in the small constellation Lyra, the Harp, found west of the Northern Cross. (Lyra, incidentally, has several double stars, the brightest of which—Epsilon Lyrae—can just barely be identified as a double by the keen-eyed observer.)

It takes precise observations, good luck, or great patience (sometimes all three) to witness these kinds of astronomical changes. For example, today we know that the scoop of the Big Dipper was nearly closed fifty thousand years ago, and that it will be wide open in another fifty thousand years, and thus, no longer a dipper at all. Just some zigzaggy lines. But the amateur stargazer, lying comfortably under a tree on a summer evening, also has the opportunity to witness some imperfections in celestial stability, variations that occur on a more human time scale. Take, for example, the many variable stars. Some of them pulsate, like Mira, the "Wonderful," in the constellation of Cetus the Whale. Mira has a period of very low brightness, during which it vanishes altogether for six months at a stretch, after which it reappears. At its brightest, Mira is three hundred times more brilliant than when its light is dimmed. The delectable-sounding red star Betelgeuse (pronounced "beetle juice"), which comprises the right shoulder of Orion the Hunter, is another notable pulsator.

Then there are the "eclipsing binaries," double stars that rotate about one another, in such a way that periodically, the duller partner shades its brighter sibling. To the naked eye, a binary appears to be a single star; therefore, when the pair of stars that we call a binary goes into eclipse, it looks as though its brightness has dimmed. To witness a good example, find Algol, in Medusa's Head, part of the constellation Perseus. Every three days, Algol dims to only one third of its usual brilliance, taking about five hours to do so; in the next five hours, it regains its customary shine. Then three days later, it repeats this predictable fade-out and return.

And for yet another example of celestial instability, there are the supernova, mind-boggling explosions by which a dying star releases more light than the normal output of an entire galaxy of hundreds of millions of stars. Events of this sort don't happen often; in fact, the last big one was observed in 1604 and can today be admired only as a faint nebula . . . that is, until the most recent supernova flamed into view on February 23, 1987. What seemed such a current event actually took place during the Old Stone Age: traveling at the speed of light, it took one hundred and sixty thousand years or so for the news to reach the Earth. To the chagrin of American stargazers, however, this *nouveau* supernova could be seen only in the Southern Hemisphere, in the Greater Magellanic Cloud.

It was quite a show. With the exception of the original Big Bang itself, a supernova is far and away the most violent event in the universe. The 1987 spectacle released, in each second, more than one hundred times the total energy that our sun will radiate in its entire, four-billion-year lifespan. For more than a year, it astonished the traditional mariners of the South Pacific (the world's greatest star navigators), to whom it appeared somewhat brighter than Jupiter, while delighting astronomers in Chile, Australia, and South Africa, to whom it offered clues on the origin of the heavier elements, the birth of the Big Bang, and the process by which some stars self-destruct.

Even those of us not versed in such astronomical arcana as pulsating stars, eclipsing binaries, or supernovae would not find our world view severely shaken these days by additional evidence that the stars are not in perfect harmony, that sometimes the music of the spheres is a bit discordant. The poet Heine once suggested—without benefit of astronomy—that perhaps the stars appear to be so fair and pure simply because they are so faraway: if they were nearer, he proposed, we would know more about their private lives and would, therefore, be more aware of their imperfections. Lacking such intimacy, we often take it for granted that they must be marvelously sublime, like a movie-star idol who never defecates.

We also take it for granted that the Earth goes around the sun, even though we still speak (and wittingly, often think) as though the Earth is the center of all creation. Thus, we use phrases such as sunrise, sunset, as well as the rising and setting of the other stars, knowing full well that we—not they—are doing most of the moving. But of course, not too long ago, nearly everyone was convinced that the sun, moon, planets, and stars all circled the Earth. It may be impossible for us to appreciate the shock that followed the demonstration, by the Polish astronomer Copernicus and the

Italian, Galileo, that in fact it is the Earth that moves around the sun.

Tycho Brahe, a brilliant student of the heavens, to whom the great astronomer Kepler was at one time apprenticed, provides a remarkable example of how even highly intelligent scientists can indulge in wishful thinking. Brahe suggested an alternative to the Copernican, heliocentric world view, an interesting example of a very human foible: a grudging willingness to accept new facts and interpretations (if they are undeniable), combined with a stubborn persistence everywhere else. Brahe could not refute the Copernican system, in which the known planets—Mercury, Venus, Mars, Jupiter, and Saturn—revolved around the sun. So in his proposed model, they were allowed to continue doing so. But he also couldn't stomach demoting his beloved home planet to such a secondary status. So, in the Brahean world view, the five known planets revolved around the sun . . . but that system (sun plus planets) proceeded to circle the Earth!

It should be emphasized that this was not a simple compromise, in which two contending parties might agree to split the difference. Rather, it exemplified our curious stubbornness: giving ground only reluctantly to information that disrupts an old way of thinking, while still clinging tenaciously to our most cherished beliefs. Adjust to reality, if need be, by making minor concessions at the margins, but keep the core of your preconceptions intact.

Brahean solutions are not unique to astronomy. Thus, upon hearing Charles Darwin's infamous theory, the wife of the Bishop of Worcester exclaimed, "Descended from monkeys? My dear, let us hope that it isn't true! But if it is, let us hope that it doesn't become widely known!" Today, we generally accept the truth of evolution while still insisting that despite natural selection and our shared evolutionary heritage with all living things, our own species is uniquely blessed with spiritual essence, the apple of God's eye. We accept the laws of physics while believing ardently in free will. We accept that the Earth's resources are finite, while continuing to exploit them unmercifully. We recognize the danger—to ourselves and to the entire planet—posed by nuclear weapons, but we are so wedded to the ancient idea of weapons in the first place that we seek to achieve safety not by renouncing them but by building yet more and calling it "strengthening deterrence," or "strategic defense." Tycho Brahe would understand. And lying under your tree, looking at the stars *moving* through the sky, you can, too.

To witness a truly unspoiled natural scene, we have to go far out to sea or perhaps to a national park or wilderness area . . . or we can look up. The Milky Way is best seen in all its pristine glory on a clear moonless summer night. It is brightest at its center, toward Sagittarius (the Archer) in the southern horizon, whereas it continues in an impressive band especially through Cygnus, the Swan (better known as the Northern Cross). Although dimmer in winter, the Milky Way is still worth noting, especially near Cassiopeia and Orion.

But just as there are roads in national parks and hamburger stands in paradise, there are human artifacts in the sky as well, "stars" that move more rapidly than most and twinkle less. Their movement is in fact much too fast for stars, but too slow for jet planes. They aren't stars at all, but artificial satellites, of which the sharp-eyed observer can see dozens in a single night. Not uncommonly, they will abruptly disappear while you watch. They aren't burning up or falling to Earth; rather, as they pass into the Earth's shadow they undergo a kind of eclipse in which the Earth blocks the sun's light, leaving the satellite briefly unilluminated, until it reappears again. It would be a kindness to stargazers if governments would coat their effluvia with nonreflecting paint.

On the other hand, some space junk can be particularly beautiful and, on occasion, destructive. Consider "falling stars," for example. A falling star is actually a meteor, a rapidly moving piece of hardened space debris, generally made either of stony material or of metal, most likely iron or nickel. While in outer space, meteors are invisible, but if they enter the Earth's atmosphere, friction with the air causes them to heat up and to burn, producing dramatic, short-lived streaks against the sky. Typically, they are first visible at about sixty five miles above the Earth, and they nearly always burn themselves out by twenty miles (above one hundred thousand feet).

Meteors are actually fairly common, and the shooting star aficionado willing to go without sleep can pretty much be guaranteed to see several on any clear night. There are also certain times when they come in predictable bunches, so-called meteor showers. In the Northern Hemisphere, the Perseid meteor shower is undoubtedly the best; it can be counted on to spray streaks of fiery light, at a rate of about one per minute, during the second week of August, year after year. Few experiences are more cozy than to be tucked inside a sleeping bag, as far as possible from competing light, on a warm August night, and to watch the sky light up with celestial tracer bullets.

Shooting stars aren't always so benign, however. Sometimes, they become falling stars that reach the ground before being destroyed. When they do, they are known as meteorites and can be extraordinarily destructive. An immense one—the so-called Tunguska meteorite—smashed into Siberia in 1908. People saw it during full daylight nearly five hundred miles away, and it shook the ground like a serious earthquake more than fifty miles from its point of impact. It probably weighed several hundred tons when it hit the ground, scorching twenty square miles of trees and flattening dense forests over an even wider area. Very long ago, before historic time, the continental United States was apparently victimized by another, even larger meteoric monster: the great Meteor Crater in Arizona, between Flagstaff and Winslow, is nearly a mile across and 570 feet deep. (I write "apparently" because the remains of the meteorite have not been found, leaving us a puzzling case of celestial—or rather, terrestrial—*habeas corpus*).

Although one's chances of being flattened or incinerated by a rampaging meteorite are vanishingly small, it is hardly reassuring to know that the Earth is estimated to gain about one thousand tons of matter per day, from falling meteorites.

* * *

> Twinkle, twinkle little star,
> How I wonder what you are.
> Up above the world so high,
> Like a diamond in the sky.
> Twinkle, twinkle, little star,
> How I wonder what you are.

Wonder is perhaps the most common—and almost certainly the healthiest—of all stargazer reactions. Sometimes wonder leads on

to poetry, or inquiry, or just plain rumination. Thus, Hamlet sought
to reassure Ophelia as follows:

> Doubt thou the stars are fire
> Doubt thou the sun doth move
> Doubt truth to be a liar,
> But never doubt I love.

It may tell us something about the state of Elizabethan star-lore
that Ophelia subsequently committed suicide.

The stargazer, unaccompanied by telescope, insensitive to the
intergalactic emanations of quasars or pulsars, lacking the electro-
magnetic paraphernalia of radio telescopy, cannot really penetrate
very far into heavenly truth, at least as scientists define it. But even
astronomers are curiously handicapped with they look at the stars
and wonder "what they are." Astronomy is an observational science; it is nonexperimental. The stars are real enough, large
enough, and important enough to be worth investigating, and since
star stuff is not fundamentally different from our own terrestrial
clay, it is amenable to the basic tools of physics and chemistry. The
only problem is that they are so far away. So they twinkle or shine,
pulsate and wobble, expand and contract, explode or collapse
upon themselves, all the while keeping a more-than-Olympian
aloofness. Sitting there, imperturable as behind a thick glass window, they invite us to look, but not to touch.

A lot can be learned this way, however. Consider the case of
Uranus, Neptune, and Pluto, final planets in our solar system. The
English astronomer William Herschel discovered Uranus[11] in
1781, apparently by accident while he was just looking around in
an odd corner of the heavens. First, he thought he had found a
comet. Since it takes Uranus eighty four earth-years to orbit the
sun, it took a while for specialists to determine its orbit, and so, it
wasn't until two years later, 1783, that Uranus was found to deviate

---

11.   One of the more regrettable cases of linguistic hyper-delicacy occurred dur-
      ing news accounts of a recent unmanned space probe that transmitted the
      most accurate data yet received on the composition of Uranus. Suddenly,
      broadcasters began putting on Victorian airs, calling that venerable planet
      "*yer* enis," with accent on the first syllable, and refusing to acknowledge the
      hard "a" sound of the middle. Like it or not, folks, the planet's pronuncia-
      tion is Uranus, as in "your *anus*." Not mine.

from the path that Newton's laws prescribed for it. And now came one of those events that give us confidence in science, even purely observational science like astronomy: namely, prediction. Astronomers began asking the question, what if the orbit of Uranus was "wrong" because there was yet another planet beyond it, whose gravitational pull was causing the observed deviation? John C. Adams and Urbain Leverrier calculated where this mystery troublemaker should be, sent the coordinates to Johann Galle and his young assistant H.L. d'Arrest, who had good eyes and better telescopes, and sure enough, there was another planet, right in the predicted place. They called it Neptune.

Then it happened again. Neptune, it turns out, was also acting funny. Percival Lowell, an American astronomer, showed that Neptune's delinquency could be explained by yet another, more distant planet, pulling on it. This planet turned out to be so cold, dim, and small that it wasn't found until 1930, fourteen years after Lowell died. But patient, eagle-eyed Clyde Tombaugh discovered Pluto, right where Lowell's calculations said it would be.[12]

Despite the power of today's telescopes and the array of techniques available to modern astronomy, it is remarkable that no other planets, beyond those of our own solar system, have been discovered. Or perhaps it is not so strange after all, since planets can only reflect light, not generate it like a star. And given that even the nearest star—aside from the sun—is 4.3 light-years away, we can understand why only extra-systemic stars, and not planets, have so far been detected. (That star, by the way, is Proxima Centauri, which is a little-known component in the relatively renowned, triple-star system called Alpha Centauri. These stars, which appear to the naked eye as a single bright point in the sky, can be seen only in the Southern Hemisphere. They weren't discovered until the seventeenth century when some astronomically

12. There is no evidence for any other planets, beyond Pluto, but one is warily reminded of Oscar Wilde's observation: "Large fleas have smaller fleas, upon their backs to bite 'em; and so it goes, *ad infinitum*."

inclined missionaries took a break from the African heathens to
explore the African heavens.)[13]

Nonetheless, it is a virtual certainty that when we look up at the
stars, not only those stars but also many planets are looking back at
us. It is, admittedly, a bit discouraging that at least for now they
cannot be seen, nor can we deduce their presence by their gravitational effects on other heavenly bodies, a la Neptune and Pluto:
such planets would be too small to exert a noticeable pull on anything as massive as a star, and furthermore, at celestial distances,
deviations would have to be substantial to be noticeable. But there
must, in fact, be billions of planets out there. Astronomer Fred
Hoyle has estimated that there are so many objects in the Milky
Way alone that right here in our own neighborhood galaxy, there
must be more than a million planets "on which you might live
without undue discomfort."[14] For now, though, it seems a safe bet
that they can't see us, just as we can't see them. But it is fun to try,
especially on a summer night, surrounded by the chirping of crick-
ets, when the ground, still heavy with heat from the departed sun,
seems to be reaching gently upward for something more, through
us and by us.

At such times, what we see is actually less than what we get;
rather, what counts is *how* we see. Walt Whitman contrasted two
ways of seeing, as follows:

> When I heard the learn'd astronomer,
> When the proofs, the figures, were ranged in columns
> before me
> When I was shown the charts and diagrams, to add,
> divide and measure them,
> When I sitting heard the astronomer where he lectured
> with much applause in the lecture-room,
> How soon unaccountable I became tired and sick,
> Till rising and gliding out I wander'd off by myself,

13. Neither Greeks, nor Romans, nor Arabs had named most of the Southern
    constellations, and so, eighteenth-century astronomers got to do what I had
    attempted in the 1950s: create a new pantheon of constellations. They were
    more modest than I, however—and also, more successful—carrying on with
    the tradition of ancient mythology. The Centaur is one of these modern-
    mythic constellations now recognized south of the equator.
14. Fred Hoyle, *The Nature of the Universe*.

In the mystical moist night-air, and from time to time,
Look'd up in perfect silence at the stars.

He was wrong. The stars are for wonder *and* for study. Both the
professional astronomer and the awestruck midnight gazer breathe
the same night air, whether cool, scientifically precise, and rarified,
or mystical moist. And science needn't be sickening; in fact, a contempt for science is even more nauseating, and dangerous as well.
It is a kind of blasphemy that today more people study astrology
than astronomy, although it is worse yet that harmless childhood
dreams of Star Travels and Star Treks are being transmuted daily
into hideous visions of Star Wars. Knowledge is good, whatever the
poet may claim, even if it can be abused. But of course, wisdom is
even better. One could do worse than to look up in perfect silence
at the stars.

Birdwatching

What an Enskyment!

Few outdoor activities are as misunderstood as birdwatching, the most scientific of sports or the most sporting of sciences, take your pick. First, there is the problem of nomenclature. As with horseback riders, who prefer to call themselves riders, birdwatchers commonly designate themselves as simply "birders." And they do not go birdwatching, but rather, "birding."

Second, there is the problem of demographics. In the public mind, birders are more than a little eccentric, often little old ladies in tennis shoes, to boot. The former perception may have some legitimacy, since birders are indeed idiosyncratic, and generally proud of it (one ornithologist has defined birding as "a mild paralysis of the central nervous system which can be cured only by rising at dawn and sitting in a bog"). As to the latter, birders come in all ages, sexes, shapes, and sizes. And tennis shoes, once worn only by tennis players (and birders, presumably), have now been transformed into running shoes and who wears them? Just about everybody.

Third, there is the problem of motivation. Why would any sane person chase about a dank marsh after some half-heard mumbling noise from a creature that would just as soon poop on you as be seen by you; or get up while it is still dark just to walk through rainsoaked brush in hopes of glimpsing—and briefly, at that—a tiny speck of feathered insouciance; or spend hours on the tossing deck of a small boat, hoping for a long-distance peek at a gull, differing from what the noncognoscenti call a "seagull" only in the merest color of its bill or the tip of its wing?

There are other problems, as well, yet birding thrives. In the United States, in fact, birding has generally been doing rather better than the birds, with the lamented exception of certain gull species and those unwanted and superabundant immigrants, the starlings and English sparrows. But why? "A bird is singing in my brain," noted James Russell Lowell, and for some of us, that singing, chirping, twittering, calling, flying, diving, soaring, perching, climbing, hopping, and hovering is almost constant, not just in our brains but also in our souls.

It seems likely that primitive human beings watched birds, just as they watched other animals, if only in hopes of securing a meal. More recently, the flights of birds and the arrangement of the entrails were thought to provide auguries for the future, perhaps because by the unquestioning certainty of their travels and the unwavering vigor of their lives, they seemed to reflect a deep and primitive wisdom.

Then, of course, there is flight. An escaped pet mynah recently made the news by tormenting prisoners at San Quentin with "I can talk, can you fly?" Not all birds fly; penguins, ostriches, and the weird, nocturnal kiwi of New Zealand are notable among the flightless variants. But the great majority are airborne. Recall the old saw "free as a bird." Thanks to today's ethologists[1]—many of them birders as well—we know that most animals (birds included) are spatially restricted to some degree. Yet like most saws, whatever their age, this one is not entirely toothless. Birds have unparalleled freedom of movement, leaving us far behind. Some, like the hawks, eagles, and vultures, can soar for miles without a flap, whereas others like the swifts and swallows perform dazzling and intricate high-speed aerial maneuvers, without a glide. The hummingbirds resemble miniature helicopters, hovering motionless for seconds which, because of their improbability, seem like hours, whereas herons and ravens fly heavily but strongly, their great wings rowing the air with seemingly unstoppable assurance.

1. Students of animal behavior.

Whatever their style, once they are blessed with flight, even the least impressive members of the class Aves have a hold on the human imagination. In his poem, "Vulture," Robinson Jeffers reprimands a hungry, circling bird: "These old bones will still work; they are not for you." But then the poet comments, regretfully, "How beautiful he looked, on those great sails . . . I tell you solemnly that I was sorry to have disappointed him." And he meditates on what it might be like to have been eaten by the great bird and to become part of it, to share its wings and its flight: "What an enskyment." From Daedalus to the Wright brothers to today's astronauts, people have yearned to fly. Our dreams, from Peter Pan to Superman, have soared aloft, and the highest praise has come when imaginations—if not bodies—have "taken wing." We can talk, but the birds can fly.

Small wonder, then, that we have noticed birds, both for themselves and as symbolic extensions of ourselves. We need elaborate technology to do what they do unaided. They can fly, and we cannot. But we can watch them.

And as we do so, we not only satisfy a primitive curiosity about living things, nor do we simply experience, albeit vicariously, the freedom of air as a navigable medium. We also validate our animal aliveness. A cardinal, with its flash of shocking blood-red against the somber green of a stand of spruce, may constitute less than one billionth of the woodlot's biomass, but without that precious few ounces, the whole scene is deadened.

Maybe some of it is recognition, a gut-level identification of animal protoplasm with itself. Some of it, too, is nothing less than amazement. Look, just look, will you, at the preternaturally bright, almost illuminated white patch on the head of a bufflehead duck, or the sharp black mask and precise, unruffled neatness of a cedar waxwing, or the vast, looming black body and great, garish naked red head of a turkey vulture, perched there on a dead branch and telling us that somewhere the Old Gods still live. Can these things really be going on, we ask, right here in our carefully controlled world of television game shows and prepackaged dinners? Hold your breath, lest the apparition disappear. Because few things are as startling as one's first sight of a bird, closeup, through a pair of binoculars. The careful detail, the freshness of color, the precise perfection of form, all combine to make the watcher downright humble, and happy . . . happy to be alive and witness to such life.

"The setting Sun will always set me to rights," commented John Keats, in a letter to a friend. "Or if a Sparrow comes before my Window I take part in its existence and pick about the Gravel."

As a biologist, perhaps I shouldn't say this, but I can't help feeling that it is true: a live bird is exceptionally alive, more so than a fish, an insect, or a reptile, even a mammal. And a dead bird—crushed on the highway, pickled in formaldehyde, or stuffed and mounted in a museum display—is tediously and unrelievedly dead, deader by far than a doornail, a dead snake, a toad, or even a fellow mammal. Keats, again: "Thou wast not born for death, immortal Bird!"

Perhaps it is the incongruity that moves us, such large enthusiasms in such small bodies. We have all of us met any number of Saul characters Bellowing for "more life." Birds actually live that way. In the words of John Burroughs, sage/naturalist of the nineteenth century Catskills, a bird is "hot, ecstatic, his frame charged with buoyancy and his heart with song."[2] Such creatures demand our attention.

Snake-, lizard-, frog-, turtle-, or salamander-watching is—let's face it—boring. Most of the time, the cold-blooded critters simply don't *do* very much. And as to mammals, although their behavior may sometimes be vigorous enough, there are problems. Mammals are typically shy, nocturnal, and drab. With the exception of the widely (and unfairly) disliked bats and the (underappreciated) squirrels, our fellow mammals generally live on the ground; hence, they are difficult to observe. Their migrations are limited (elk and mountain goats descend into river valleys during winter and climb back to alpine meadows in summer) and don't hold a candle to their avian counterparts: hundreds of thousands, indeed millions, of birds of all sizes, all shapes, rivers of life flowing across the skies above our continent twice each year.

And they can be found almost everywhere: multipatterned warblers in an evergreen forest; brilliant orioles and tanagers in tulip trees of the Old South; ruffed grouse drumming on a fallen log in a northern oak forest; elegant and archaic long-legged waders in salt marshes, bayous, and swamps; rows of delicate, earnest little san-

2.   Quoted in Joseph Kastner, *A World of Watchers* (New York: Knopf, 1986).

derlings and sandpipers parading along sandy beaches between the oncoming waves; hawks balancing lightly on thermals rising above a hot canyon; murres, gannets, and assorted ocean-goers crowding the rocky cliffs above a crashing surf; whippoorwills, meadowlarks, and bobolinks welcoming a prairie morning; owls sounding no less rhapsodic about a woodland night; ducks, mergansers, and grebes floating serenely on quiet inland ponds; great, noisy flocks of starlings, blackbirds, and grackles roiling up the evening sky before heading in eerie, bickering unison for their roost under a bridge, in a grove of trees, or alongside an abandoned barn.

Even in our biggest cities you can find them: nighthawks soaring from their rooftop nests; swifts by the thousands spilling from an unused chimney into the fluorescent flickering of a warm urban night; and occasionally—wonder of wonders—the peregrine falcon, among our rarest and wildest birds, whose dive has been clocked at two hundred MPH to the ruin of many a fast-flying, a wild-living duck. The peregrine himself, apostle of the free, untrammeled life, has actually been seen pursuing the abundant, popcorn-eating, solid burgher pigeons among the chasms of New York City's financial district and even nesting (albeit rarely) on the skyscraper ledges that mimic its preferred cliffs. Upon visiting the Jamaica Bay National Wildlife Refuge, within the confines of New York City and reachable even by subway, the birder can regularly spot an exuberance of animals, including the glossy ibis, a garish-looking creature whose long, sharp, down-curved bill and exotic mien seems more at home in Egyptian mythology than under the roaring approaches to Kennedy Airport.

In his classic *A Guide to Bird Watching*, ornithologist Joseph Hickey noted that birding is marked by "a ready exchange of experience, by a high regard for truth, and by a conviction that wild birds express the most spectacular development of nature." This may be amended: Whether in their technicolor extravaganzas of the tropics, or the raw power and numerical abundance of the Arctic, or the exiguous survivors and tired migrants of a great city, or the welcome, semi-domesticated visitors to a backyard feeder, birds *are* nature.

Birding is rich in movement, in color, in sound. Whether pursued actively, as an exhausting sport with long days characterized by strenuous hikes through difficult terrain, or inactively as a leisurely pastime; whether professional or amateur, social or solitary, scientific or aesthetic, birds bring joy to millions of people. When mystery writer Margaret Millar was asked what difference birding had made in her life, she replied, "The days don't begin quickly enough, and never last long enough, and the years go by too soon."[3]

Consider the joy of lists. Admittedly, some birders may get a bit carried away in this department. For them, it is not so much bird-*watching* as tallying. Birders will commonly keep several kinds of lists: daily lists (the number of species seen or heard during a given day), seasonal lists, annual lists, and lifetime lists. The human psyche delights in counting and categorizing, and also in the taking of trophies, keepsakes, mementos, souvenirs, or scalps. The birder gets both to name the quarry—hence, to possess it in a primitive and satisfying way—and to keep a box score over which he or she can ruminate, celebrate, and compare notes with others. All the while, the animals are untouched and (symbolically, at least) one's hands are clean.

Birds are far and away the most prominent wild animals to be seen in any terrestrial environment. Sometimes, the only ones. Go to Texas, or Maine, or Kansas: you are far more likely to encounter painted buntings, black-throated green warblers, and bobolinks, respectively, than peccaries, moose, or bison. Or go to Hawaii, South America, or Africa, to seaports or bazaars, manufacturing centers or cemeteries: no matter how diverse or strange the human environment, by observing and knowing the birdlife, one can achieve the odd sensation of knowing at least some aspect of the country better than many of the locals. It is easier to fathom the birdlife of India, for example, than its *Homo sapiens* counterpart. (Whether it is more gratifying is another question.)

But the rewards of birding are not limited to the world traveler. "The invariable mark of wisdom," wrote Emerson, "is to see the miraculous in the common." Consider some of the most pedestrian North American species: the overgrown mandibles of the aptly named crossbills, the delicate spidery legs of an avocet, the stag-

---

3. Margaret Millar, *The Birds and the Beasts Were There* (New York: Random House, 1967).

gering red and black sharpness of the scarlet tanager . . . such precise definitions of shape and color can be almost too much to register dispassionately. Even the "common" can be not merely
miraculous, but downright shocking; seeing may be disbelieving.

Seeing the pert blue-and-black exactness of a Steller's jay—really *seeing* it, not just absentmindedly registering its existence—or
the astonishing orange slabs of an oriole, or for that matter, the
glossy coat and bright yellow bill of a starling, or the trim black bib
of a chickadee or an English sparrow, may lead to an instantaneous
flash of admiration and wonder. To see a thing in itself, any thing, is
to enter the luminous, even mystical, world of physical existences.
To see an animal in itself is to pass into yet another dimension of
that physical world, since the creature's vitality mirrors and magni-
fies our own.

It is said that once, when his creative juices were flagging, the
poet Rilke was advised by Rodin, his friend and mentor, to go to
the Paris zoo, choose an animal, and watch it. "For how long?"
asked the poet. "Until you really *see* it," replied the great sculptor.
"Several weeks should do." The result was "The Panther," perhaps
Rilke's finest work.

Had he looked at a free-living bird instead, several minutes—
even a few seconds—might have "done." Birds will repay several
weeks of watching or a lifetime. They can also provide an instantaneous moment of epiphany, temporary escape from the humdrum
of row upon row of tidy houses set righteously on their asphalt
grids, not to mention the noxious lines of commuter traffic and
neon beltways, the rank and vile.

You might forget your first car, your first apartment, your first
job, even your first lover, but not your first warbler. Not if, like
Rilke's panther, you have really *seen* it. And not only poets need
inspiration in their daily lives. On a birding field trip, led by a
prominent Audubon Society veteran, I saw—for perhaps for the
hundredth time—one of America's most abundant and easily recognized warblers, with its unmistakable salmon and black patches
alternating on wing and tail. Half butterfly and half bird, it flitted
constantly, spreading its tail, drooping its wings, agitated lest it be
unable to squeeze a complete repertoire of movements into every
ten-second interval. Thinking of her acolytes' lifetime, annual, or

daily lists, the group leader asked, "Does anyone need an American redstart?" I sure did.

A very important thing happened to American birding around the turn of the century. Binoculars replaced guns as the chosen instrument for the study of avian natural history. Previously, the only sightings considered reliable were those made along the barrel of a shotgun. With the recognition that real-life observations can be every bit as valid as a lifeless corpse (and often, a good bit more interesting), the naturalist-observer replaced the marksman, and gradually, a niche opened up for the recreational observer as well. Birding has grown astronomically; all to the better, because watching birds—rather than shooting them—seems likely to lead to a more gentle world.

"The ornithologist is almost always a good fellow," wrote Witmer Stone, himself one of America's most renowned birders. "He can hardly be otherwise . . . the elusive grace and charm of the wild bird is not for the morose or mean man. Of course, the ornithologist is a good fellow: he cannot help himself."[4]

Only two pieces of equipment are necessary for the aspiring bird enthusiast: binoculars and a guidebook. The former allows visual access to what is otherwise glimpsed fuzzily, at a distance. Seen through a glass brightly, however, that world is changed. And it is never the same again. Virtually all birds look better up close than at a distance, often dramatically so. The bay-breasted warbler, for instance, seems to be nothing more than a dark-looking little twitter, seen at a distance or in poor light. Through the binoculars, it is revealed to be a sartorial show-off, with maroon cap, sides, and throat, surrounding a velvet black eye-mask. (On the other hand, it must be admitted that a small minority actually look better at a distance; for example, the wood stork from Florida's Everglades, so slim and elegant from afar, is seen up close to have a shockingly naked head and neck, grotesque and downright pterodactylian.)

Whereas binoculars open the portals to avian Truth—showing us the ornithologic world as it is, for better or worse, generally better—a good field guide opens the world of human Knowledge, or at least, nomenclature. It gives us the ownership that only a

4. Witmer Stone, *Cassinia* (1909).

name, the correct name, will provide. It allows intellectual access to what is otherwise likely to be kaleidoscopic confusion, empowering us to say with confidence, "I know that creature, it's a——." It is no coincidence that the English verb "to know" implies both identification—and thus, formal knowing—and familiarity, a subjective knowledge. (The French distinguish these as two different words: *savoir* and *connaître*. For the birder, objective, nomenclatural knowing in the sense of *savoir* is a prerequisite for knowing in the more personal dimension.)

Probably no one has done as much to spread birding savoir faire as naturalist, artist, and author Roger Tory Peterson, whose *Field Guide to the Birds*, first published in 1934, has gone through numerous reprintings, revisions, and imitations. Peterson introduced a simple technique for field identification, emphasizing certain characteristic "field marks" by which even the novice can distinguish one species from a seemingly look-alike cousin.

Eye-ring—present or absent; tail—square or indented; back—solid or striped; bill—yellow or black . . . this is how one species of gull, woodpecker, finch, or hawk is told from another. Such is the stuff of birding, a fussy attention to detail that is easy to poke fun of and whose satisfactions are difficult to convey in words, but equally difficult to ignore once experienced.

Armed with field guide and binoculars, you are ready to begin.

You can go alone or with others. Local bird clubs, which exist just about everywhere, are a good way to start. You get to know the nearby marsh where night herons reliably roost, the sandbar where a few bald eagles spend the winter, the patch of evergreens frequented by peripatetic troops of warblers looking for the world like traveling clowns and minstrels, the prairie owned by meadowlarks in the morning and whippoorwills in the evening.

It is humbling to be in the company of an experienced birder. The woods and fields, bushes and seashore literally come alive, places to be reckoned, depths to be plumbed. Hearing and vision are ratcheted up; every sound is pregnant with meaning, every flutter a signature. To walk the shoreline, streamside, forest edge, or open prairie with a knowledgeable birder is like visiting the Prado with an art historian or touring the Grand Canyon with a geologist; there are more things under heaven and above the earth than any one person can dream or philosophize about, never mind understand or even recognize. But it is captivating, and sometimes a bit unnerving, to try.

There is also no better way to learn the ropes. Thus, instead of "unknown reddish fellow with white cheeks," you register "male red phalarope," and instead of "robin-sized mystery with long upright tail," you immediately solve the mystery: "brown thrasher." And the next time you hear a staccato rattling from high on a dead branch, you won't even have to spot the rust- and gray-banded chest, or the tousled head crest pointing rakishly upward from an inordinately thick, pointed bill to know "belted kingfisher." Far easier to remember the clues once the culprit is clearly apprehended, and the mental connection has been made.

The expert also has certain tricks up his sleeve, such as calling birds. Without taking a postgraduate course in animal communication, many different species can be summoned, as though by Dr. Doolittle himself. In some cases, it takes a rather precise imitation of just the right territorial call to provoke a resident male to dispute with an imagined interloper. For example, knowing that a family of indigo buntings once nested by a particular roadside, you can call them down with about the same reliability that you can phone a friend "up." In others, a high-pitched, generalized squeaking—resembling the typical predator warning sound—will bring down a whole host of curious onlookers. If you wish, you can buy an Audubon Bird Call, inexpensive and specially designed for such communication. I prefer reaching out and touching someone the old-fashioned way: by kissing noisily and juicily on the back of my hand. Irresistible.

During much of the year, and particularly the breeding season, a birding expedition should start early. For reasons unknown even to the experts, most birds do not keep banker's hours. They are likely to be most active just before dawn and for a few hours after; a lesser peak occurs within a few hours of dusk. What to do with the rest of the day is up to you.

Actually, there are some glaring exceptions to the rule that the early birder gets the list: Ocean and shorebirds can be seen at pretty much any time of day. Similarly with the long-legged marsh dwellers, as well as the ducks and geese. There is also a notable exception here to the sufficiency of binoculars. For watching ducks, grebes, mergansers, and the other waterbirds on a lake, marsh, or out beyond the surf, a spotting telescope offering about twenty power magnification is much appreciated, plus a tripod. When it comes to binoculars, anything greater than nine power cannot be held steadily in the hand, and the field of view is generally too restricted for following an active animal.

Even if you aren't parasitizing an expert, you are likely to find more birds if you go with a few others rather than alone, simply because more eyes and ears are available. But for one of the world's most frustrating experiences, try directing someone else to a pert but only semi-visible little being in a tree or on a distant hedge or in a particular clump of grass a quarter mile away across an open prairie. The world, you quickly find, isn't neatly divided into coordinate grids, with letter and number indicating every spot, as on a highway map. Instead, it is more like "Over there." "Where?" "About halfway down the fourth—wait a minute, the fifth—dark green tree." Or, "Go three quarters of the way from here to the gray barn, then left maybe two hundred yards." Or try, "Out in the water, about halfway between here and the horizon."

Even worse than trying to give such directions is trying to follow them, especially when everyone else is oohing and aahing with delight at what they are seeing: "Right there, by that bump! Don't you see it?" Or maybe, "Over to the left, in the tree!" ("Which tree?" you ask yourself, looking over an infinite forest.) Or better yet, "Oh wow, he's gorgeous! He's right there in the bushes. No, he just flew. How could you miss him?" Easy.

Just as some people are never able to find anything in a microscope, others (perhaps the same hapless folks) just don't seem to have the hand-eye coordination, or the good luck, to find things with binoculars, either. (Wielders of a spotting scope are generally more successful in sharing their finds, if only because the targets are usually more sedentary, and the scope can be aimed, before the view is passed around.)

But when it is successful, the quiet communion of watching the same elusive animal, simultaneously, is a sharing indeed. In a sort of triangulation, two people bouncing photons off the same yellow-headed blackbird are also making contact with each other: "Look at *that!*" Most of the time, though, silence suffices. And I'll never forget the face of my eight-year-old daughter lighting up, literally *lighting up*, when she first saw the little black plume nodding comically up and down from the head of her first California quail.

As in most activities, there is considerable tension, however, between the theory of birding and its practice. Especially in the early stages, it is easy to pour over dozens of books, offering literally thousands of illustrations, range maps, identification marks, even—for the truly devoted—genus and species names. Then there are the birdsong records, admirable aids in their own way, but counterproductive when—like a surfeit of books—they intrude upon the opportunity and sometimes even the inclination to get outside and find out what's there, for yourself. And even out "there," wherever that may be, it can be tempting to glimpse a bird, then spend ten minutes or so trying to match your recollection with the right illustration and verbal description. Worth remembering: The book is unlikely to disappear into a thicket or fly away. The bird is less dependable. One in the bush is worth several in the book.

The novitiate birder also learns some early, valuable lessons, such as the fact that to bend down with a pair of binoculars dangling from a leather strap around one's neck is to invite said binoculars to swing in a radius that is only slightly less than the Olympic record for the long jump and with a velocity and impact rivaling a ballistic missile reentering the atmosphere.

If you like keeping records, and for reasons I don't quite understand most serious birders do, a notebook and pencil will also be toted about. Alternatively, various Audubon societies often publish pocket-sized lists of local birdlife to be checked off during an outing. (The ink from most pens tends to run when wet, and if you are a serious enough birder to keep lists, you are probably serious enough to get wet in the process; hence, pencil.) In addition to noting the species encountered, many people like to estimate numbers. This can be of great value in comparing year-to-year population trends, thereby assessing the effects of pollution, habitat destruction or augmentation, and hunting pressure. It can also help satisfy some birders' craving to count things, perhaps because in counting—as in naming—there is mastery. But just as it is surprisingly difficult to give verbal directions to a particular branch, rock, cloud, or wave, the number of birds in a flock can be stubbornly resistant to human needs.

When small birds are densely packed—as, for instance, a flock of swallows combing the air for mosquitoes—the visual impression is of fewer than there are. With large birds, by contrast—such as Canada geese invading a cornfield for the leftover stubble or crows about to retire to their nocturnal roost—the opposite holds: the observer, impressed perhaps by the sheer abundance of biomass, usually overestimates the actual count.

There is, to be sure, more than one way to get to know birds. In addition to the active style of vigorous pursuit, there are more passive techniques: getting the mountains to come to Mohammed. Bird feeding regularly accounts for hundreds of tons of grain, fruit, and suet per year, and such winter provisioning may be responsible for the northward range extension of such breeding species as the cardinal and mockingbird, plus the more northerly wintering of white-throated sparrows and rufous-sided towhees, animals that might not otherwise find themselves spending cold, snowy months as far north as New York or Michigan. Backyard birdfeeders give the opporunity for closeup observation, and better yet, from the warm side of the window.

Hummingbirds—those buzzing, iridescent busybodies, resembling large needle-nosed bumblebees dipped in liquid jewel-paint, but invariably too fast-moving to be fully appreciated—can be enjoyed at leasure while they congregate around a tube feeder which dispenses red-dyed sugar water. (Although the Southwest is hummingbird heaven, with upwards of a dozen different species to be seen at a single feeder, at least one species, the ruby-throat, is found throughout the East, and our smallest, the calliope, breeds as far north as Montana.)

Feeders don't usually get much action during the summer, when natural food, especially insects, make for stiff competition. Birdbaths, however, are a popular attraction throughout the year. And for some reason, few birds can resist the appeal of dripping water. But even bird feeding has its downside, such as: building a veritable four-star restaurant of a feeder, outfitting it with the most gourmet of avian delights . . . and having no one show up. Or the problem of being too successful, overrun by English sparrows and pigeons while the more elegant species remain either intimidated or aloof . . . or having a single hyperaggressive jay or mockingbird monopolize the goodies . . . or finding that your ornithological ambitions notwithstanding, you have become the designated provisioner for the neighborhood's rats, squirrels, and skunks.

Take heart. There are those who consider mammals more manly than birds. After all, they have more red meat.

"What kind of bird is that?" And what difference does it make? The swallow, executing delicate maneuvers as it pursues its mate through the air, is no less real, no less wonderful, even if we don't know what species it is. To be sure, our appreciation is enhanced if we get a good look and can admire the gracefully forked tail, but so what if we didn't, and therefore couldn't identify it as a barn swallow? (Which is surely what it is, because no other swallow has a forked tail.) And what of knowing whether a small, grayish-brown seedeater is a tree sparrow or a field sparrow? (The former has a black dot on its breast, the latter does not.)

In short, what's in a name? What can the taxonomists and ornithologists add to the suchness and instantaneousness of the creature itself? And conversely, why should not knowing the name result in a tortured frustration? If a ruffed grouse by another name would taste as good or drum as assiduously on a dead oak log during the splendor of a northeast autumn, then who cares if we mistake it for a quail, or a partridge, or for that matter, a pear tree? Many bird names are virtually meaningless anyhow: Lucy's warbler was named for the thirteen-year-old daughter of its discoverer's friend; the Cape May warbler, first found on Cape May, New Jersey, has almost never been seen there since; the house finch is more purple than the purple finch and less likely to be found on or near houses. So long as we are seeing it, why does it matter that we know what we are seeing?

To some extent, the affixing of names is secondary. The important thing is in fact the animal, the seeing it, sensing it, experiencing it, knowing it.[5] But we *Homo sapiens*, although perhaps impoverished in our ability to perceive much of our surroundings—after all, we are insensitive to the honeybee's ultraviolet, we lack the dog's olfactory prowess, or the eagle's visual acuity—have been blessed with a capacity for perception that includes understanding, that uses our remarkable brains to energize our hearts. Biologist Ernst Mayr reported that the people of a remote New Guinea

5. As distinct from knowing *what* it is.

forest, without benefit of modern ornithology, had identified 363 different kinds of birds in their homeland, where a zoological expedition subsequently identified 364. Apparently, the inclination to classify and identify runs deep in our own kind. It is how we strive to make the world manageable, by making it at least somewhat orderly and comprehensible. Most of us no longer live in close association with wild things, but the joy of knowing lingers yet.

When it comes to birdlife, such identification is not always easy, even for the well-studied avifauna of the United States. Birders quickly learn to recognize family groupings: whether a bird is a gull, or hawk, or woodpecker, etc.. Flycatchers, for instance, can be recognized by their habit of perching upright high in a tree, vireos by their oblique posture, often with head down. Sparrows can be known by their heavy, seed-cracking beaks, as opposed to the narrow-beaked, insect-eating warblers. Even if the quarry is not clearly seen, other hints can help narrow the field. A small bird flying in a roller-coaster, up-and-down pattern is likely to be a finch, whereas woodpeckers, for example, fly in more gentle undulations. Hawks soar with wings held straight whereas among vultures, the body is kept somewhat lower with the wings bowed up on either side. The ducklike grebes can be known by their peculiar ability to force air out of their feathers and body cavities, which allows them to float partially submerged, like submarines slicing the water at periscope depth. Even at a distance, it is easy to identify a cormorant, with its dour, snaky neck, perched unmoving on an island stump in a marsh, looking like some prehistoric flying lizard.

Getting to know the birds, one also gets to know how to observe. Oblivious to detail, all small birds look alike at first. Then, the finer points begin to emerge: color of head and breast, shape of wings and bill, presence or absence of an eye-ring or spots on the side. Sight is a bequeathal of our anatomy and physiology, of corneas and optic nerve. *Seeing*, by contrast, is not something that we are born with. It is a learned skill.

Having decided whether your quarry is a sparrow or warbler, tern or gull, you are much of the way home. But the private name of many birds, their species, can be more elusive. Three species of flycatchers, for example—the least, alder, and Acadian—look indistinguishable and can be told apart only when they sing. In poor light, blues may appear black, whites appear yellow, gray seems green . . . and vice versa. (At a suitable distance, many a discarded beer can has temporarily made pulses race with the promise of some African or South American exotic, perhaps a Ballantine barbel, a Hamms hornbill, or a Coors curassow.)

It often takes an expert, or a highly motivated puzzle-solver, to discriminate the many different species of gulls, typically lumped together by the casual non-observer as mere "seagulls." (Many of them have little to do with the sea.) And the abundant busy-legged little shorebirds, collectively known to the frustrated birder as "peeps," constitute a challenging advanced course in bird identification.

Knowing the females is harder yet; males generally sport the brighter plumage. A novice can easily learn to distinguish the various puddle-duck males: mallard, pintail, shoveler, bufflehead, blue- and green-winged teal. But it seems to take a male duck to be fully confident about a female. Even then, errors occur; hybrid ducks are not uncommon.

In the autumn, especially during migration, even some males lose their panache. Peterson devotes several colored plates—unsuccessfully, as far as I have been concerned—to distinguishing the "confusing fall warblers." And when it comes to juveniles, sometimes the task is downright hopeless. Most gulls, for example, have several years of speckled, mottled, dirty-looking immature plumage before breaking out into their white, black, and gray splendor. The little blue heron, easy enough to identify when adult, is snowy white—very much like a snowy egret—when immature. (Be patient. Wait until either one picks up a foot: the egret has golden slippers whereas the heron's toes are dark.)

The process of elimination is also helpful. For example, take Peterson's account of the five different Eastern thrushes: "In the lowlands of the Southern states only one stays to nest, the Wood thrush. The student in Georgia, knowing this, does not bother about the other four in the summertime, once having ascertained the bird to be a thrush. In like manner, on Long Island all five occur in migration, but in winter any thrush could be called, with almost complete certainty, the Hermit thrush." And so it goes.

Knowing the most abundant local species is not, in fact, all that difficult, precisely because they are local. It isn't necessary to memorize all the obscure field markings of all the world's bizarre and exotic animals. The woods, fields, and waterways of home offer mystery, diversity, and excitement aplenty, but not so many different species to be intimidating.

Saul Alinsky once offered the following advice (although the context was political, not ornithological): "Think globally, act locally."

On the other hand, avid birders interested simply in seeing a new and different species may quickly exhaust the nearby opportunities, resulting in a jaded palate, and dreams of vacations to Colombia (with more bird species than any other country), or impatience for the next fall hurricane which just might deposit European (if East Coast), Hawaiian (if West Coast), or Central and South American strays, such as the yellow-billed tropic birds sporadically spotted as far north as New York. Great excitement was occasioned late one winter when a vermilion flycatcher—brilliant embodiment of black and red, only rarely seen north of the Rio Grande—somehow wandered nearly two thousand miles off course, to be spotted eating insects alongside a small creek in the Pacific Northwest town of Redmond, Washington. The news of its appearance was spread by an Audubon Society Rare Bird Hotline; within days, however, there was a cold snap, and the spectacular southern stray was gone, probably dead of exposure.

There are about seven hundred different bird species that breed in North America (about eight thousand six hundred worldwide) and knowing them all is next to impossible; on the other hand, only about a hundred or so are found within a fifteen-mile radius of most of us, making it feasible that anyone who so aspires can learn the local avifauna. A sought-after goal, attainable only by the knowledgeable and energetic, is the "century day," in which one hundred different species are catalogued during a single twenty-four hour period, typically beginning with owls before dawn and closing with owls again, after dusk. On the popular Christmas Day bird counts, thousands of enthusiasts fan out to assess the local avifauna, with an atmosphere both celebratory and competitive. Those seeking to participate in national records—generally in excess of two hundred species—may want to go to Freeport (Texas), Cocoa (Florida), or San Diego (California) to get in on the high points of December's birding action.

The birder's dilemma begins when the locally abundant birds are all tallied, and even the "unusuals" and "occasionals" become old hat. Rarities are in fact, rare. For sustenance, birding must then become more than bird spotting or species scanning. Rather than merely dismiss a species as a check on a list, the bird-watcher, if he or she truly wants to *watch*, must linger awhile. By doing so, new worlds open up, domains that challenge our observational powers and our wits, and that offer gratifying rewards. In addition to identifying birds, in short, one can begin to watch their behavior; that is, not just what they are, but what they do.

Here are a few possibilities: Take courtship, which among birds is relatively easy to observe, extraordinarily varied, and sometimes quite elaborate. Sparrow hawks may take turns, appearing to play tag through the stratosphere, with one member of a courting pair dropping a grasshopper or small mouse, after which the other catches it in midair, then repeats the performance. Grebes actually exchange ritual food offerings, generally as part of a detailed dance that will find both partners skittering along the surface of a pond. Around April, in the deciduous forests of the eastern and central states, the hour after dusk is the special property of a peculiar, drab-looking bird with a long bill that actually opens up at the end, to enable it to grab earthworms: the woodcock. But the woodcock's renown lies properly not in its bill but in its courtship ritual. Each spring, the male woodcock is transformed from mere worm-eater to the premier dancer in the sunset sky, giving his curious "peenting" call and hovering hundreds of feet above the female, only to plummet back to earth and repeat the performance. Woodcocks are said to be tasty; maybe so, but their courtship is downright scrumptious.

The prairie chickens and sharp-tailed grouse of the Midwest, and sage grouse of the Far West, establish so-called "leks," where the males strut about for the benefit of the females, "booming" air in and out of their brightly colored throat pouches. In the jungles of New Guinea, several species of bowerbirds have long fascinated ornithologists with their penchant for constructing special display arenas—bowers—and adorning them with a diversity of flowers, stones, and leaves. But right here in our own backyards, even in distinctly nontropical North America, the great crested flycatcher sometimes adorns his nest with abandoned snakeskins, eggshells, fish scales, cigarette packages, and other treasured delicacies.

Consider also the seemingly mundane business of eating. Most woodpeckers really do peck wood, extracting adult insects as well as their eggs and larvae; but the red and yellow-shafted flickers prefer to promenade about the ground, eating ants, and the red-bellied woodpecker has become a nuisance to citrus farmers because of its inclination to puncture oranges and suck the juice. The shrike is technically a songbird, but it has taken up a vigorously predatory lifestyle, as evidenced by its common name "butcher-bird," occasioned by its gruesome habit of impaling its victims— grasshopper, lizard, small bird, or mammal—on a larder of sharp thorns. Or watch a boozy bunch of Bohemian waxwings, made more than a little tipsy by gorging themselves on naturally fermented berries. The waxwings (when sober) are, by the way, the perfect gentlemen of the bird world, in their dapper dress and calm deportment; by contrast, witness the most unseemly table manners of the black vulture or its turkey relative . . . then consider the phrase "eat like a bird." Or watch a flycatcher catch flies, an osprey feed on fish below a dammed river only to have an eagle steal its catch, or notice how acorn woodpeckers store acorns by the thousands in holes bored in a dead tree. And note how it is food that keeps the tiny body of a black-capped chickadee so intensely preoccupied, and able, somehow, to maintain a heartbeat of five hundred per minute and a body temperature of 114 degrees throughout the bitter winters of the northern Adirondacks of New York State, or Minnesota. And when it comes to food, enter into one of the more intriguing minor mysteries of the animal world: Consider the clownlike, ocean-going puffin, so often seen and photographed with three or four small herrings limply lying crosswise in its parrot beak . . . and then ask yourself how on earth (or in the water) the bird manages to hold onto the first while adding the second.

Even the straightforward business of moving from place to place reveals a diversity of behavioral techniques. Notice how a crossbill uses not only its feet, but also its bill, in regular progression, when moving up or down in a tree or feeder. The brown creeper invariably feeds along the trunk of a tree (never out on the branches or leaves), starting at the base and spiraling upward; whereas the white-breasted nuthatch reverses the procedure, starting high and circling down. The water ouzel or dipper is smaller than a robin, and even less dramatic looking, but the drama is enhanced when you see it striding matter-of-factly into the coldest, quickest-flowing mountain streams, whereupon it walks along the bottom, calmly feeding on insect larvae, then emerges unruffled as though to say "Doesn't everyone make a living this way?"

The brown-headed cowbird is a nest parasite, laying its eggs in the nests of other birds, which may or may not then raise the interloper as its own; red-headed ducks do this, too (sometimes). How does a young cowbird or red-headed duck, growing up as a foster child and never seeing its real parents, know what it is and—when the time comes—with whom to mate?

Grackles, crows, and some species of blackbirds form enormous winter roosts, occasionally numbering in tens of thousands. And no one knows why.

Unlike most mammals, many of our songbirds are monogamous, and often both male and female cooperate in provisioning the young. In such cases, watch for nest-relief ceremonies when one parent replaces the other. In other cases, such as the red-winged blackbird, males are polygynists, maintaining territories within which they may have four or five different mates. But some males, of the same species, have only one female; why the difference? Indeed, the diversity and observability of birds has been such that many of the most intriguing discoveries in animal behavior and ecology come from careful study of their lives, study that requires nothing more than patience and inclination.

Chekhov watched a mediocre, middle-aged actress eat a partridge for dinner, observing in his *Notebooks*, "I felt sorry for the partridge, for it occurred to me that in its life it had been more talented, more sensible, and more honest that the actress." Some bird-listers would probably agree, but ironically, patient bird *watchers*—of the sort who might focus on the talent, sensibility, or honesty of their subjects—are likely, on reflection, to conclude otherwise. After all, as Andre Gide noted, "Fish die belly-upward and rise to the surface; it is their way of falling." And birds, like fish or people, live the only way they know how. The bliss of the birder is that to some extent he or she may get a glimpse of how, too.

If there is a special affinity between people and birds—and I believe there is—it may be due in part to the fact that we experience the world similarly. Human beings are mammals, but unusual mammals in that we lack the potent sense of smell so important to our furry cousins. (If in doubt, reflect on the different meaning of a fire hydrant to a dog and to its master.) But we also have something that most of our fellow mammals lack: color vision. Among the mammals, only the primates can see the blue sky, a red sunset, or an orange's orange. Indeed, mammals are overwhelmingly drab and lacking in color, since it makes little sense for an animal to bedeck itself in wavelengths to which its fellows are not sensitive. So, while we are tone-deaf to that crucial mammalian signal, odor, the mammals are even more insensitive to our penchant for color.

Birds, by contrast, share our sensitivity to technicolor, and their bright colors are a source of unending delight . . . to us, if not to them. (Why people are not multicolored is something of a mystery; significantly, we make no small use of dyes and pigments, multihued minerals, and even bird feathers, to make up for this deficiency.)

We and most other mammals "see" the outside through different windows. We just don't "relate to" the typically mammalian pharmacopoeia . . . at least, not with the precision and insistence that most of our furred cousins do. But with relatively few exceptions (including notably the vultures), birds are again like us in being more or less indifferent to the sense of smell. But—once more like us—they are closely attuned to sounds. And so it is that people are especially likely to perceive and be beguiled by birds, not only for how they look, but also for what they have to say. In the manic, burbling trill of a red-winged blackbird, we heard the throbbing heart of spring, alive with all the bursting sap and energy of the breeding season; the raucous calls of gulls do more to evoke the sea, with its loneliness and wildness intertwined, than any number of boats inside bottles; and as the shrill, drawn-out "tweeeeee" of the broad-winged hawk dwindles eerily, we know that the feathered thunderbolt is hungry and hunting, leaving a prickle of goose bumps even among those mammalian bipeds like ourselves, too large to fear instant death from its beak and talons.

Birds are often more easily heard than seen, and in fact, the expert birder will make a large proportion of his or her "observations" by identifying a bird's song. You are much more likely to make the acquaintance of a bittern by hearing its gulp than by meeting it face to face, and thousands have heard the eerie, prolonged quavering whistle of the varied thrush for every person who has ever seen one. Nonetheless, many of us remain preeminently visual; hearing a bird may be lovely, but not entirely satisfying. To possess, if only by name, one must see the creature as well.

Nonetheless, many bird sounds are distinctive. The upland plover gives a long, drawn-out whinny, which explains why it is sometimes known (incongruously to anyone who simply looks at this inauspicious, medium-sized sandpiper, perching on a prairie fencepost) as the "flying horse." The saw-whet owl dutifully says "saw-whet," but screech owls hardly ever screech. Only about one half of the North American owls, in fact, actually hoot or say "Who," although some of our largest and most impressive, the barred and great-horned, obligingly do so. The barn owl, for example, musters no more than a sneeze. For those who would perceive owls, however, vocalizations are nonetheless especially important, since owl "watching" is mostly owl "listening." Nor is this asymmetry limited to owls; birding at night is the realm of ears, not eyes. Mockingbirds not uncommonly sing all night long, and others, such as the whippoorwills, nightjars, night herons, and bitterns sing almost exclusively after dusk and before daybreak.

There is something strange about sounds at night. It takes surprising courage for a person to yell, alone, into the empty, receiving darkness. Perhaps because we are, at heart, diurnal primates—hence, incidentally, different from most other mammals, which tend to shun the light of day—we hesitate to announce our presence to the unseen nocturnal predators that haunt our dreams. At most, we might be up to a bit of whistling in the dark, leaving certain birds and mammals, as well as the unsavory frogs, insects, and others to scream, genuinely scream, in the dark.

Students of bird noises like to suggest, in English, what a bird is saying—not so much linguistic imperialism or anthropomorphism as a search for mnemonic devices in a kaleidoscopic sea of auditory confusion. Hence, the ovenbird is reported to say "teacher-teacher-teacher," and the rufous-sided towhee, "drink your tea" (with emphasis on the beverage). The chestnut-sided warbler announces "I want to see Miss Beecher," whereas the white-throated sparrow waxes reminiscent about its northern breeding grounds:

"Ah, sweet Canada, Canada, Canada." The song sparrow seems to stutter at first, as though uncertain, but then waxes with religious enthusiasm, "press, press, press, Presbyterian." And the kiskadee flycatcher owes its name to someone's effort at translating its song into French: "Qu'est-ce qu'il dit?" (Appropriately, but less onomatopoetically, "What's it saying?")

Sometimes, however, despite the fortuitous overlap of human sounds and bird speech, the latter simply cannot do justice to the former. For example, the canyon wren's voice, sometimes rendered into a kind of English as "tea-you, tea-you tea-you t'you t'you t'you," is far better captured by Roger Tory Peterson's implicit recognition that some things can be described more readily than imitated: "a gushing cadence of clear curved notes tripping down the scale."

Mockingbirds have the habit—only rarely appreciated by would-be sleepers rudely recruited into bird listening—of singing in the southern moonlight, a far-off, dreamy, liquid melody, poured out upon the magnolia blossoms. And the prairie-dwelling horned lark burbles vigorously on the wing, although not as melodically as the European skylark, which, according to Shelley, pours out "his full heart/ In profuse strains of unpremeditated art."

Poets have long been impressed by the singing of birds. Browning remarked on the "fine careless rapture" of the thrush, and Shakespeare took birdsong more personally yet:

> My state
> Like to the lark at break of day arising,
> From sullen earth, sings hymns at heaven's gate.

When, three centuries later, the (human) singer in *Finian's Rainbow* announces, "I hear a bird," the conclusion seems only natural: "it well may be, it's bringing me a cheery word."

But not all birdsong conjures up images of a bright and shining Gloccamorra. Take the loon, for example. This low-slung bird is heavy-bodied like a battleship, and battleshiplike, it almost never ventures onto land. Rather, there is something primitive about the loon, less like a modern naval vessel than like that early Union ironclad, the Monitor, half submerged even when it swims. Although a strong flyer, the loon's immersion in its northern ponds and lakes seems so complete that the transition to air is laborious and even comical, since the poor loon needs a long running start, skittering and splashing across the surface for what seems like a quarter mile before finally lifting off. But this isn't what makes the creature seem so loony. Rather, its voice: a wild, hysterical laughter that evokes—no, epitomizes—the loon's cold, forbidding haunts in spruce and tamarack bogs. There, not surprisingly, tales are told of an insane mother, frantically searching for her lost child, who falls shrieking into a dark, mist-shrouded lake. Her mad cry echoes even now in the heavily bearded moss of our own, supposedly sane imaginations.

And finally, as the loon so clearly shows, not all bird sounds are birdlike. Even beyond the raucous jays and gulls, the curious gulping of the bittern, the imitative pyrotechnics and complexity of mockingbird, catbird, and brown thrasher, some birds just don't sound at all like anyone's conception of a feathered being. On Broadway and Forty-second Street in New York City, or Chicago's Loop, that loud snapping "Crack" at dusk is not a car backfiring but rather a nighthawk, arresting its antic tumbling dive to the city pavement by suddenly snapping out its wings. The incredibly low-pitched and persistent booming heard across the central Wisconsin prairies during an April dawn is not a misplaced water pump needing adjustment, but rather a congregation of prairie chickens, with the males defending their little territories and displaying crazily for the edification of their female consorts, pumping air in and out of their personal plumbing, brightly colored air sacs that look more like birthday balloons than nuptial adornment. And that startling buzz, appearing it seems from out of nowhere, loud and almost annoyingly insistent, is neither the world's largest bumblebee nor a miniature, radio-controlled helicopter, but rather, the smallest bird, humming not with its throat but its frantic wings.

Just when things seem settled, the seasons change, and with them, the occupants of North America's land and water. *Homo sapiens*, that most restless and transient species, is actually rather sedentary compared with the birds, whose annual ebb and flow washes over the human population like a tide over rocks. And just as tidal rhythms are crucial to ecological renewal, the rhythms of bird migration bring diversity and rebirth to the more sessile human beings who witness them. In midwinter, gulls and terns make their appearance as far inland as Nebraska, salty old mariners on shore leave, bringing the spirit of the sea, the soul of the beach wrack, to frozen cornfields. Geese, barking like dogs, string their perfect V-lines across the skies, and in isolated woodlots, hordes of jewel-like warblers give to the temperate zone in April and May a glimpse—tantalizing, fleeting, intense—of the tropics.

For many birders, seasonal records are crucially important: Within birding circles, special dignity and honor is accorded the first-arriving robin in Vermont, and no reading of tarot cards can be as meaningful as the initial autumn departure of the first North Dakota meadowlark. Even while basking in an Indian summer, or berating a late-arriving spring, no one can be deceived as to the true progress of the seasons so long as there occurs the undeniable congregations of ducks and geese along the great Atlantic and Mississippi flyways, pointing to the waxing or waning of warmth and light. To generations of Americans, the bluebird was a sign of spring (before it was all but crowded out by the immigrant house sparrows, which have appropriated their nesting cavities). Even before the grateful settlers, the Iroquois venerated the bluebird and its return, noting that it was made of blue sky, red earth, and patches of white snow left over from the departing winter.

Perhaps the most extraordinary migration spectacle, however, is one little known except to birders. (In years past, it was renowned among hunters as well; thankfully, they have largely been excluded today.) Every autumn, literally thousands of hawks—and some eagles as well—make their way south, following the ridgetops of Massachusetts, southern New York, and eastern Pennsylvania. Sitting on the huge boulders of a ridge at Hawk Mountain Sanctuary, near tiny Drehersville (north of Reading and west of Allentown), the observer can watch the procession of sharp-shinned, red-tailed, and especially broad-winged hawks, sometimes thousands in a single day. Also in the crowd: turkey vultures, Cooper's hawks, golden and bald eagles, sparrow and marsh hawks, osprey and peregrine falcons. To see these medium to large-bodied predators—generally so fiercely independent and almost never "flocking together"—crowding the airways, almost wingtip to wingtip, moving steadily in the same direction in response to their own internal proddings and seemingly oblivious to each other, is to sense the enormous power of the migratory urge.

Migrating birds also teach us something of risk, of willingness to take chances, to stake everything on a wild flight into the future. A chickadee, wintering over in the same woodlot where he may subsequently breed, can take back a premature song by lapsing into silence. But a migratory warbler, arriving too late at its breeding grounds in Canada may be forced into a non-territorial, nonreproductive limbo because all the choice real estate has already been appropriated; arriving too soon, however, and finding the branches on those same breeding grounds to be iced over, with no access to the insect larvae and eggs sealed inside, it can only die. And all this, of course, assumes that just a few ounces of living fluff can successfully traverse more than a thousand miles of hostile terrain, through wind and water, heat and cold.

Much of the admiration (or at least some of it) that flows so automatically to the noble, white-headed eagle or the brilliant songster, might legitimately be expended on behalf of the drabbest, most inconspicuous sparrow or sanderling, traversing the world's great oceans and landmasses, thankless testimony to the boldness and perseverance of life itself.

One consequence of migration is that the human observer is exposed to an ever-fresh, seasonally varying menu of birdlife. Summer residents—which typically breed—are replaced by autumn transients, just passing through. Then come the winter occupants, those who reproduced farther north, where, of course, they were the summer, breeding residents. Next, the spring transients, once again passing through—but this time, going from south to north—and then back to the summer residents once again. The residents, summer and winter, are easiest to learn and identify; the migrants are trickier. Their tenure is so much shorter, sometimes they hang around for only a few hours, and they are unlikely to give voice to complete, recognizable song. Moreover, migrants are less fussy about where they seek rest and rehabilitation en route, so tree dwellers might be found in bushes or streamside residents might set themselves down miles from the nearest water.

The regularity of birdly replacement is both reassuring for those who detect the seasons by natural, animate rhythms and convenitent for those who seek to track its changing pulse. In Southern

California, for example, there are predictable substitutions: The Wilsons, yellow-and black-thoated gray warblers of summer, are replaced by the Audubons, Townsends, and myrtle warblers of winter; Swainson's thrushes (summer) give way to hermit thrushes (winter); and western tanagers and black-headed grosbeaks, breeding residents, head south in the winter, making room for the purple finches and ruby-crowned kinglets, who bred in the northern forests and who arrive expecting what will be for them a very mild winter.

Whereas some migrations are predictable, others are less so. For instance, large numbers of tanagers, or towhees, or nuthatches may come through a given region one year, not to be seen again for a decade or more. Waxwings, siskins, and crossbills, typical winter residents of Canada, may occasionally clatter down as far south as North Carolina and in large numbers. Most dramatic of all, however, are the periodic "snowy owl years," in which thousands of these great birds temporarily abandon the Far North because of a shortage of lemmings—their preferred food—and appear as far south as St. Louis, looking like hoary totems of another time and another world . . . which to some degree, they are.

Some natural movements occur more gradually than the seasonal repetition of migrations or the irregular irruptions of hungry owls. Cardinals (along with their southern sidekicks, the opossums) have been inching their way northward. Among the most dramatic cases of natural-range extension has been that of the cattle egret, a miniaturized replica of the great, stately American egret characteristic of our warm, southern marshes and swampland. During the 1920s and 1930s, for reasons best known only to themselves, pioneering cattle egrets made the Atlantic crossing from Africa to British Guiana and then began their northward trek. Now naturalized Americans, they are found especially in dairy pastures from New Jersey to Texas, feeding on insects turned up by the cattle, just as they used to associate with buffalo in their native Africa.

Another, lesser-known natural-range extension has also been occurring in the northwest corner of Alaska, where the bluethroat, a small perching bird with a thin bill, has been making a beachhead in the New World, although it still returns to the Old during the winter. If only it was more widely acknowledged, the delicate bluethroat would go a long way toward dispelling the myth of Soviet Siberia as a place of uniform drabness: on its brilliant, iridescent blue throat and breast there is superimposed a conspicuous, bright red spot. The surrounding white belly make this welcome immigrant look downright patriotic.

Thoreau recounts in *Walden* that a friend questioned how he would occupy himself during his forthcoming season in the wilderness. He replied, "Is it not occupation enough to watch the progress of the seasons?" Birders would agree.

The trick to seeing a moderately large number of birds is to expand your horizons: spread yourself out in time (of day and season of year) and space (places explored). This is both good advice for the birder and part of the charm of the enterprise. Each season is special. There are relatively few birds during the North American winter and not very many species. Hence, those on hand are easy to learn, especially the waterfowl which obligingly don't even require getting up early. Since they are not consumed by the breeding season with all its agitating privacy, winter birds are also tamer, as well as more likely to come to a feeder since their preferred foods, notably insects, are either lacking or harder to obtain.

Spring and early summer are times of passage and migration, with progressively more and more activity, culminating in the frenetic pace of bursting, burbling, burgeoning, and breeding, a time when living things make their clearest statement, when they achieve an existential advance against an uncaring universe. After all, the rest of the year, they barely hold their own and, in fact, lose ground to the hazards of predators, drought, wind, cold, and starvation. But by reproducing, they thrust themselves—or rather, their offspring—forward into the future. From winter through spring, there is a steady increase of things to watch and admire; typically, a few birds in January increasing to a great flood in June. Then, the diversity gradually shuts down again through the fall migration, time of departure and hunkering down, as the living world gets ready once more for the relative dormancy and sparseness of winter.

Different species are also encountered at different times of the day, and particularly, in different habitats. It is ironic that birders are often thought to be quaint and distracted, out of touch with reality, whereas in fact, to be a watcher of birds is to be delicately yet deeply in touch, attuned to the sights and sounds of our most fundamental reality, the natural habitats of which our planet is made. Indeed, more than any of the outdoor lovesongs considered in this volume, birding is plugged into environments and habitats. Marsh, grassland, mountain, seacoast (rocky or sandy—they are quite different), coniferous forest, desert, and on and on . . . each offers a different supporting cast.

When natural environments are humanized, they are typically homogenized as well. Lawns, telephone poles, automobiles, roads: these can be found almost anywhere, and are virtually inter-changeable from Louisiana to Bismarck, Palm Springs to Burlington. And to be sure, some of the birdlife has become equally interchangeable: starlings, English sparrows, and increasingly, robins. But the roadrunner of southern Arizona simply will not be found in the Minnesota forests, and an oyster catcher of the Maine coast probably wouldn't even be caught dead on the prairies of Illinois.

Even a narrow taxonomic focus repays our attention. The birder will quickly learn that for summer tanagers, explore cottonwoods by a stream (where you may also find the delicate parula warbler); scarlet tanagers, on the other hand, are more likely in higher, drier oaks; and for western tanagers, try evergreens.

To see a great flock of shorebirds, whirling with astounding pre-cision—first white overhead, then dark, depending on whether belly or back is facing the observer—is to be in touch with the seashore. To watch a green heron, stealthily stalking a fish; to catch a glimpse of a sora rail furtively feeding in the cattails; or to follow a phalarope spinning crazily for her supper . . . is to be in touch with a marsh. To hear the strangely sad, bell-like tone of the thrush or trace a warbler's path in the hushed, cathedral-like gloom of an evergreen forest .. is to be in touch with the northern woods. Similarly for meadowlarks, bobolinks and the American prairie; or auks, gannets, murres and the rocky ocean coast; mallards, pintails and the inland lakes; roseate spoonbills and the Florida Ever-glades, or ruffed grouse and bluejays in the once-great eastern deciduous forests of oak, maple and elm.

There are many ways to know a nation: its government, industry, language, folk culture, or climate, to name a few. For the birder, a trip across the United States, say from east to west, reveals something else. Indigo buntings are turned in for the lazuli; rose-breasted grosbeaks and scarlet tanagers for black-headed grosbeaks and western tanagers; red-headed woodpeckers for white-headed; red-shouldered and broad-winged hawks for the Swainson's and ferruginous, and so on.

The birder learns also that there is truth in the old notion of transmutation of species. Although dirty rags don't become rats, or salamanders appear magically from fire, bugs do in fact become birds and dead wood transforms into a nest and eggs. The trees grow, make seed, lose branches, hatch birds (like bluebirds or the gaudy wood ducks), and eventually die, to be replaced by other trees and other birds. And when the Baltimore oriole, resplendent in orange and black, seems to be transporting a bit of the tropics to the eastern seaboard, the truth is that after his winter sojourn in the Caribbean or Venezuela this is exactly what he is doing.

Yet, for all the worldwide connectedness that birds have to teach us, perhaps the most fundamental unity they offer springs from the identification of animal with place, an identification to which the attentive human being is in no way immune. Winter residents and seasonal migrants are interesting diversions, but give us the breeders, those who elect to perpetuate their kind in canyon, field, or marsh, in broad-leafed maple or towering redwood, to define their habitat, and our own. No matter how exotic the animals we may see, or yearn to see, there remains something special about the birdlife of home: perhaps a raven or Steller's jay to the Puget Sounder, a bobolink to the Nebraska wheat farmer, or a herring gull to the Long Island commuter—these are not just the symbols of home, but its reality. God may or may not be in heaven, but all is right with the world when the gold and blue prothonotary warbler is in its tree overlooking the Potomac, or the heron is in its marsh, looking oddly Oriental in its motionless patience, giving a zenlike lesson in the Art of Watchful Waiting, and the Hungarian partridge still bursts with a fluttering explosion from its brushy hiding place in a Utah canyon.

Regrettably, birding in the United States may be developing its rightful numbers just as the birds are losing theirs. To be sure, certain species have been prospering—the generalists like gulls, starlings, and robins, capable of taking advantage of garbage heaps and suburban lawns. But the more interesting specialists—like the Everglades kite, which eats only snails, and just one species at that, or the spotted owl, which needs extensive stands of old-growth coniferous forest—are in precipitous, perhaps permanent, decline, largely because of pollution and habitat destruction. The mourning dove is still abundant, saved paradoxically because of its more or less solitary habits compared with its relative the passenger pigeon, which once darkened the eastern skies in flocks that may have numbered in the *hundreds of millions* and were therefore easy targets for the gunner. The pileated woodpecker is astounding enough, with its large size and sharp red crest; its relative, the ivory-billed (even bigger than the pileated) may be gone forever. Believe it or not, there even used to be parakeets native to North America—the Carolina parakeet, descending in clamorous, iridescent flocks on moss-laden cypress trees—and great auks, larger than the biggest penguins, in the cold waters of the North Atlantic.

Right now, today, the songbird populations are being decimated by the clearing of tropical forests in South and Central America, much of it to provide beef-cattle pasturage for American fast-food joints. Our warblers, orioles, thrushes, and kinglets can't find a safe place to over-winter, and the result, increasingly, is silence in North America's springtime forests. For now, at least, the issue isn't extinction, but rather, a subtle, continuing change in the texture of life, as many of our best-known songsters simply fade away.

Today's starlings show no regret as they oust the native bluebirds from their potential nest-sites, and precious few people shed any tears when the last dodo was killed on the island of Mauritius, or the last heath hen on Martha's Vineyard. But part of our dignity and worth as a species may be discernible by our regret at the passing of the passenger pigeon, Carolina parakeet, great auk, and yes, the comical dodo, as well. Moreover, we may even earn some measure of redemption by whether we choose to protect the whooping crane, the peregrine falcon, and the California condor . . . no less than by whether we actually succeed. And whether we choose to forgo a few swallows at MacDonald's in favor of a whole skyful of swallows.

Not very long ago, miners took canaries with them down into the shafts because the birds—more sensitive than people to noxious gases—would give warning when the air became contaminated by dropping dead. But gradually, the message is getting out, to birder and nonbirder alike: All birds are canaries, and so are we.

Chopping Wood

Eco-guilt, Dirty Dancing and How a Tree Is Like a Lobster

The ancients were wrong. There are five primal substances, not four: earth, air, water, fire—and wood. Wood is the hearty emanation of our planet's roots, reaching literally up out of the earth, toward the sky. With its meaty, fibrous solidity, wood is the embodiment of life made substantial, in its literal meaning of *substance*. And splitting wood is a way of revealing its inner aspect, delving into its secrets and thereby coming to terms with it.

Wood is remarkable stuff. It is heavy, yet it floats (except for ironwood and a few other peculiar species). It is (or was) alive and yet to be "wooden" is to be stolid and inert. It is extraordinarily strong, yet it can be carved and cut, whittled and sawed, shaped and sanded, and it holds a nail or screw like nothing else. It is the soul of trees, and, of course, we human beings owed much of our early primate evolution to trees, although we subsequently abandoned wood as a medium of movement and a fundamental habitat. It is now a stranger to us, and yet, every child yearns to climb trees, and adults love to see them, or just to rest under them, and to run their hands over the smoothness of polished wood, to admire the beauty of grain and texture. It is blocky and without movement, and yet it is also the primordial stuff of fires—or at least, fires as people have made them for thousands of generations.

149

"A tree stands there," writes Annie Dillard, "accumulating deadwood, mute and rigid as an obelisk, but secretely it seethes; it splits, sucks, and stretches; it heaves up tons and hurls them out in a green, fringed fling. No person taps this free power . . . "[1] No, dearest Annie, you're wrong there. I tap the power of trees, by cutting them down, chopping them up, and burning them away, right before my own astonished eyes.

We can be assured that people have been reducing large pieces of wood into smaller chunks for the express purpose of providing heat for a very long time. (In an age of Three Mile Island and Chernobyl, the injunction, "split wood, not atoms" makes particular sense.) Wood makes us warm, in many ways. Cutting down a tree, it warms us. Cutting the log further into sections ("rounds"), it warms us. Chopping the round sections, splitting the body of the trunk into convenient, burnable pieces, it warms us. Stocking the split firewood, it warms us. And so, by the time we sit by the campfire, stove or fireplace, experiencing what is supposed to be the *raison d'être* of the woodchopper's labor, experiencing the release of sunshine long ago captured in the living structure of a tree, that final warming seems almost beside the point.

Almost, but not quite. If winter is a time of reflecting, of hunkering down, of making it through on the vitality of the rest of the year, burning wood provides the light and the warmth to do it by. Much of the time in winter, we live by releasing the memories and wisdom of earlier times, reexperiencing what went before; the wood fire does this literally, releasing the energy gathered from earlier days of sun and rain and dirt. Moreover, it is an elemental presence, almost, a household god.

Most Americans—especially urban dwellers—cannot situate themselves in the natural ebb and flow of earthly rhythms. How many of us can tell the phase of the moon, the height of the tides, the times of sunrise or sunset? Maybe it's eleven o'clock, but do you know what time it *really* is? Is it sunspot time, sea-turtle spawning time, time for the goldenrod to blossom? Even the progression of the seasons makes barely a scratch on our exterior: air conditioning and central heating make summer and winter virtually interchangeable, asphalt doesn't actually turn to ice in winter

1. Annie Dillard, *Pilgram at Tinker Creek* (New York: Harper & Row, 1974).

(it just seems to) or mud in the spring, and concrete and steel do not have leaves to turn color or to shed. There is little to "stock up" for winter, nothing to plant in the spring or harvest in the fall.

Maybe this is why chopping wood feels so good, and not only the doing of it. For woodchopping is a preparation, a getting ready for the next swing of the seasons, like the bear laying on fat, or the redwings heading south. The bear doesn't fret over how much adipose tissue to accumulate, the redwing knows how far to fly and when to start doing so. But as to how much wood to chop, people tend to look for omens, consulting others who are wiser than themselves: the patterns on wooly-bear caterpillars, the thickness of muskrat fur in October, the height of the spider eggcases. As a child, I once went fishing in northern Quebec, guided by an Algonquin man named Tomas Laframboise (all the Indians for miles around, for some reason, were named Laframboise, "raspberry" in English). His ancestors had lived in the woods of northern Canada for many generations, hunting moose and catching walleyes and northern pike in the cold, dark waters of what is now La Vèrendrye Park. It was late September, and Tomas said matter-of-factly, "Hard winter comin' on dis year." I asked how he knew, expecting to be told some new and engaging bit of native lore, but instead I learned "You know fer shur dat winter be hard when white man stack up lotsa firewood."

Chopping, sad to say, isn't all sweetness and light and warmth and sweat. There is also a dark side, something that we might call eco-guilt. Eco-guilt is the self-conscious guiltiness of the ecologically aware: by what right, we ask ourselves, do we kill trees for our own warmth and satisfaction? Who are we to do this thing? How can we justify deforestation, whether it be of our own woodlot, local ecosystem, or the entire continent (and ultimately, the planet), with the soil erosion and destruction of wildlife habitat this so often implies?

When it comes to woodchopping, eco-guilt looms larger than with the other outdoor lovesongs here considered: certainly, stargazing is not environmentally destructive and organic gardening only minimally so, if at all. But backpacking exacts its toll on the backcountry, for example, as does cross-country skiing (to a lesser extent), or even birdwatching. And to my knowledge no one has ever argued that horse poop, despite its undeniable organicness, adds to the aesthetic quality of environment, whether human or equine. In most other cases, it takes gasoline even to begin appreciating the out-of-doors, and gasoline itself is a nonrenewable resource, whose combustion creates pollution and whose refining and transportation leads to awful oil spills and other despoliation.

There can be little argument that the adverse environmental impact of burning wood or a small amount of gasoline pales in comparison with such major insults as creating thousands of tons of nuclear waste, lethal for the next hundred thousand years, poisoning the land with broad-spectrum toxins, or driving whole species to extinction. But nonetheless, the eco-guilt of the home woodsman or the most well-meaning nature lover is not only real, but appropriate. It is part of the larger human dilemma: how are we to live on this planet, in a humane, sustainable and sensitive manner?

A big topic, that, and beyond the scope of this book, whose goal is much more modest: to share the joys of the planet Earth, to sing of love, and thereby to help evoke some of the caring and appreciation that will be needed if this larger question is ever to be resolved. In the meantime, even the most ardent lover of the outdoors must make his or her peace with the tragic truth that there may not be any truly good way to live equitably with our heritage. Perhaps we simply cannot live off the interest; maybe we have no choice but to eat up our capital. It may take one hundred years, for example, to grow a maple that will warm my family for just a few weeks.

Many of us in the United States of America are able to live relatively well. Living good, on the other hand, is much more difficult. It has been said that to be human is to suffer. Maybe so, but it is more certain yet that to be human is to be a burden to the natural environment. Aldo Leopold, patron saint of American conservation and the country's first "wildlife manager," once wrote that it is the sad fate of the ecologically aware to "live alone in a world of wounds." Awareness hurts. And so does eco-guilt. It hurts the environment, and it hurts the environmentally sensitive. But it is better than obtuse insensitivity, or—worse yet—a Panglossian optimism that actually extols ecological destruction in the interest of "progress" and in the naive (and often, in the short term, self-serving) hope that our planet is infinitely enduring and self-regenerating. Although there may be no perfect way to live, let me propose that eco-guilt should at least be minimal when life is pursued on a minimally destructive, human scale, employing renewable resources whenever possible, and avoiding excess and irreparable damage. We have as much right to exist as a maple tree or a Bengal tiger. In the course of its life, a maple tree will doom other plants to wither in its shade, just as the tiger will consume its animal prey. But unlike the tree or the tiger, we have the ability to be destructive far beyond our meager, biologically given capacities; hence, we have a special obligation to live with tact. Unlike the tree or the tiger, we also have the ability, and the duty, to know what we are doing, to be mindful of our actions.

The alternative to wood heat—with its dead trees and air pollution—is to heat with electricity, or oil, or natural gas, all of which have environmental drawbacks . . . or to live only in the tropics. In fact, wood makes more air pollution than does natural gas, for example, so that combusting it is not necessarily more moral. We can avoid gas-guzzling cars, and we can use public transportation, but most of us still have to get from place to place, just as we can insulate our homes, but we still have to heat them as well.

Perhaps we should only chop those trees that have fallen for other reasons: natural blow-downs, for instance, or those felled by fungus infections. But the wind is more likely to topple trees at the edges of (man-made) clearings, and in any event, by appropriating the fallen wood, we deprive the soil of the nutrient replenishment that it would otherwise receive.

Most scars, however, do heal. Trees (so long as they are not irreplaceable first growth) really do renew themselves; a balanced sustainability, not just in wood but in all resources, is not just a dream but a goal. Maybe even an attainable goal. It is possible—it must be possible—to walk softly upon the land, mindful of our imprint, minimizing our impact, aware of our responsibilities to the present environment as well as to future generations. In the meanwhile, we must admit that not all lovesongs are ecstatic. Sometimes lovers sing of mourning, of loss, of betrayal. Even in the joy of union, there may be the ache of separation, a painful awareness of transience. And as the cliché has it, we always hurt the one we love.

The best part of chopping wood is the actual splitting, that penultimate step in the journey from tree to fire in which the stocky cylinders, perhaps eighteen inches long and as far around as the tree trunk from which they came, are subdivided into their component chunks. Few activities in life are more satisfying. (Few are more peculiar as well, in that one is left with an apparent increase in volume when the job is complete: like eating a lobster or an artichoke.)

In the eighteenth and nineteenth centuries, intinerant woodchoppers used to knock on the doors of rural America—especially in the autumn—offering their services in return for some money, or perhaps a meal. I would not have prospered in those times: seeing a glorious jumble of great hulky blocks piled invitingly and waiting to be deconstructed, I would have paid the owners for the privilege of splitting their wood.

There are two ways of doing it. For smaller pieces, an axe or driving maul will do. The latter has something like a sledge hammer on one side of its business end, and a narrow axe-head on the other. Axes are lighter than mauls and can be swung horizontally if need be. A maul, by contrast, is too heavy to strike in any direction but straight down. It is also too heavy to be actively powered, even on its downstroke. Ninety-nine percent of the woodchopper's effort is simply concerned with raising the head of the maul, smoothly above the shoulders of the chopper, then *guiding* it, not *propelling* it, letting gravity and weight provide the momentum and do the rest of the work. By a gentle swaying of the body and a rhythmic dancer's wiggle that begins in the legs and carries in an undulating wave up through the back to the shoulders and arms, a maul can be raised smoothly overhead, the sinuous sweep punctuated by a gratifying crack as the sharp end bites into its target. If the round is the right size, then one good shot will do it. The victim lies at your feet, neatly cloven in two.

Robert Frost knew what it was like:

> Good blocks of beech it was I split,
> As large around as the chopping block

And every piece I squarely hit
Fell splinterless as a cloven rock.[2]

It is important not to make apologies for this power trip; after all, it's him (her?) or you. This is mortal combat. Winner takes all. No holds barred. No quarter asked, none given. Maybe it is possible to chop wood gently, and with kindness, but I have never discovered how and don't especially want to. Doing it firmly and even a bit roughly leaves me cleaned out, and, I suspect, more likely to be gentle and kind in my interactions with others, whose sensibilities may be somewhat more delicate than a block of wood. On the other hand, it is possible to chop wood lovingly and with appreciation for its solidness, sensitive to its suppleness, grateful for its compelling combination of resistance followed by smooth, utter, instantaneous capitulation.

Axes aren't really used very much in woodchopping these days; rather, they make their appearance mainly for clearing limbs or making kindling. Only rarely are they employed for felling trees, or "bucking up" logs once they are on the ground. Chain saws have taken over. Chain saws are among those things that are immensely useful and timesaving, but utterly obnoxious. Unfortunately, there is virtually nothing good that one can say about a chain saw. Even without Texas Chainsaw Massacres, they are dangerous, ugly, smelly and unforgivably loud.

If the piece of wood is too large, or too dry, or too knotty, even a good smooth stroke with a driving maul will not be enough. Then comes the awkward part: with the head driven deeply into its still-unsplit target, the maul itself is useless, and the woodchopper, helpless. If you have the strength of King Kong, you can try picking up the whole mess and smashing it down into the ground (usually this drives the head in only fractionally farther, not enough to do any good), or you can hit the sledgehammer side—the part sticking up, out of the wood—with another hammer, thereby using the maul's head as a wedge.

The best solution is to use a wedge and a sledge in the first place.

---

2. From Robert Frost's "Two Tramps in Mud Time," with permission from Henry Holt & Co.

Place the wedge against the wood, set it in place with a few light taps, and then the stage is set. If there are any natural cracks, go with them; the wood sometimes announces where it would most like to separate from itself. Progress is made with each successive, rhythmic whack. Unlike so many other things in life, there is no backsliding. The wedge can only go deeper. It is on a one-way trip, boom or bust.

Listen to the rhythm, when the hammer first hits the head of the wedge with a high, sharp, metallic ring; and then, about a second later, after rebounding several inches into the air, it bounces heavily with a lower, echoing thud onto the block of wood being split: *TEE*-bum, *TEE*-bum, *TEE*-bum. (How obliging of it to provide support and cushioning for the instrument of its own demise!) Now add the rhythmic body movement, as well as regular, loud exhalations—or should we call them exhortations—like squeezing of a bellows in a wild, organic forge, as time goes on and the chopper heats up. *TEE*-bum-huh, *TEE*-bum-huh, *TEE*-bum-huh.

This is dancing at its best, a primitive and practical percussion. Robert Frost again, as he remembers:

> The weight of an ax-head poised aloft,
> The grip on earth of outspread feet,
> The life of muscles rocking soft
> And smooth and moist in vernal heat.

If the wood is fairly green, then the first good shot or two elicits a faint oozing of sap on either side of the wound as the wedge plunges home. The pungent odor of tree-blood swirls about the chopper, while sawdust, wood chips and leaking sap combine in a rich, wholesome amber to which everything adheres. Next come the first unmistakable signs of surrender: small, freshly formed cracks, lines of least resistance extending from the wedge toward the periphery. As they grow, lengthening with every stroke, zigzagging on their unique and visible faultline, the appetite is whetted, and triumph is assured. In some particularly delicious cases, the wood sings along, creaking or whining as the fibers groan and complain . . . and then finally, let go.

But most satisfying by far is the actual moment of splitting—the piecè de résistance (or better yet, the coup de grace)—when a clean, culminating shot ends the suspense by neatly bisecting the block and, if everything is truly perfect, sending the wedge zinging smoothly into the innocent ground beneath, standing proudly erect in that revealed space between.

I like to think that it is a triumph for the wood as well, that deep in its fibrous heart, it really wants to individuate, to emerge into the sunlight, free of encumbrances, just as guru Meir Baba used to claim that we did flies a favor by swatting them, since they weren't really happy in that particular incarnation.

But some wood, sad to tell, is less than obliging. Oliver Wendell Holmes was a great admirer of trees, notably elms, which he considered the most graceful of all. He would travel for hours to view a particularly noble specimen, to revel in its urnlike perfection. But when it comes to splitting, elms are far from perfect. Unlike most trees, whose fibers typically run in only one direction, and which, therefore, facilitate splitting of their wood, elm fibers are a dense feltwork of strands, each an individualist, going in a different direction. As a result, elm doesn't split. It just absorbs wedge after wedge, smiling smugly as it gulps them down . . . the first one followed by numbers two and three, sent to rescue the ones that went before. It can only be sawed or maybe pulverized.

Chopping wood is a kind of enforced futurism, since wood is most easily split when it is green, but should not be burned until it is dry, perhaps six months later. So to chop wood is to think ahead, to barter current effort for future heat; for the time being, the warmth of the doing will have to suffice. On the other hand, you can always get wood delivered, precut and presplit. I suppose you could also order ashes by the truckload, wood that is preburned as well. Or you can have a "fireplace" that "burns" artificial "logs," or that features the easy, predictable flicker of natural gas. No mess, no smoke, no wood chips in your hair, no singing in your ears, no fragrance of pine or maple, no reassuring weight of handle in hand, no sore back, no coolness of wedge or axe head, no spark of steel on steel, no sweat, no callouses . . . no thanks.

Cross-Country Skiing

Snow, Silence and Leopards in Carpet Slippers

"Think snow," we are exhorted. Yet most of us never really do, even the ardent devotees—skiers, for the most part—who proudly display those approving, optimistic bumper stickers. Snow is rarely a cause for meditation. More often, we take it for granted: a nuisance and an inconvenience, a danger or a delay, or maybe a welcome excuse to stay home from work or school. Even the mobius strips of our asphalt highways—those continuous ribbons of modernity, intruding everywhere in sinuous lines yet going nowhere—may not only be paralyzed but for a time, blotted away. Snow offers us the opportunity for snowmen and snowballs, as well as the sometimes delectable predicament of being snowbound . . . that is, slowed-down, whether we like it or not.

Snow also generates a unique eye-pleasing spectacle, a transformation of the world unimaginable to the resident of the tropics. And it covers our sins, binding the scarred land made ugly by ruts, clear-cuts, and stubbled fields, applying a soothing poultice of wholesome, purist white. At the same time, it covers not only the scars we impose and the effluvia we create, but also the harsh

reality of an otherwise difficult season. One of the enduring contrasts to be found on this planet is the tender caress of snowfall on
jagged, anguished land, smoothing and softening the rough, win-
ter-hard earth, saying "There, there now, everything will be all
right."

And of course, snow offers recreation: something to throw, to
build snowmen with, but most important, snow is to slide upon.

But rarely do we stop and Think Snow. Of all substances, only
water occurs naturally in all three states, as gas, liquid, and solid,
and it should occasion no surprise that we take the first two forms
for granted. After all, water vapor is often invisible; even as a
cloud, we rarely encounter it closeup, except for our own very
pedestrian exhalations on a frosty day. And as for its tenure as a
liquid, water is so commonplace that it has taken on the virtual
definition of liquidness.

As a solid, however—snow or ice in any of the myriad forms of
crystal structure that have been identified—hardened water merits a good deal more wonder, or at least thought, than it generally
receives. After all, about the same proportion of the Earth's surface
that is farmed (roughly ten percent) is permanently covered by
snow and ice. Another ten to twenty percent is predictably whit-
ened every winter, an amount that increases to approximately fifty
percent, at least on occasion. More than three-fourths of the
world's fresh water is locked up in solid form . . . and yet, if we
didn't know it so well, the periodic occurrence of such fluff, falling
from the sky sometimes thickly, sometimes just in ragged snatches,
would seem the stuff of wildest science fiction. And that this stuff
should pile up occasionally in great quantities (more than one
thousand inches per year, for example, at Mount Rainier in the
state of Washington), change its consistency to that of powder,
sugar, corn, slush, or hard ice, then melt away into a liquid and
disappear—all this would be too strange to believe.

Throughout most cities, snow rarely if ever gets to run through
its natural life cycle. Usually it is melted by salt, sprinkled with
sand, besooted and exhausted, scraped, shoveled, compressed,
piled, dumped, and heaped someplace other than where it has
fallen: out of "the way." At least in the past, however, snow has long
had a utilitarian side as well. In the "good old days," snow was
considered helpful for travel rather than a hindrance. When lakes,

rivers, and inlets froze, they could easily be crossed; much more easily, for example, than during the summer when the water ran freely, or several months earlier, in April or May, when the sloppy springtime ground of the far north swallowed wheels up to the hubcaps and beyond. Even today in parts of Scandinavia and the Soviet Union, snow is compacted on roadways, rather than cleared. In fact, at one time throughout the northern United States, municipalities deployed simple but enormous rolling machines for tamping down the snow. Now, we struggle to scrape it off the land and haul it away.

Human beings evolved in sub-Saharan Africa, and our bodies still carry the unmistakable signs of tropical warmth: as mammals go, we are just about hairless, and when overheated, we exude moisture onto our naked skins, which then evaporates and cools us. Our sweating and our nakedness work admirably in disposing of excess heat, but do not suit us well in cold climates. We require all sorts of cultural adaptations just to survive in the so-called temperate zones. Even an overdomesticated and seemingly helpless cocker spaniel can easily spend the night outdoors in almost any month of the year. No blanket? No problem. But the dog's owner, if similarly undressed, might well succumb to exposure even during the summer. Yet it was cold—sometimes very cold—for a bit more than one-half of the 500 thousand years that made up the Paleolithic, or Old Stone Age, of earliest human history.

During our more recent past, the fourth and last major Pleistocene glaciation began about seventy thousand years ago, lasted for tens of thousands of years, and gave rise to the renowned Ice Ages, during which our ancestors, seeking to get away from the cold, earned the name cavemen (and women). Under the exigencies of winter, they discovered fire, the use of animal skins for clothing, and probably the drying and salting of meat and storage of nuts. It may even have been during the interminable blizzards that we began to amuse ourselves making artwork, telling stories, and otherwise employing our minds in response to the enforced inactivity. In any event, it seems likely that winter—no less than the balmy tropics—has had an impact on the human species.

The story is told about the ruler of an ancient kingdom who was much distressed. It seems that this kingdom had many stones and other sharp objects, which bruised and tore the bare feet of the inhabitants. So the compassionate king ordered that his entire land should be covered with the skins of wild animals (fur side up). At this point, a wise counselor perceived that the king's plans, although high on empathy, were low on common sense and would lead to financial ruin (not to mention the extinction of the local fur-bearing animals). So she proposed a better solution: instead of covering the entire countryside, why don't we simply cover a much smaller area, namely the bottoms of everyone's feet. Thus were shoes invented.

In much of the world, the ground is regularly covered, not with sharp and painful objects, but with the opposite: a blanket of snow, whether soft and powdery or thick like ice cream or concrete. And not surprisingly, people have responded with common sense and ingenuity. They have put various shoelike things on their feet, so as to get around, although not always without pain.

The early inhabitants of North America favored webbed devices of various kinds: generally round, oval, or shaped like a teardrop, made of wooden frames between which they stretched strong, thin strips of animal hide or gut, in a crosshatched pattern not unlike a modern tennis racket. These snowshoes greatly increased the surface area over which the walker's weight is distributed, thereby allowing the snowshoer to stand on top of the snow, even the fluffiest powder, without sinking in. Along with dogsleds, snowshoes were long the primary means of travel in the Canadian North. (Surprisingly, Eskimos made less use of snowshoes than did the more southern, forest Indian peoples.) Although they make an impression that is shallow and temporary in the powdery whiteness, snowshoes are deeply and indelibly associated with the early fur trade in North America.

Meanwhile, on the other side of the globe, long before there were rope tows, T-bars or J-bars, chairlifts or heated gondolas, lift lines and $25-per-day tickets—not to mention plush resorts and orthopedic specialists in spiral fractures of the tibia—there was also something called skiing. Unlike the New World and its snow-*shoeing* people in the Old World discovered something a bit more nimble: snow *sliding*. They found that if they attached themselves to long, flat-bottomed strips of wood, they could glide along on top of the white stuff. Indeed, sometimes they could move rather quickly.

The first skis have been carbon-dated to about 2,000 B.C. Not surprisingly, they were much closer to those used in today's cross-country skiing than to downhill. The skis were quite long—about ten feet—and they permitted the heel to be raised while walking, although the foot could also rest flat on the boards when gliding or sliding down a hill. Finally, nearly four thousand years later, after a regrettable romance with downhill, or so-called alpine skiing, enthusiasts are rediscovering the roots of skiing, generally known as cross-country, Nordic, or ski-touring.

Nor surprisingly, the origins of American cross-country skiing are strictly practical, a way of getting from here to there. In the mid nineteenth century, a young Norwegian immigrant, Jon Torsteinson, saw an ad in the *Sacramento Union*, with this understated headline: "People Lost to World! Uncle Sam Needs Mail Courier." Recalling the ease with which people made lengthy journeys across the snow-covered country of his native Norway, Torsteinson volunteered for the assignment. On skis, he made the ninety-mile trip from Placerville to Carson City, Nevada, in the area of today's Squaw Valley ski resort, in just four days, carrying packages and mail. The journeys became routine—thirty to thirty-five round trips each winter—and the young man, his name Americanized, became a legend: "Snowshoe Thompson," renowned in the annals of winter travel. He had been born in the Telemark province of Norway, a region that has since left its name on the most graceful of cross-country ski turns. More than anyone else, Torsteinson introduced Americans to the Old World art of ski-touring, and in so doing, he introduced the New World to a new world indeed.

Usually, if we want to experience a different land, not to mention a new world, we have to get off our butts and go someplace. Snowfall changes this. Overnight—or even in an hour or so—it changes everything, making our old world new, sometimes scarcely recognizable. We go to sleep, or simply lose ourselves in a book, a meal, or a television show, then look outside, and *Voilá* everything changed. Like Gandalf in Tolkien's *The Hobbit*, adventure comes knocking uninvited at our door. And sometimes it stays quite a long while. Until spring, for example.

But let's not romanticize snow. Beyond its magical qualities, snow is also cold, often wet, surprisingly heavy, and potentially dangerous. And it happens most often during winter, which as everyone knows, is downright cantankerous. There is no getting around it. But listen closely, for I shall now announce one of the great, heretofore unspecified advantages of winter: it makes no demands on us, other than survival. It does nothing to make us feel guilty about staying indoors, sleeping late when we can, keeping warm, and dry. Winter doesn't lure us to bask, to savor, to photosynthesize or to reproduce, to sow or to reap. It doesn't even insist that we go outside very much at all. Quite the opposite, in fact. It drives us inside, where crackling fire, hot toddy, soothing bath, good book, a warm friend, and perhaps a stereo set will do quite nicely. And so, when we do venture outdoors, either out of boredom or defiance, or aesthetically impelled to experience that snow-changed, snow-charged world, only to find that we *enjoy* it, we have every reason to be proud: we have really pulled one off.

In the past, people responded to winter and its snows with misery[1] or resignation, with audacity (like Snowshoe Thompson) or timorousness . . . very rarely with elation. Maybe, therefore, there is such a thing as true progress, after all, if only in the fact that modern civilization has given us winter as something to be enjoyed and not just endured.

Confronted with snow, it is hard to resist sliding. Indeed, snow is for sliding just like water is for splashing. Although winter survival is serious business for animals, sometimes even they get into the act. A quiet, backwater riverbank in the Adirondack mountains of New York State had been the site of a boisterous game of slide-down-the-mud-into-the-water, performed by a family of river otters. Several months later, the same track was transformed into a luterine luge run, with the watery plop of summer changed into a slippery runout on flat, smooth ice. (The snow had been pretty much cleared away, perhaps intentionally, but more likely just as a result of many repeated slides.) Not content with just one trip, each animal would scurry repeatedly back to the top, perhaps twenty-five feet up, place its paws on either side of its head, then shove off with its hind feed, on a short, wild ride back to the bottom. The yearlings were less restrained than the adults; after

---

1. "Great God!" explorer Robert Scott wrote in his diary at the South Pole, "This is an awful place."

scrambling back up, they often didn't have the patience to turn around and face downhill. Pushing off prematurely with their front legs, they would slide feet first down the well-worn rut.

Penguins will sometimes belly flop while traveling long distances on well-packed snow. Occasionally, so do polar bears. But human beings favor the intervention of at least some technology. And for those employing skis, there are basically two choices: cross-country or its glitzy, high-tech sibling, downhill skiing. Some people have been rejecting this either/or approach, trying to keep both options open. On a winter vacation, for example, they bring both downhill and cross-country gear. But the activities are actually quite different, appealing to dramatically different sensibilities.

Comparisons are odious, a wise man once said. But sometimes they are necessary, or at least helpful, in owning up to my own heartfelt biases. Cross-country skiing is to downhill as green is to chartreuse, as a flannel shirt is to a nylon bodystocking, as the Little Engine That Could is to the SST. Downhill skiers replace the jangle and stress of working days with even more jangle and stress on holidays. Northwest outdoorsman Harvey Manning wrote that "The snow calms the land, and those who walk there." It does little, on the other hand, to calm the denizens of our downhill ski resorts. And the alpine-skiing industry labors not to calm the land, but to clear it.

Downhill skiing itself is a series of alternations: riding uphill on your behind, followed by a free fall back down the mountain. Up and down, up and down—a good life, if you're a yo-yo. By contrast, cross-country skiers move under their own power, wherever they want to go. They ski uphill as well as down . . . and to the yo-yo skier's amazement, the ski-tourer is often more comfortable doing the former than the latter. Downhill skiing, especially on weekends or during holidays, is hurry up and wait: down the slopes in a hurry, then wait on a line (sometimes an hour or more) for the privilege of being carried back up to do it all over again. The downhill skier flees the crowded city for crowded slopes and even more crowded liftlines. Occasionally, a ski slope is so densely peopled that it is even necessary to wait on the way *down* for the crowd to thin out. It never does.

By contrast, there are essentially no crowds in cross-country skiing because the skier is free to wander about *ad lib*, instead of being forced to use the same preprocessed descents. And since there is no lift, there are no liftlines. It is easier to ski cross-country where others have already skied, following in the parallel tracks of your predecessor. But it isn't necessary. True to its name, the cross-country skier goes across the country and that generally means pretty much anywhere.

Doubtless some people go downhill skiing for the sheer joy of the experience, but the truth is that most downhillers spend an awful lot of time watching each other, trying to look good, and fearing to look bad. Downhill skiing is necessarily an exhibition sport; the attention devoted to the terrain is often exceeded by the attention directed toward each other's form and style. (In fairness, all this mutual regarding is at least partly because downhill skiing, when done by an expert, is surpassingly graceful.) Spectator-participants bunch up just above any particularly difficult spot, waiting for someone to be so bold, so indifferent to public judgment, supremely confident, or just plain cold or bored enough to proceed to the next downhill staging and viewing area, where it all starts again.Cross-country skiing, by contrast, is done for one's self, almost never for, or with, a crowd. Actually, it is possible—and according to most experts, desirable, for safety's sake—to go ski-touring with others. And in fact, a small group of cross-country enthusiasts can generally count on being together as much as they want: pausing at the scenery, watching an animal or deciphering a track, eating a snack, or just plain talking and perspiring in unison as they glide along. Downhill skiing, on the other hand, although infinitely more crowded, is paradoxically more isolating as well. The mechanical lifts restrict interaction with your partner on the chair, and the wind and speed of the downhill run makes conversation dangerous, if not impossible. The loneliest crowds are on today's ski slopes.

In certain places—notably, the environs of popular downhill resorts—landowners will charge the ski-tourer a small "trail fee." And some resorts that specialize in cross-country and that maintain miles of groomed trails will also insist on a modest payment. But the expense of cross-country is a different order of magnitude from that of downhill. This is especially true of the equipment: perhaps five hundred dollars to get started downhilling, as op-

posed to one hundred dollars for cross-country. Downhill equipment employs rigid, form-fitted boots that are firmly attached to
wide, heavy skis with hard, sharp, metal edges (all the better to
bite into a steep slope, my dear). Cross-country skis, by contrast,
are longer, much thinner and more flexible, lighter and very
skinny. The "boots" look more like track shoes, and are attached to
the skis only at the toes. Poles are longer, to facilitate pushing off
when going uphill, and as to clothing, anything goes. Aerodynamic,
form-fitting jump suits—so chic in the downhill world—have little
place in the much slower-paced world of skinny skis, except for the
serious racer.

"If you can walk, you can ski." Such is the claim, at least, for
both forms of skiing. Don't believe it. Downhill skiing requires not
only fancy equipment, but some fancy technique, as well, such that
ski lessons, all by themselves, have become a major industry. Numerous books and videotapes dispense advice for novices all the
way to experts, and ski magazines are filled with "tips on technique." Alpine skiing is not easy, and there is a great premium on
doing it well. By contrast, in John Caldwell's excellent guide to
cross-country skiing,[2] the chapter on technique begins with the
following remarkable piece of advice: "If you want to do your own
thing and ski your own way, just skip this chapter and no one will
be the loser." He means it. The goal in cross-country, you see, is
simply to get out in the snow and be self-propelled, to go, literally,
across the countryside meeting the terrain and the winter-world
on its terms. To be sure, competitive racers are concerned—sometimes obsessed—with technique, but for more of us, ski-touring is
doing what comes naturally.

Injuries are legendary among downhill skiers; indeed, the risk
may well be part of the appeal. This is at least partly because speed
is so important to downhillers, getting from point A to point B as
quickly and as stylishly as possible (with the space between A and
B typically measured as vertical drop rather than horizontal distance). Downhill equipment is a self-referential, pessimistic proph-
ecy: lower leg, ankle, and ski are held so rigidly that when the skier
takes to the slopes, he or she already appears to be wrapped in a

2. John Caldwell, *The New Cross-Country Ski Book*, (Brattleboro, VT.: The
Stephen Greene Press, 1971).

plaster cast, even before the injury. And when a tumble occurs, there seems little question which will break first, layers of high-grade steel with epoxy and fiberglass reinforcements, or human bone.[3] By contrast, when the skinny-ski enthusiast takes a tumble, his or her ankles are less likely to break than are the skis themselves. moreover, because these skis are affixed loosely to the skier (toes only), with the ankles free to flex and the heel lifting up with each step or glide (or fall), the limbs of the cross-country skier have many more degrees of freedom, and the orthopedists, many fewer patients.

Then there is the silence. This may have little to do with physical health, but everything to do with mental health., Away from chair lifts, lines, automobiles, and snowmobiles, the world under white wraps is quiet, organically muffled; puncturing the thin hiss of wood on snow, the skier's breathing may seem so loud as to be obscene, but it only underscores how very low is the cross-country decibel level. And don't forget the peace. And the connectedness to the winter-world, not as a recreational industry has made it, but as it is. The cross-country skier sees close up and in detail what the yo-yo skier glimpses only at a distance and in quick photoflashes, if at all: the play of diamonds on a frosty meadow, the lie of the snow on a fir branch, the brittle, crystalline tracery of fern fronds encased in a shellac of ice.

Animals are difficult to see at this time of year. Many are hibernating, or sojourning in the south, or dead and represented only in proxy by their dormant eggs. In the summer, it takes an expert tracker to read the guest book that has been inscribed on the warm, solid ground. On the other hand, although the world in snow is depauperate, it takes its citizens more seriously, preserving and then revealing the imprint of whatever has passed: a hollowed-out scoop where a quail spent the night, the distinctive quadrilateral of a rabbit, the deep, strangely sharp imprint of a family of deer, their high heels sinking awkwardly into yesterday's snow.

Sometimes, you see the animals themselves. And when you do, it is with the stark haiku clarity of oriental ink drawings on white parchment: "I remember the smell of the pines," wrote Ernest

---

3. It may still be possible to find downhill skis made of wood, someplace other than at an antique shop, but I haven't.

Hemingway, recalling his cross-country ski experiences in Austria, "and the sleeping on the mattresses of beech leaves in the wood-cutters' huts and the skiing through the forest following the tracks of hares and of foxes. . . . Above the tree line, I remember following the track of a fox until I came in sight of him and watching him stand with his right forefoot raised and then go carefully to stop and then pounce, and the whiteness and the clutter of a ptarmigan bursting out of the snow and flying away and over the ridge."[4]

To be sure, there are other ways to experience the joy of snow. When it comes to speed, for example, the downhill skier excels. But with all that concentration on the *doing* of it, the natural context gets shortchanged: trees and bushes, animals and other people become things to avoid rather than to savor, and the scene that flashes past could just as well be projected on a screen. The world is made peripheral, secondary to the goal of getting down the mountain, quickly and well. Moving along on skinny skis, however, the cross-country traveler knows little of speed, but much about the purity of powder underfoot, the twitter of a flock of chickadees looking desperately for insects in a hawthorn bush, the deep, sudden thump as an overloaded limb deposits its burden on the forest floor, the quiet play of morning and evening shadows alternating with the brilliant glitter of sunlight on diamond-dust, the smooth, gunmetal gray of a blanketed night, and the unexpected dividends of high clouds obscuring the sun: soft, luxuriant folds of rich velvet vanilla ice cream down on the ground.

If done as a sport rather than an activity, cross-country can be very demanding; indeed, it may be the best of all aerobic exercises, with expenditures of eight hundred calories per hour. Not surprisingly, cross-country racers are the world's best endurance athletes, as seen by their ability to absorb oxygen into the bloodstream. Soccer players average less than fifty milligrams uptake of 0_2 per kilogram of body weight per minute of exercise. Middle distance runners, rowers, and swimmers are a bit over sixty two, marathon runners clock in at seventy-five and cross-country racers, over eighty! And even those of us whose oxygen uptake is more modest

4. Ernest Hemingway, *A Moveable Feast*, (New York: Charles Scribner's Sons, 1964).

can profit from the smooth gliding and stretching, which is far less stressful on one's joints than the heavy footfalls of running, for example.

The latest rage in competitive cross-country skiing is "skating," which resembles ice skating, only with very long "blades." American Bill Koch won the World Cup by skating, and skating on skis is now a recognized Olympic cross-country event, generally known as "freestyle." However, skating requires a carefully prepared track, one that is wide, smooth, and firmly packed down. It also takes great balance and coordination, skills that must be honed like those of the downhiller. Most cross-country devotees slide along pretty much like their Nordic predecessors have always done, flat on the skis, pushing off along two straight-ahead parallel tracks, from one leg and the alternate pole, to the other, and then smoothly back again. You just shift your weight rhythmically from one ski to the other, springing lightly, as one instruction book puts it, "like a leopard in carpet slippers."[5]

Going downhill in cross-country gear is a bit more challenging and less feline. The epitome of cross-country skill is the graceful Telemark turn, by which the skier alternately swoops from one bended knee to the other, while carving a series of gentle, linked "S"s down a wide, open slope. If the descending route isn't wide and open (it usually isn't), then the skier is reduced to a V-shaped snowplow, often with many brief halts . . . occasionally upright, but not always.

Fortunately, when it comes to cross-country skiing, a little bit of snow goes a long way; unneeded is the fifty-inch base of a commercial downhill development. Just a few inches will suffice, enough to cover the stubble in your neighbor's field. It takes surprisingly little to smooth and gentle the angles, sharpnesses, protuberances, and bumps of autumn. With the world made round at last, friction is overcome, and the fun begins.

Cross-country skiing can be done anywhere there is snow, not just in the Alps, or certain "developed" resorts in Vermont, New Hampshire, or the Rockies or Sierras. Cow pastures are good. Golf courses are even better, transformed from cultivated domesticity

5. Art Tokle and Martin Luray, *The Complete Guide to Cross-Country Skiing and Touring*, (New York: Holt, Rinehart & Winston, 1973).

to stretches of delightful mini-wilderness. Forests can't be tackled until the snowfall is heavy enough to penetrate to the ground, but bridle paths and logging roads are often superb, just the right width and devoid of traffic. (In the Pacific Northwest, which is particularly disfigured by logging clear-cuts, winter is the time when our environmental sins are least painfully apparent.)

Except for children eager for snowmen or snowballs, nearly everyone prefers dry snow to wet. When it squeaks underfoot, conditions are perfect. When it crunches, look out for ice. And under the ice or snow, look out for streams, still flowing sneakily and quietly, waiting to engulf the bottoms of your skis and transform them from frictionless surfaces into great globs of concrete, weighing several hundred tons apiece.

And now, a word about waxing. The cross-country skier asks a lot of his or her ski bottoms: they must glide smoothly forward, but resist slipping back, a trick that is all the more difficult (and all the more important) when the skier is pushing off from one ski onto the other. Wax has these wonderful properties because it is magically able to "set up" firmly and briefly after each slide through the snow. There may or may not be science at work here, but there most assuredly is a whole lot of art. Waxing is to the cross-country skier as the tying of lures is to the ardent fly-fisherman: a source of infinite attention and debate. Devotees happily spend hours discussing the relative merits of green versus blue hard wax in moderately dry old powder when it is eighteen degrees outside, or whether to use silver or red klister on wet, granular snow at forty degrees. Being "into" waxes requires being "into" snow in all its various transformations and idiosyncrasies, and since cross-country skiers are, by definition, going (out) into the snow, a certain degree of snow-consciousness comes with the territory.

There are waxes for every conceivable condition: dry snow or wet, fine powder or crusty ice, warm or cold, or in between. And of course, it matters whether your route will take you primarily downhill, on a climb, or pretty much level. A friend once insisted that the optimum wax depended on her most recent meal, whether large or small, high or low in carbohydrates. And as conditions change, it often helps to change your wax as well. This is not an irrelevant obsession: the right wax can make an enormous difference, between a dreamlike glide with just enough bite underfoot to propel the skier forward . . . and a lot of hard work and frustration as you stride forward only to have your legs slip backward instead, or find yourself immobilized with globs of snow balled underfoot, caught in the grip of that fierce Nordic undersnow ski-grabber, the subsurface snow-troll with the strength of Thor and the inclinations of Loki.

Especially in regions where the snow tends to be consistently wet, growing numbers of cross-country skiers have been using nowax bottoms, relying on the wonders of fish-scale finishes, oblique steplike surfaces, or some other mechanical contrivance to rescue them from the mess and concentration of waxing. Like a one-way valve—or a good waxing job—the idea is to facilitate movement in one direction only, while inhibiting it in the other. "Climbing skins" are based on a similar principle: by attaching animal pelts beneath one's skis, with the nap of the fur running front to back, the skis are encouraged to slide forward, while backsliding is discouraged. The wax enthusiast is typically a bit disdainful of no-wax shortcuts, just as the wind sailor looks down on his or her motordriven ("stinkpot") cousins, or indeed, cross-country skiers collectively view the yo-yos . . . most of whom don't bother very much with waxes at all.[6] Somehow, waxes have taken on the aura of being acceptably "organic," probably because they 1) have a reputable history, 2) are administered by hand, and 3) require a degree of woodsmanlike skill. It seems a good guess, however, that the exquisite days of precise waxing are numbered and will soon be limited to high-level competition. On the other hand, some of us thought the same would apply to the clutch and stick shift once automatic transmissions became widely available.

Sliding in and out of trees, playing tag with the long winter shadows, happily in touch with the world around them, most skiers nonetheless remain somewhat removed from ecstatic out-of-body communion. It is almost impossible to lose one's self entirely, since every kick and slide, every hummock and uphill climb or downhill dip is a little bit different. Sometimes, perceptions are assailed by continual evaluations, especially the pervasive awareness of how well or poorly one's skis are catching the snow's surface for each

6. Climbing skins are "in," however, largely because they are used in steep terrain, where they are essential.

little kick, and how smoothly they slide forward in response to each gentle prod from the opposite ski. Was that a little catch there, about halfway through? Is it time to change wax now, or at least to check for ice adhering to the bottom, maybe under the heel of the right foot? Or is it the toe of the left?

But most skiers also notice other things, such as the dazzling glare of sun on unbroken whiteness, the way the snow sticks to one kind of tree bark and not another, and how orphaned feathers of loose powder whip crazily above an iced-over pond, its surface like the face of a homeless old man, punctured by a ragged beard of stiffly frozen rushes. They may also wonder at how unevenly the snow is piled: mounding about the trunks of trees in the lee of the wind, blown nearly clear of the flat surfaces nearby. They watch as a hyperactive squirrel tries to cram in just one more mouthful of seeds, while balancing its fat gray body above the thin white dusting on a rich brown limb. They marvel at how, on an overcast day, the luminous ground actually seems to be brighter than the sky . . . which is impossible, we know, because the sky is the source of all that light, of which the snowy ground merely reflects back a portion. (It must be that we are so accustomed to the ground being dark that when there is light emanating from below, our minds go reality one step better.) And cross-country skiers, when not dazzled from below, or above, or within, may well have time and inclination to marvel at how low the sun rides along the horizon, and how cold it gets when you stop moving or when the sun goes behind a cloud, noting also, with appreciation ever-renewed, how effectively a chocolate bar turns up the interior thermostat.

But even when the waxing is perfect, the weather is ideal, the terrain is diverse, and the chocolate bar is Cadbury's (with almonds), anyone skiing cross-country on anything steeper than a cow pasture or golf course has something to worry about. As Hunter Thompson might put it, the mood can "turn ugly," and in a hurry. Snow—that widely accepted symbol of purity, serenity, and peace—can go from Jekyll to Hyde in an instant of demonic transformation. In the Andes, a blizzard is known as "el tormento." And blizzards are bad enough, especially a "whiteout," in which sky and snow blend together into a single featureless amalgam, a kind of homogenized horror. But there is something worse yet, the arch villain of the winter slopes, the avalanche. Just as Christmas has the Grinch, cross-country skiing has avalanches.

Only, avalanches are real.

Snow on a steep incline is actually nothing less than a suspended storm. The energy of position is there, just like Humpty Dumpty ready to have his great fall or water about to thunder over Niagara. It can be released slowly by gradual melting, or suddenly, in the terrifying fury of angry snow and ice roaring downhill, sometimes literally taking to the air and flinging itself through space. A single cubic yard can weigh nearly a ton. The savage snow of an avalanche can hardly be imagined until it has been experienced and not very many who have had the experience live to tell of it. When it comes to avalanches, there are very few living veterans.

Perhaps the most dramatic thing about an avalanche is the nearly instantaneous dividing line between heaven and hell. One instant, all is peaceful and quiet; then the world is swallowed up in a shiver of monstrous, deadly power, accompanied by anything from a gentle hiss to a deafening roar. For all their unpredictability, however, some avalanche patterns can be anticipated: slopes that are steep and relatively bare, for example, are far more likely to avalanche than those that are thickly treed. This is because trees tend to damp out the early recruitment of snow crystals by other snow crystals, the preliminary, rapidly accumulating snowball effect whereby a small slide eventually becomes a potential killer. (Once underway, however, trees are no protection whatever. Large-scale avalanches toss them about like toothpicks.) But a healthy growth of timber does at least indicate a place where avalanches haven't recently come through. By the same token, incongruously bare slopes should be suspect, since these may be so-called "avalanche chutes," regular conduits for rampaging snow. Lightning is neither more nor less likely to strike twice in the same place. Avalanches are.

Snow is programmed to fall when circumstances permit (even after its initial fall, to the ground, has been achieved). And, depending on the weather, it is also programmed to adhere to other bits of snow that are going in the same direction. For an unlikely, but useful analogy, consider the computers that increasingly dominate Wall Street, just as snow dominates our winter mountains. Like the preprogrammed snow crystal, stock market computers have been programmed to sell when circumstances call for it.

On October 19, 1987, something extraordinary happened: computer-generated "sell" orders elicited additional "sell" instructions from other computers, which, in turn, caused yet more selling . . . and all the while, horrified onlookers could do nothing but watch as the system snowballed out of control, gained increasing mass and momentum and plummeted, not quite to the bottom, but terrifyingly close. A similar process, structured out of snow crystals rather than ticker tape, takes place even more often out in the real world where the mountains are white and the laws are written by gravity rather than people.

Just as the accumulated financial resources of Wall Street can be thrown into a tailspin by a hiccup in interest rates or a sneeze from the chairman of the Federal Reserve, the accumulated snowpack of a winter season can be disrupted and sent into a panic, equally downhill. At that special, delicate point, when the world hangs quivering between stability and instability, almost anything—even a loud noise, certainly a passing skier—can set things off. Like the freestyle investor who has wandered away from traditional financial paths, the cross-country wanderer, venturing away from groomed slopes, is far more likely than the downhill skier to encounter avalanches. A little discretion will, therefore, go a long way. For example, it doesn't take a Ph.D. in avalanchology to insist on getting reports on snow conditions before setting out and to avoid those days when heavy snowfall and a quick freeze has just followed periods of relatively warm weather. In such cases, the new, wet snow may well be lying uneasily, unbonded to the icy slopes just beneath, waiting for an opportunity to "let go." But dry snow can avalanche, too, especially if too much has fallen, and there hasn't been enough opportunity for it to consolidate.[7]

Some other suggestions: when possible, stay on ridge crests or in valleys. If you must travel through avalanche terrain (and frankly, there is very little reason for anyone to do so) then in early winter try to make it in midday, thereby avoiding the rapid, destabilizing temperature changes of early morning and late afternoon. As winter turns to spring, on the other hand, the opposite time of day may be safest, that is, early morning and late afternoon, when

7. Additional stock market analogies are tempting, but shall be left to the reader.

temperature is lowest and the snow is the most firm.

The hiker follows a trail, the canoer or kayaker can only ply the one-directional flow of a river, and the downhill skier is limited to the designated slope of a groomed mountain. But the cross-country skier is free to glide at will, to poke around and explore, to plot a new route every time. Sensitivity to the land really pays off, and not only in keeping out of harm's way. For example, you can set yourself against the flow of the land and tough it out, or you can mold your route to the existing terrain with a kind of navigational jiujitsu. This applies to the microgeographic no less than the macro-, route-planning stage. Sun cups (pockets in the snow perhaps two feet across and sometimes almost as deep) can be a challenge or an opportunity, depending on how they are navigated; likewise for logs, ridges, ravines, and thickets. A sharp eye for structural nuance (as well as the likely weather) comes in handy here, not only for fun but also for safety: the mountains are bad places for the unwary or the insolent. This is even more true in winter, when getting lost is no picnic. Fortunately, however, deep snowmarks usually last a day or more, unless it is snowing very hard or melting very quickly. So, do not begrudge your outbound tracks: they can become a lifeline back, like Theseus following his trail of string out of the Minotaur's labyrinth.

It is easiest, however, to follow preexisting tracks, both out and back. And here comes a confession, at the risk of permanent expulsion from the ranks of cross-country purists: I like snowmobile tracks. (I also like Hostess Twinkies, but find them more resistible.) Snowmobile tracks are about the right width, and more than one outing has been saved by discovering and following the nicely packed route of some motorized couch potato-cum-snow jockey.[8] Deep, newly fallen snow may be picture-perfect, but it can also be very difficult going. For that reason, cross-country skiing—unlike downhill skiing, hiking, or horseback riding—puts a special burden on whomever goes first. The trailbreaker's lot is not an easy one. In unskied snow, therefore, follow-the-leader is a good game to play . . . for the followers, that is. Since leadership on a cross-

8. Sad to say, many other outings—probably many more, in fact—have been despoiled by the grinding roar, the stinking exhaust, and the plain inconvenience of having to get out of the way of those damned machines! It is the tracks that I appreciate, not their creators.

country trip is such a mixed blessing, one of the advantages of going in a group is the opportunity to take turns. Forty-five minutes or so at "point," then you can drop back to reap the rewards of someone else's labor. (This is very much what wild geese do, in their long-distance migration flights: the animal at the front of the "V" has a somewhat more difficult time than the others obliquely behind, who profit from the slipstream produced by the leader's wings. Every so often, they switch, with the leader dropping back into line.)

Usually, a few hours is more than enough for an entire trip, especially if the pace is quick, or if there is fresh snow, not packed down by others. Unlike the downhill skier, cross-country tourers typically carry a small backpack or hip belt with them, containing some extra clothing, food, and drink. (Wine is the classic, but not always the smartest choice, since the heat and energy it provides is only temporary and an inebriated snooze in the snow is not generally recommended.) Recently, cross-country guide services have been springing up, and at least in the West—in particular, the mountains of Utah, Colorado, and British Columbia—it is now possible to go on multi-day trips without having to carry more than a few personal items. The key player is the "yurt," a large, sturdy tent somewhat resembling a rounded teepee. For centuries, yurts have been used by nomads of the high, cold Mongolian deserts. Now, they provide shelter for a new breed of modern-day cross-country nomads in North America.

Perched on a substantial snowpack (and often largely covered by additional snow, as well), the yurts that increasingly dot the backcountry of wintertime North America cause virtually no environmental impact and are removed every spring. They make for a lovely combination of wintertime wilderness plus relative comfort. Whatever hosannas one may sing to cross-country skiing, the fact remains that it can involve some rather strenuous exercise.[9] Insofar as I am concerned, this is all to the good. When it comes to overnight trips, however, the problem is to be graceful, safe, or just even-tempered while also carrying fifty pounds on your back! The

9. It doesn't have to, but the option is certainly there for anyone who wants to go particularly far, or high, or quickly.

advent of the yurt hasn't eliminated all vestiges of this dilemma, but it has certainly helped.

Genghis Khan would doubtless be proud to know that along with the hordes of wealthy Caucasians who regularly overrun the world's downhill ski resorts, his tribesmen's favorite domicile has also been making a successful invasion, all the way to the New World.

We decided to start early. For a typical midwinter cross-country ski trip, that is around nine o'clock. Breakfast was huge: pancakes and bacon, eggs and toast, orange juice and coffee—lots of coffee, pungent and black, even if it meant lots of yellow snow later in the day. Our route would be a twelve-mile loop, through an upper New York State sampler of old fields, across a frozen lake, along two different icy streams, and through forests both deciduous (bare branched in January) and heavy dark spruce, as well as up and over one of the ancient, rounded knobs of the Adirondacks. Anticipatory eating is one of the great pleasures of such an enterprise; you eat because you know that you will soon appreciate the warmth and the calories, and also because the exertion to follow gives you permission to do so, without prospect of remorse.

Yesterday had been unusually warm; then last night it went down into the low twenties. Not a good prognosis. And not surprisingly, the snow had a hard, unfriendly crust. But the sky was a cheerful blue, and the dryness made even the air feel brittle and sharp. In the tropics, there can be an overpowering sensation of the air as a *substance*, perfumed and heavy; in the wintertime north, the feeling can be exactly opposite. On this day, the crisp chill of the outside felt like the purest vacuum, a clear void between objects, nothing material at all. Our breath, in fact, was the only thing floating between earth and sky. It was a day to be outside, but one to keep moving.

We started right from my friend's back door, across his orchard of unpruned apple trees, feeling a little ponderous and stiff. After the first, rather tentative slides to assess the waxing job—not great, but then again, we had agreed that in this stuff nothing goes really well—we were soon going a bit too fast, full of anticipation and a little too eager to do it all, as though in one great stride. Or to work off the bacon, and quickly. The coffee sloshed inside. (Perhaps that last cup had been one too many.) And the damned wool knickers made themselves felt as a solid itch, from knees to crotch.

The sun glittered sharply on the neighbor's field, and the breath of her beef cattle was the only thing moving . . . except for ourselves. Some jays called overhead, and a few light clouds (nonthreatening) began to form in the southern sky. Within an hour, the hard crust had begun to crumble, and as our skis bit more reliably into its surface, our mood improved to match the weather. Which was just as well, because we were starting to climb along the unrelentingly steep, hillside forest that marked part of the Adirondack Preserve. In the sunny meadow, there was broken crust underfoot; when we ventured tentatively into the trees, it was not only dark and cold, but the footing felt like solid rock. The trees would have to wait. But the meadow had some delicate offerings of its own: clumps of grasses leaning together like miniature teepees, each sheltering a tiny nest of snow, held precariously a foot or so above the surface.

About a thousand feet higher, the crust gave way to genuine powder snow on a firm base. Apparently, at this altitude, yesterday's warm weather hadn't been so warm, and the top layer of snow had remained unmelted. Breakfast was long gone, turned into our own striding and breathing and warming all over. (Even the knickers stopped itching.) Sunglasses came out, and the windbreaker came off, although my thermometer still showed only twenty-six degrees and the wind had picked up, chasing a bouquet of oak leaves in a crazy, rustling dance, spinning crazily, fully two feet above a patch of frozen milkweed. But the clouds floated serene and unmoving. We headed west, the sun warming our backs.

The lake was a popular fishing spot in summer, almost never visited in winter: too far from any road for ice fishing or skating. Compared to its unearthly flatness, even the relatively smooth expanse of meadow seemed disrupted and rank. We slipped over its serene surface, leaving a parallel set of tracks that were so out of place on the lake's unbroken expanse that it looked like they might be a permanent scar. About halfway across, there was a sudden reminder that what appeared so solid was actually changeable: a pressure ridge, where conflicting patterns of expansion and contraction had met and pushed up a long jagged line, a kind of upthrusting fault of the sort that makes enormous mountain ranges.

Only this miniature escarpment was about four inches high.

On the far side of the lake, just where our route skirted an enormous rocky dome that had been blown clear of snow, we could trace the busy, incredibly precise little footprints of shrews or field mice, appearing and then disappearing as they popped in and out of their invisible tunnels. We had already come about five miles, and except for the lake traverse, it had been steady climbing all the way. Lunch, we therefore decided, was earned. Skis went tailfirst into the snow as sentinels to our endeavor, and our bodies sprawled gratefully on the surprisingly warm surface of the barren dome. A few mouthfuls of wine to go with the salami, bread, cheese, and apples, and the gratitude was even greater.

Before pushing on, I bent down to examine a tiny seedling, a perfectly symmetrical cone of green sticking a few inches out of the snow. Carelessly putting my foot alongside, it burst through the snow and dangled about ten yards above the ground: that "seedling" was actually the top of a middle-sized tree, nearly buried in an enormous drift and with only the faintest skeleton of snow distributed around its trunk. The tree's inner body had absorbed enough of the sun's heat to melt out much of the nearby snow, while the top remained snow-covered except for the very tip. Rocks can be similarly dangerous, absorbing heat even on cold days, then acting as radiators that dispel the snow around their periphery and leave a nasty surprise for anyone who steps carelessly at the margin.

Nearby was a jumble of pumpkin-sized boulders, each ornamented with a unique wrapping of velvet snow. Each could be examined, revealing up close, an immense and ancient solitude of crystal upon crystal . . . and yet, each pattern must have been formed just a few days ago.

Another two miles to the top, a broad mountain that had lost most of its upper tree-cover to a fire thirty years before. The last few hundred yards were too steep to be tackled directly. So it was time for the aptly named herringbone, an uphill climbing maneuver with toes pointed out, weight on the inner edges, and heels together, one pole downhill of each ski, waddling upward like a pregnant duck. (Pausing to catch your breath and admire your progress, you see that the fresh tracks look almost exactly like the skeleton of a giant fossil fish.) Just below the summit, some snowshoers come trudging by, having ascended by a different route, the one we were about to follow on the way down. They added a new pattern—waffles—to our gradually lengthening fish fillet.

Whereas skiers glide in almost constant motion, relying on momentum and a lack of friction for their progress, snowshoers do the opposite. They pause for a split second and consolidate their gain after each step, letting their webs bite into the snow before stepping out again. And whereas skiing—even cross-country skiing—involves at least minimal technique, snowshoeing requires virtually none, except the ability to avoid stepping on your own feet. This is best achieved by walking bowlegged and carefully. When the route is steep, snowshoers—even with their heavy, plodding gait—can outpace skiers, for whom a little bit of friction has become a valued and scarce commodity. Sliding down a hill, backward, when you are trying to go up, just isn't much fun. Moreover, snowshoes make for an easier time getting over or through trees and maneuvering in tight corners, in heavy brush or very deep powder.

These people were moving well, and cheerfully, carrying ski poles like ourselves. One of them wore a traditional trail model, each shoe about five feet long, with graceful, upturned tips and pointy tail. (Excellent for straight walking in deep snow.) The other had "bearpaws," symmetrical little ovals that do particularly well on steep slopes and where fancy footwork is called for. We converged at the top, shared pleasantries, chocolate bars, and the view, which included at least two more frozen lakes as well as a little lumber town trying to hitch its future to the manufacture of woodstoves, specially designed to work underwater in hot tubs (no kidding!).

The descent was quick, a little too quick, since we got a bit carried away, allowing ourselves to drop down several hundred feet alongside a sprightly, fast-flowing stream that laughed a lot and seemed to know where it was going, and that promised a good time, with no regrets. Besides, there was no good way to cross it, clamber up the ravine, and continue descending more gradually as we should have. With the sun relatively high overhead, shadows were less pronounced and depth perception was seriously compromised. Each procession of hummocks became a special challenge, with guesses becoming more uncertain as fatigue increased. So I

fell. Actually, it was more of a toppling-over than a heroic extravaganza (no harm done, but a warning that another rest stop was in
order). In such conditions, one appreciates the existential wisdom
etched onto the bottom of my old Peugeot's rearview mirror, WARN-
ING: THINGS ARE CLOSER THAN THEY SEEM.

Eventually we had to abandon the meadow nymph and climb
again, doing penance for our descent into sin, until we met the
tracks made by the snowshoers on their way up earlier that same
morning. After a few miles of easy, gentle descent, we parted company with their spoor, becoming once again the only people in the
world.

Then we were seduced once more. Earlier, it had been that
laughing stream beckoning us downhill. This time, it was an elderly matron: a mature forest of oak and hickory, whose large,
heavy trunks were obligingly spread, revealing wide, parklike
spaces that were simply irresistible. Creamy, rich snow flowed
smoothly underfoot, like the finest vanilla ice cream studded with
chocolate chips: last autumn's leaves. I knew this forest, from another time. During its leafy season, it has a brooding demeanor,
like a great, dark building. But it was very different now: the so-
lemnity of its summertime canopy had fallen to the ground, in a
crash of snow instead of plaster. As though wreckers had sliced the
roof off a cathedral, hidden surfaces were exposed to a prying,
irreverent light. But the forest interior, bare yet healthy, did not
seem so much violated as liberated. Mostly, we think of winter as a
time of darkness and heavy forests, as filled with foreboding. But
not always. Indeed, this time the effect was downright sprightly,
with the midafternoon sun dancing on the exposed branches,
spraying mischievous sunbeams where in another season, sobriety
reigned.

By the time we got back into open meadow, the shadows were
lengthening once again. The valley snow, whose early morning
crust had been so troublesome on our way out, had melted slightly
during midday and was now a soothing slurry. Legs were going on
autopilot by this time, and the previous smoothness of arm and
shoulder had become a dull ache. But no matter: we could see the
fireplace smoke rising from where—long ago, it seemed—breakfast had been consummated, and the day begun.

Later, there was an ominous coldness in the air. That morning the temperature had actually been even lower, but it had been an upbeat coldness, obviously transient and energized with the promise of warmth to come. Now it was different. With the sun beginning to set, the world was slipping back into its natural condition, which in midwinter in upper New York State is forbidding. The wind was also picking up, and I wasn't looking forward to the drive home, since the roads would be icy. Our little excursion had been just that, a very brief and tentative journey into a very large universe that winter had made larger yet and not entirely friendly. Much as I had enjoyed the trip, I was glad that it was a memory now. The cross-country world at twilight is the domain of self-doubt, of frozen goblins and ice princesses, howlers in the darkness. I paused between the illuminated warmth inside the house and the familiar well-lit inside of my automobile, to sniff and shiver at the darkened outside in between. But only briefly. It was no longer a place for me.

On the other hand, there was this cheery thought: Tomorrow is another day. And maybe it'll snow.

Backpacking

The Travail of Trails, or Adventures in a Pasayten Place

Something there is in the American psyche that finds backpacking strangely compelling, yet at the same time confusing and even forbidding. After all, human beings have generally made it their business to insulate themselves as much as possible from the natural world; in fact, our success as a species is largely due to our effectiveness in overcoming natural obstacles. Moreover, Americans in particular are proud of having carved a nation out of the vast, uncaring, and often dangerous North American wilderness. Going intentionally from our hard-earned civilization back into that wilderness, therefore, seems a bit unappreciative, even perverse.

But on the other hand, there is something attractive about heading off on foot to confront Mother Nature, something that appeals to our beloved image of rugged individualism as well as the growing sense that wilderness—once something to be feared and defeated—is now to be protected and enjoyed, even savored.

Imagine the scene: a ten-year-old boy, on one of his family's several cross-country summer vacation drives during the 1950s, dutifully admiring the scenery at a roadside viewpoint in some beautiful national park—perhaps Yosemite, or Yellowstone, or maybe Mount Rainier, it doesn't really matter—when two rather dirty, woodsy-looking fellows toting dun-colored backpacks materialize from a mountain trail nearby. With several days' growth of beard, and heavy, dusty boots, metal cups, and jackknives clanging from their belts, they seem like creatures from Mars among the bright-clad, camera-toting tourists in Bermuda shorts. And yet they, not the tourists, have just emerged from what must have been a very intimate association with the more private parts of the planet Earth. They also smell faintly and appropriately of smoke and sweat, and their sudden appearance creates something of a sensation among the tourists, several of whom ask if they would pose for a photograph or two . . . with the mountains in the background. And when asked (from a respectful distance, upwind), one of them mutters something about the lovely "backcountry" they had just visited "out there." Then we drove off in our station wagon.

But the image lingered, a faint whiff of things to see and do, away from the usual tourist roads, trailing a mysterious promise of unspecified "backcountry," beckoning the imagination like Bali Hai, or Davy Crockett, or Robinson Crusoe. Even from the road, you could see that there was an "out there." And these people had been to it. The mountains, apparently, could be more than background.

Living now in Seattle, the backcountry is very real and blessedly accessible. More than once I have found myself in the position of those woodsy apparitions of my youth, seen myself (now grown up, bearded, aromatic with smoke and sweat, rattling my own cup and walking heavily in my own dusty boots) reflected in the wondering eyes of ten-year-old boys from the next generation of carbound city dwellers—congruous with the backcountry, incongruous in a parking lot, emerging from the wilderness. Admittedly, sometimes there is more than a little self-appreciation in backpacking. Contrary to the mystique of solitary grandeur, it's fun to end a backpacking trip at a crowded parking lot, with an audience of curious onlookers.

Seattle is blessed with some remarkable nearby mountain ranges, such that local residents occasionally become a bit nonchalant about their bounty. Consider that Mount Adams, more than twelve hundred feet, and Mount Baker, more than ten thousand feet, both massively glaciated and awash in rivers of snow and ice, have essentially no federal protection, and that superb Mount St.

Helens, the Fujiyama of North America, was equally ignored before she blew her top in 1980, perhaps in indignation. Imagine that
just one of these had been on the East Coast—let us say, New
Jersey—instead of in the Northwest: the great snow-capped mountain might well have become the national symbol, and entire religions would have revolved around it.

In any event, life in the Northwest isn't uniformly glorious, despite the mountains. Although the winters are mild by eastern
standards—even a few inches of snow, for example, are rare—they
are also dreary and damp. Between October and June, blue sky is a
treat. So when summer comes around and Seattle's nine-month
rain festival drizzles to an end, the locals begin drying out their
gills, wiping the moss from between webbed toes, and looking toward the mountains, not with fear or reverence, but with anticipation. (Correction: We can *look toward* the mountains all year; it's
just that we can't *see* them until summer. In a tale much beloved of
Seattle lore-guardians, one film crew is said to have spent more
than forty days, at the cost of several hundred thousand dollars per
day, waiting for Mount Rainier to appear through the midwinter
clouds. It never did.)

For many of us, then, summer is repayment for enduring nine
months of gloom. During the winter, it is even perilously possible
to forget the great ice giants marching just outside the Puget
Sound metropolis, veiled by cloud and fog. In short, it is easy to
forget about what lies beyond reach of the station wagon and a
healthy pair of legs, easy to get depressed.

Unlike other parts of the United States, spring and summer
aren't heralded in the Northwest by the onset of green; it is always
green. What is born in spring and summer isn't so much flowers or
even foals, but rather, the mountains. They actually *appear*, just
when we are beginning to give up on them. As the clouds abate, an
unseen hand puts the mountains back where they belong, whereupon the backpackers begin thinking about where *they* belong. If
one is neither a skier nor a masochist (some would say there is no
difference), it is easy to stay out of the mountains during the winter
when they are less than inviting and when they don't seem to exist
anyhow—although it is vaguely reassuring to know that (ostensibly,
at least) they are nearby. But for the backcountry hiker who has
tasted the summer's delights and also "paid his dues" during the

long winter, it is almost impossible to stay put once summer finally arrives. (Sometimes, sad to relate, it never seems to; Mark Twain noted that the warmest winter he recalls is the summer he once spent on Puget Sound.)

But a facsimile of summer generally can be found. And then, sight of the snow-capped mountains glimmering cool and inviting on a warm June day can generate a series of ruminative peregrinations through old maps and hiking manuals (especially the regional backpacking bibles, *101 Hikes in the North Cascades* and *102 Hikes in the South Cascades, Alpine Lakes and Olympics*), redolent with memories, squashed mosquitoes, and spilled beef stroganoff.

Actually, the backpacking subculture already permeates much of America and, to some extent, the world. On the New York subway or the Chicago Loop, at West Palm Beach or the Texas Panhandle, even the most sedentary American may be seen wearing hiking boots, down jackets with rip-stop nylon (increasingly, Gore-Tex), and most especially, backpacks of all shapes and sizes and for every conceivable purpose. But for the backpacker, these aren't style, but rather, substance. And for those of us fortunate enough to live near the mountains, healthy enough to get to know them, and obsessional enough to make sure that we do so, the annual mountain *hejira* is recreation in the truest sense: re-creation indeed.

After more than twenty years of backpacking and nearly ten thousand miles—much of it in the Cascades—I recently took my longest trip ever, a ten day, 105-mile walk through northern Washington's Pasayten Wilderness Area, with my wife Judith and high expectations.[1] For years, we had talked about doing it, but had never before been able to combine enough free time for both of us with the necessary logistics of transportation.

Some hikes end where they begin; others end somewhere else. The latter are most difficult to arrange, requiring two cars, a ride from a friend, or a hitchhike back to your car. And the former are also of two kinds. Those that simply retrace their steps, exiting the way they enter, and the "loop trips" that return without traveling the same path twice. Not surprisingly, loop trips are universally

---

1. For backpackers, high expectations generally means the expectation of getting high in the mountains . . . no drugs needed.

preferred, but difficult to find. Although it isn't necessarily a bad thing to spend half one's time walking the same trail in the opposite direction—after all, you get to see the other side of the tree trunks that way—it is nonetheless distinctly more gratifying to cover new terrain all the way. Some of the nicest loop trips in the Cascade Mountains begin with a boat ride on long, narrow Lake Chelan, which reminds the easterner of New York's Finger Lakes, except of course, for the snowy mountains just inland. The Chelan backpacker leaves his car at dockside, then takes a tourist boat, the *Lady of the Lake*, to one of the drop-off points up-lake. Upon returning to the shore, the final step is to flag down the Lady on one of her return journeys. Most trips, however, aren't so conveniently arranged.

Indeed, most long trips do not end where they begin. Typically, in fact, they deposit the backcountry traveler some distance from the beginning . . . and ours was to be no exception. We wanted to start at the far eastern end of the Pasayten, then walk west for about 80 miles. After approximately eight days (ten miles per day, on average), we would reach the Cascade Crest which divides western Washington from its very different eastern self, then head south along the knife-edge of the crest, a final twenty-five miles or so. Fortunately, we found some generous people who agreed to meet us at our car (deposited at the southwestern exit point) and drive us around to the starting place, in return for our willingness to deliver a lecture at the local school the evening before we started.

So, on July 9, we drove from Seattle over the North Cascades Highway to Winthrop, Washington, a town of about one thousand people which has staked its hopes for a tourist bonanza on a self-proclaimed Wild Western ethos: nineteenth-century signs, dusty street with hitching posts, and storefronts that might have been lifted out of an MGM studio, if not Dodge City. Of the three east-west highways that traverse the Cascades (Snoqualmie Pass, Stevens Pass, and the North Cascades Highway, going south to north), the North Cascades Highway is the highest and also the newest. Driving inland from the Pacific coast, the mountains change dramatically at the Cascade Crest—dark green trees, mainly Douglas fir, western hemlock, and western red cedar, heavily hung with black lichens and often wreathed in fog and mist,

suddenly give way to blue skies and the lighter yellow-green needles and toasty brown bark of Ponderosa pine. Even the smell is
different on the east side, more pungent and open, less brooding
and portentous. Less rain makes the east-slope mountains different, too: not as much snow and ice, more dry rock offering good
climbing but less other-worldly glitter in the high reaches.

The east side of the Cascades is also warmer in the summer, too,
and colder in the winter. When the weather is good on the west
side (something that is never guaranteed, not even in summer),
backpackers scurry to take advantage of the rare treat, exploring
the pleasures of Glacier Peak, for example, or the Picket Range,
wonderlands of snow and gleaming ice, remarkable spectacles
which, because they are only rarely accessible, cry out to be enjoyed when they can. Even the names are formidable: Mount Defiance, Mount Terror, Forbidden Peak. The east side, by contrast,
is less outstanding, but more reliable.

Our particular trip began at Irongate, several hours' drive across
the dry eastern plateaus on roads of progressively deteriorating
quality. Every trail begins at a "trailhead," a word that could accurately be applied to many backpackers as well. The journey of such
human trailheads to their own chosen trailhead is itself a gradual
narrowing of technology and, hence, velocity, starting in most
cases with a superhighway that eventually turns into a two-lane
road, then degenerates into gravel, then dirt, with progressively
more ruts and bumps as civilization gives way to a more ancestral
condition. Accordingly, by the time the hiking starts, it often feels
more like a logical regression in time than an abrupt departure.
Having driven as far as possible, first quickly and then more and
more slowly, the next step is to abandon one's car, as the road
becomes too narrow and too rough, whereupon it is finally time to
set out on foot. (One problem with roads in eastern North America, as opposed to their western counterparts, is that they hardly
ever *end*.) Sometimes a backpacking trail takes off from right near
a superhighway, but this is blessedly unusual; such a transition
would be too abrupt, like suddenly dousing the lights in a theater
while instantly illuminating the stage. As it is, the transition from
asphalt to wilderness is usually gradual, allowing the mind to en-
compass what the body is about to do.

My wife had been feeling some pain in her knee, compliments of another, shorter trip a week before, on which she had tried too energetically to condition herself for the bigger one to come. And so, I did penance for this earlier exuberance, carrying seventy-five pounds on my back, while she danced along with a mere twenty-five or so. If you sense a mixture of pride and irritation here, you are correct. Backpackers are notoriously ambivalent regarding the weight of their packs: hating every ounce, and yet reveling in their accomplishments and as inclined as fisherfolk to exaggerate them. For most hikers, the Big One That Got Away is the overweighted pack, often enhanced by memory. Unlike the classic fish story, however, backpacker tales of too-heavy packs are typically recalled not so much with regret as with a kind of benighted wonderment, as in "Boy, was I stupid on that trip!"

As I staggered along the first few miles, feeling more like a beast of burden than a summertime athlete, I remembered that Irongate was near Toat's Coulee (an abandoned aqueduct, constructed—by Toat, we may assume— some decades ago). I was Judith's coolie, a bit unsteady on my feet with weight that seemed to pull backward as well as pushing down, but secretly enjoying the martyrdom.

Actually, long backpacking trips offer a guaranteed surcease: with the passing of each day, the pack gets lighter, as the food is used up. Very few people actually plan to live off the land. With proper planning, the food runs out simultaneously with the itinerary, and whereas it is debatable whether anyone actually gets stronger during such a trip, you certainly *feel* stronger as the load diminishes. Beginners often err by carrying much more food than they need, prodded by fear that if they lose their way or are otherwise delayed, security lies in something to eat. To some extent, of course, this may be true, but in fact, starvation almost never accounts for hiking tragedies; the likely killer instead is hypothermia, since the human body is remarkably able to do without food, but unable to maintain 98.6 degrees unless it is dry and adequately clothed. And one thing about being in a wilderness is that you can't turn up the household thermostat or climb into a hot tub.

The really important and potentially life-saving provisions, therefore, are not so much food as warm, water-resistant clothing, which regrettably does not get any lighter as the trip goes on, but which does stay warm even in the rain, or if accidentally immersed in a river. In this respect, wool is infinitely superior to cotton, and goose down—unless it is carefully protected from rain—can be almost useless and certainly inferior to artificial fibers. Wet cotton clings to the body, wicking the warmth away, and wet down becomes a thin, soggy mess without any loft and hence, without value. On really cold, dry days, however, jackets, mittens, hats, sleeping bags, or jockstraps made of goose down are what my grandfather used to call a *machiah*. (Denim jeans, by the way, are about the worst possible clothing to hike in, regardless of the weather; they transmit the cold and stay wet indefinitely.)

I once helped locate the bodies of several teen-agers who had started a backpacking trip at Obstruction Point in Olympic National Park. The trailhead is unusual for most North American hikes, in that the beginning is alpine and the trail initially *drops* several thousand feet. On that tragic hike, it had started to snow and rather than remain at Grand Lake where they were initially camped (three miles away and fifteen hundred feet down), the kids panicked and sought to get back to their car. As they climbed into the storm and the snow grew thicker, they apparently panicked yet further—perhaps because of incipient hypothermia, which cools judgment along with the body—and actually discarded their packs, which contained their warm clothing. Had they stayed down by the lake, snug in their tents and warm in their sleeping bags, they could easily have weathered the storm, suffering nothing worse than perhaps some boredom.

The following observation, by the British sage John Ruskin, can be found at the Visitor's Center in Banff National Park, in the Canadian Rockies: "There is no such thing as bad weather, only different kinds of good weather." Mr. Ruskin, it seems, didn't spend much time in the mountains.

One of my most cherished hiking memories revolves around a surprise storm during a day hike in the French Alps, in which I had climbed energetically several thousand feet above the tiny Alpine village of Bessans, in Vanoise National Park, near the Italian border. It began as a beautiful day in early summer, not a cloud to be seen. By midday, however, the wind had picked up and soon the sky was an angry gray. Immense, wet snowflakes began falling at an alarming rate. It wasn't even possible to find—not to mention follow—the route back down, so I huddled under a tree, put on all the clothing I was carrying (quite a bit, fortunately), and prepared to spend a safe, if miserable night. Then, a wisp of smoke curled from behind a ridge, and I made for it, through snow that was already more than six inches deep.

A tiny shepherd's hut, of the sort that might be occupied by Heidi's grandfather, clung to the alpine hillside, heavy rock walls topped by a confidence-building roof made of great thick slabs of slate. I was welcomed by a heavily bearded, bearlike man named Jean-Claude, who warmed my insides with the hottest, blackest, sweetest, and altogether most delicious coffee I had ever tasted, drunk from soup bowls, not cups. It turned out that an American airborne operation, staged near the town at a place called Col de la Madeleine, had rescued a detachment of Free French toward the close of World War II; and I was the beneficiary, more than thirty years later, of Jean-Claude's gratitude. By the time we were done talking, the storm had subsided, the sun was out again, and the snow had even melted enough so that a strategic retreat down the mountain was not only possible but downright fun.

So, despite the overriding importance of warm, dry clothing, food does come in handy. Hot drinks, in particular. And warm, dry shelter is even better. Overnight hikers—backpackers—carry their own overnight shelters. For day hikers, like myself on that Alpine adventure, it is catch as catch can.

Fortunately, that first, seventy-five-pound day on our Pasayaten hike was brief, since we didn't reach the trailhead at Irongate until about three o'clock in the afternoon, and our first night's goal—a huge, friendly, rolling subalpine meadow known as Horseshoe Basin—was only about five miles away. It was unseasonably cold and rainy when we thanked(?) our friends and started off. Surprisingly, perhaps, starting can be difficult, even on a long-planned and eagerly anticipated trip. (One time, when some relatives had kindly deposited me at a trailhead nearly fifty miles from the nearest town, I found myself asking them—only partly in jest— "Are you really going to abandon me here?")

The Pasayten country is quite unlike the rest of Washington's Cascades: Almost lacking in glaciers and generally quite dry, it is a land of wide, rolling alpine meadows with literally miles of wildflowers and the most open, cheery alpine terrain this side of *The Sound of Music*. Horseshoe Basin is among the most accessible and renowned of these meadows, and if we were somewhat apprehensive, it wasn't about the wilderness, but rather about crowds, especially after we began hearing the occasional sound of a bugle, blowing an off-key "charge" every twenty minutes or so. Apparently a Boy Scout troop was hot on our heels. But by the time we reached Louden Lake, a half mile beyond the Basin, our pursuers were gone; they must have turned off on another trail. Moreover, the weather had improved considerably, and it was even possible to skinny-dip in the delicate little lake.

The shock of cold water on a hot and sweaty body is excruciating, both painful and deliriously refreshing. It seems to precipitate a change of consciousness, as the senses—dulled from fatigue and heat by day's end—are instantly called to a unique sharpness. Some of us take a special, pseudomasochistic delight in such immersion experiences at the end of a demanding day, and indeed, this is one reason—beyond the value of having a clearly demarcated *place*—why lakes are such popular campsites.

A mile-and-a-half stroll from our lakeside camp, up gently rolling meadows, and we were in Canada, as noted by a small granite obelisk. Our route would continue to play tag with the Canadian border for most of the trip; hence, its name, the Boundary Trail. It is striking how in the absence of customs officials and border guards, one nation grades imperceptibly into the next; the mountains don't know the difference, or if they do, they keep it to themselves. Similarly, when I had gone for a week into the high Alpine Lakes region of the central Cascades (now a Wilderness Area like the Pasayten), in 1974, a beleaguered Richard Nixon had been president; when I came out, it was Gerald Ford. It mattered a great deal to me (or at least, I thought it did), but to the mountains, not at all.

From the number of cars at the trailhead parking lot, we had feared that Horseshoe Basin and Louden Lake would be unpleasantly crowded, but in fact, we could barely glimpse two tents, one red and one blue, pleasant counterpoints to the soft green meadows, hidden in the furrow of some adjoining ridges. Although overuse is a growing problem in some parts of the Cascades, where certain especially renowned meadows—like the fragile fields surrounding Cascade Pass in the North Cascades National Park—are being literally loved to death, most wilderness areas, because of their uneven, dissected terrain, can absorb remarkably large numbers of hikers. (Or at least, visual contact is often interrupted so that the illusion of solitude is easily maintained.) The most dramatic example of this is probably the gorgeous and justly renowned Enchantment Lakes, a sky-high string of shallow granite basins in the Alpine Lakes Wilderness, ringed by stunted larch trees that obligingly turn brilliant red and orange in early fall. On a nice summer weekend, several hundred cars jockey for position at the parking lot ten miles away and three thousand feed below, but somehow, the Enchantments themselves just swallow up the people, and I have rarely counted more than twenty or so while rambling about the lakes and their surrounding boulder and snowfields.

Even though wilderness lovers are agreed that too many people can literally spoil a very good thing, all the experts, guidebooks, National Park and U.S. Forest Service Rangers—not to mention the Search and Rescue Units—are also agreed on a seemingly contradictory dictum: Thou Shalt Not Hike Alone. But I do.

Anyone can twist an ankle, wrench a knee, fall and get knocked on the head, or suffer a sudden stroke or attack of appendicitis. So the experts are right. You should always hike with someone else. And you should let me hike alone. I insist on my God-given right to get away, when I want, not just from civilization but also from people, occasionally *all* people. (Even if this also includes the God-given right to endanger myself in the process.) It is wonderful to backpack with the right company: for me, this means my wife, my children, my brother. But it is also wonderful to hike by myself, luxuriating in the freedom to linger by a perfect waterfall, spend two hours tracing the pattern of a bumblebee in a field of mountain asters, and then, if I feel like it, going like a bat out of hell for the rest of the day.

Sometimes, on a solitary jaunt, the splendor of a scene (a flower, a mountainside, the swirl of water behind a rock) is just too much, and there are tears in my eyes, a bittersweet sadness that such an experience, if it is truly to be experienced and honored as it deserves, should be shared. And sometimes there are momentary panics, as when the trail disappears or I briefly feel my balance crumbling during an anxious traverse on a too-narrow ledge of rock, situations that once again call for a companion. But despite all the benefits of colleagueship on the trail, there are also the

costs; frankly, there are few things more irritating than going backpacking with the wrong person: someone who goes too slowly, or
too quickly, or too noisily, or too quietly, or is too messy or too
fastidious, or whose campside routine just doesn't meld with your
own.

Those people who regularly backpack with near-strangers,
whether because of high sociability needs, a high tolerance of others, or a strongly felt sense of The Safe And Responsible Thing To
Do, have my full admiration and respect. They'll just have to do
without my company.

Walking was much more pleasant the next day, perhaps because
we made a blessedly early start: Awake by 6:30 and afoot by 8:00.
Also, there was virtually no climbing, as the trail started high and
stayed that way for the next ten miles, through bright fields of
avalanche and glacier lilies poking their shoots directly through
the retreating snow and, in the wetter meadows, creamy white
pasqueflowers in addition to red and yellow monkeyflowers.
Above us, the brilliant blue sky was challenged only by the ethereal white of distant glaciers, and under the circumstances, we felt
rather legitimately high ourselves. Although the sun hadn't been
out for long, it was already melting the remaining snow which still
lingered on the ridges above us, and accordingly, little streams
tumbled across the trail every few hundred yards. Even when not
particularly thirsty, most hikers find it difficult to pass by these
Cascade bubblers without taking a sip or two—an act of communion with the countryside. Indeed, it seems almost sinful (at least,
ungrateful) to ignore such offerings; not surprisingly, therefore,
Cascades backpackers sometimes walk around with sloshing bellies, especially in the early summer . . . testimony to the sky's be-
nevolence and the allure of taking just one more swig from the
laughing waters.

Regrettably, there is now a fly in the ointment, or rather a proto-
zoan in the streams: *Giardia*, an intestinal parasite that produces
the disease giardiasis, also called beaver fever. As a result, it is
advisable to boil water, especially at lower elevations where the
transition from snow to backpacker's belly may be intercepted by
beavers and their fevers.

Later in the summer, the "problem" is blueberries, of a size to banish regret for the withered blossoms, and of such sweetness and abundance that hikers have been known to linger on a hillside, entrapped, for hours. The poppy fields of Oz are no more perilous, especially if one has a schedule.

Compared to other mountain wildernesses in the United States, notably the Sierras or the eastern slopes of the Rockies, the Cascades are blessed with abundant water and so, even the most hydrophile backpacker rarely has to carry any. The liquid bounty is provided not so much by rain, which runs off such steep, high country almost as quickly as it falls, as by the gradual dissolution of lingering snowfields. This is all to the good because there is something very gratifying about such a self-contained system: A snowbank melting just a few hundred feet above the trail obligingly becomes water that nourishes the grateful hiker just below. Occasionally, when the winter white-stuff is unusually scant, and the snowfields all melt away before the end of summer, water may become scarce by August, and then, the Cascades backpacker experiences what his or her Arizona counterpart has to deal with nearly all the time. (And then one discovers that water is *heavy*.)

In addition, since it can get cold in the mountains (with mornings below freezing, even in midsummer), there is a daily cycle to the streamflow: Rivulets that can easily be crossed in the morning, just by stepping on stones, may become thundering gushers by the afternoon. I have often gone to sleep surrounded by a roar of cascading waterfalls, then awakened to an eerie silence, as the night's frost turned off the faucets. But my midday, they are wide open again.

We had planned to cover about ten miles per day, but the going was so easy on Day Two that nearly eleven miles had been accounted for by three in the afternoon. To the uninitiated, ten miles may sound like a very long way, but remember, the backpacker isn't doing much else. In this respect, backpacking is unlike any other sport, except perhaps long-distance sailing or canoeing. Thus, you can play tennis, basketball, or soccer, even go skiing or run a marathon, and still have time and opportunity (if not inclination) to do something completely different during the rest of the day. Not so with backpacking, however. Once begun, that's it. You are captured, utterly immersed as long as the trip lasts. It demands total commitment: to the activity, the countryside, and your companions. If the route isn't particularly steep, two miles per hour is not a difficult pace, and therefore, ten miles isn't very far to walk in a day, considering that you have the *entire day*, morning until evening, to do it . . . and nothing else. The agenda is clear, simple, and encompassing.

Our second night's stopping place had other backpacking advantages, beyond its convenient, ten mile measure: water, a level spot, and firewood. The significance of nearby water goes without saying. The latter two attractions, however, are often insufficiently appreciated, especially by neophytes and armchair voyagers. Thus, mountains are vertical places by definition, and yet most people sleep best when they are horizontal. And many of us can't sleep unless that horizontality is utterly perfect. Moreover, it can be sheer agony to discover—typically in the middle of the night—that your head is just a teeny bit lower than your feet and then suddenly to be inundated with a severe, nocturnal case of imagined cerebral swelling as all your blood seems to drain stubbornly downhill. Even when your head is appropriately higher than your feet, if the declination is excessive, you wake up (usually several times) during the night to find that you have slipped downhill so that your feet are all scrunched against the wall of the tent.

Then there is the problem of bumps: rocks, tree roots, pine cones, stubborn clumps of grass and stems of heather, tent stakes that someone else left behind, not to mention the pernicious tendency of ground that superficially seems dry to reveal itself later as boggy, brambly or hiding one particularly ill-favored stone. So, it pays to scrutinize a would-be campsite and to venerate flatness in an angled world.

Upon these housekeeping concerns, firewood impinges—not as a necessity, but rather, a much-appreciated bonus. In the alpine meadows favored by most backpackers, wood is scarce or nonexistent, so wood fires are often prohibited or impossible. For this reason, a small portable stove, usually powered by gasoline or butane, is *de rigueur*. (My little Svea stove is pleasingly compact, has served me unfailingly since 1966, and is still going strong.) Gathering wood can be a beloved and well-earned tradition, especially when hiking with children, who particularly enjoy the pioneer, pitch-in participation. But otherwise it is tempting—and ethical, mind you—to parasitize a pile that someone else has left behind. Although most backpackers forego the marshmallows (except, once again, if children are along), it is nonetheless cheery, as well as literally warming, to cook dinner over a campfire whenever possible.

In the process, however, one must reckon with Landry's Law, named for a former professor of mine, and actually a corollary of Murphy's observation that whatever can go wrong will. Landry's Law states that wherever one sits about a campfire, the wind will always blow the smoke in your face.

My own preference is for a campfire at night, followed by a stove-cooked breakfast in the morning when the wood is often damp with dew, and when it is typically too cold to bother making a real fire, and when the perambulating wilderwalker is not inclined to linger very long, anyhow, so that a good roaring blaze would soon have to be abandoned, just when the coals are ready to burn anything—even the bleached old fossils of prehistoric alpine fir trees that seem otherwise nonflammable.

From Scheelite Pass (our second night's comfortable campsite), the trail led on through airy and abandoned mining country, along the south slopes of Wolframite Mountain to the tumbledown Tungsten Mine and one of the strangest mountain meetings in my experience, a close encounter of the survivalist kind.

We were now about twenty-five miles from the nearest road, in the largest, least-known, and most rarely traveled wilderness in the forty-eight states. A bend in the trail and there they were: Two men, appropriately bearded and pack-bearing, the first we had seen since we started. (The bugle, mind you, had only been heard.) Under such circumstances, it is usually pleasant to meet fellow human beings; indeed, although backpackers may be accused of misanthropy, getting away from *Homo sapiens* actually enhances one's appreciation of people. By a perverse, Inverse Law, one comes to appreciate our species in inverse proportion to its density: Meet someone in a crowded city and both parties typically look away. In fact, it really isn't a *meeting* at all, but rather, an avoidance, with eyes unfocused and shoulders hunched. But after walking alone on a mountain trail for several days, meetings are real. You simply cannot avert your eyes and keep walking, and wouldn't even if you could. After all, you are immersed in a similar experience, so there is much to share, such as the condition of the trail and the country ahead, information as to good campsites, and of course, the weather . . . which is of more than passing interest.[2]

But this time, as we drew closer, it became clear that something was wrong. Our fellow travelers wore olive-drab pants and camouflage shirts, baseball-type caps, and had revolvers strapped to their thighs.

Although I have no particular fear of guns, I am always a bit uncomfortable when I meet people carrying revolvers on a wilderness mountain trail. Self-defense can hardly be their reason, although I did meet one young man on a trail in Alaska's Mount McKinley National Park who was sporting a .22 pistol and who explained he had it in case of grizzly bears. When I pointed out that such a popgun would hardly stop a charging grizzly, he explained that *in extremis*, he wouldn't use it on the bear, but on himself.

These two gentlemen, however, were not planning suicide. Quite the contrary, in fact, at least as they saw it. They quickly announced that they were on "survival maneuvers." Comes the nuclear apocalypse, they're gonna make it. One of these would-be survivors identified himself as an instructor, the other lived in Detroit and had never seen a mountain before this particular "maneuver." Presumably, he will be heading west as soon as he hears the first detonations. (It isn't clear if he plans to walk . . . or run.)

These two are not all that unusual, it seems: Self-proclaimed survivalists have been gathering in the Rogue River valley in Oregon and along Washington's Olympic coast, while modern-day trolodytes are even now excavating tunnels in the mountains of Colorado and Utah. But these were the first we had met, especially in their natural habitat. They weren't evil men: as already mentioned, my wife had been suffering from a sore knee, and one of them gave her some "Tiger Balm," a sort of liniment cream. Under the condi-

2. There are also two codicils to the Inverse Law: 1) The countryside is appreciated, understood, and somehow owned, in inverse proportion to the speed with which one traverses it (the progression from airplanes to automobiles to walking is one of decreasing speed and at the same time, greater knowing), and 2) Accomplishments are often gratifying in inverse proportion to their ease—nothing makes a hike more satisfying than sweating a bit in the process. Even getting a little lost. If it comes too easily, or too quickly, it is less tasty.

tions for which they were preparing, however, they would presumably have acted rather differently, although I doubt very much that they would survive for long, even if they somehow managed miraculously to reach this Pasayten Place.

But they had the guns and we muted our disagreement. Their advice to us as we parted (warily, to be sure): Store food and put your available money into .22 caliber bullets. "After all, everyone has a .22, so think of what a great barter item the shells will be!" (Does *everyone* really have a .22?)

We went on, backpacks getting noticeably lighter, our hearts heavier. Several miles more and a long, sweeping approach to a very high, windswept outpost of lakes, rocks, and snow known as Cathedral Pass. In good weather, Cathedral Pass and its surrounding spires and other places of wilderness worship would be a sheer delight, but it had grown cold, so cold, in fact, that we were wearing heavy jackets and gloves, even while working hard and breathing heavily, climbing up to the pass. Backpackers quickly discover that walking uphill is much harder than level or downhill (although the latter, if steep, can be stressful on the knees). The connection between physical exertion and body heat also becomes very clear. The "layered look" may or may not be stylish, but as a practical matter, it is definitely "in." The layers are peeled off when ascending, then quickly replaced when resting or going downhill.

And then there are blisters: going uphill, on heels, coming down, toes. Feet are to the backpacker like horses to the cavalry, indispensable and demanding constant care and attention. A patch of "moleskin"—soft, feltlike material with an adhesive backing—applied to an incipient blister usually alleviates further damage, but it is important to act quickly, at the mere twitch of a problem, before the blister becomes flagrant. And moleskin doesn't cure anything; it just keeps it from getting agonizingly worse.

My wife the doctor pronounced the Tiger Balm moderately useful, and we huddled in the lee of a huge boulder to munch some "gorp," a universal hiker's snack made of equal parts raisins, peanuts, and M&Ms. (Gorp, it is said, comes from "Good Old Raisins and Peanuts." As for the M&Ms, they add some sugar, and of course, they melt in your mouth . . . not in your pack. On the other hand, even molten chocolate bars can be stiffened by immersion in a cold snow-melt stream, but then there is the problem of separating the newly hardened chocolate from the encroaching wrapper.)

Simplicity—whether of pleasure, purpose, or stress—is one of the special delights of backpacking. The straightforward, understandable challenge of boot on trail, the cold reality of rushing water, a glimpse of an eagle or a deer framed between swaying aspens, the real, gut-level meaning of a mile away or a hundred feet up, the legitimacy of having a large appetite when you have dispensed an equally large number of calories. Then there is food and sleep, lots of both. Perhaps less celebrated than most other rewards, but no less important or gratifying, well-earned nourishment and rest each deserve special places in the backpacker's pantheon.

Much to my continuing amazement, some people actually *enjoy* the various cooking and other campside chores. By contrast, I seek to minimize them, preferring to spend my time and energy while hiking, hiking. There are those, however, who pride themselves at being gourmet trail chefs and who will patiently boil stews for twenty minutes or more and actually bake breads and the like. But as for me, give me breakfasts made by pouring hot water into pre-designed granola mixed with powdered milk, lunches of beef jerky, cheese, and dehydrated fruits, and dinners made by that estimable firm, Mountain House of Albany, Oregon—freeze-dried wonders such as turkey tetrazini, beef burgundy, or shrimp creole—to which one need only add boiling water and wait an eternal five minutes.

Purists may sneer, but let them. After all, no one ever claimed that simplicity had to be *natural*, and certainly, there is little that is natural—or organic—about high-impact plastic tent stakes, aluminum tent poles, boots made of Gore-Tex, or mountain stoves of equally high tech.

Regardless of what you eat, or how it is prepared, it remains true that the phenomenon of food itself remains one of the greatest of backpacking simplicities. With little else to do (except to walk, and thereby burn up calories), eating becomes fascinating, as well as important. And with an early start, First Lunch might well happen by ten o'clock, then Second Lunch by two o'clock. (I've not yet been able to justify a full-fledged Third Lunch, but the ambition is there.) And of course, throughout the day, there is a constant influx of nibble and drinks—a bit of gorp before crossing a stream, a mouthful of dried apples to celebrate a particularly compelling rainbow, a chew of beef jerky to occupy the jaws while beating through an especially boring patch of riverside brush. On balance, however, for a healthy person, input tends to be closely keyed to outgo. By the end of our trip, after walking for eleven days, burning up enormous amounts of calories, and eating prodigious quantities of food, our weight—remarkably—was exactly the same as when we started. It must be possible to gain or lose weight on a backpacking trip, but I never have.

The next day we met some horsepackers, who had ridden up the popular Andrews Creek drainage. There is a curious civility mixed with mutual distrust when backpacker meets horsepacker. And for good reason: The horsepackers have it easy, too easy. They carry weird, overweight items like axes and shovels, even heads of lettuce or bottles of ketchup. Besides, they generally seem to be overweight themselves, and their steeds leave substantial calling cards that the rider hardly even sees, but the backpacker has to walk around or through. On top of that, backpackers have to give way to horses, since we can leave the trail but they can't.

On the other hand, occasionally there is something admirable— or rather, enviable—about the large tents and multiple conveniences that the horsepacker can bring. Of course, if you really want all the comforts of home, you can always just stay there. And there are many times when I wished that I had, yearning for my own bed, kitchen, and bathroom, not to mention the opportunity to stand up without hitting the ceiling or to boil water just by the flick of a switch. Such feelings of backsliding (the dark side of back*packing*) are especially likely during lengthy periods of bad weather when a small backpacking tent can be a cramped, miserable prison, with the occupants asking themselves, ruefully, "Is this really something we are doing on purpose, to have fun?"

Once, when my wife and I huddled miserably in our tent, feeling very small and vulnerable while the world's worst storm howled and raged outside, casting enormous one-thousand-decibel lightning bolts that undoubtedly were aimed right at us, and also feeling more than a little stupid for not having replaced the waterproofing in the tent floor, we—well, I suppose I should be honest—we began to fantasize how nice it would be to do our "co-cooning" at home, in front of the VCR.

The self-reliant (some might say, masochistic) American way of backpacking, interestingly, is not shared by most Europeans. The Alps are magnificent hiking country, at least as splendid as anything on the North American continent, although there is nothing comparable to America's wilderness areas. Signs of human habitation are everywhere in the Old World: grazing sheep, sturdy shepherd huts built to survive hundreds of years of avalanches, and often the sight of ski developments or aerial tramways. Anyone carrying a fully packed backpack on a European mountain trail is almost certain to be an American. By and large, the Europeans either make do with day trips (made more feasible by the fact that most Alpine trailheads begin at or above timberline), or even if a lengthier trip is in the offing, they carry only personal clothing[3] and some money, navigating from one backcountry hostel to another.

These structures, variously known as *refuges, huttes,* or *refugios* (depending on whether the environs are French-, German-, or Italian-speaking, respectively) each have a unique character, but are generally rather sturdy, multi-story buildings, often with extensive sleeping accommodations and remarkably good food—including wine—at low prices. The essence of incongruity is a miniature grand hotel, complete with gourmet cuisine, ten miles or more from the nearest road, and reachable only by an extensive trek across a steep snowfield, perhaps after shimmying up a two-hundred-foot ladder, bolted into vertical rock. If you haven't tried it, don't knock it.

But we were in the USA, land of rugged individualism; the only comforts—or necessities—for us were the ones we carried along. The trail eventually climbed back up, to Bald Mountain and the most spectacular flower fields we have ever seen: literally miles of dazzling color, hip high and calling out not only to be seen, but somehow experienced. Would that we could have imbibed the flowers like the streams. Higher yet, toward the gentle summit, they grew shorter just as the streams grew thinner, and there was no resisting the temptation to leave packs by the trail and romp a

3. Sometimes *very* little clothing; one of the pleasures of Alpine hiking is to encounter a party of Europeans—especially, French—the ladies wearing nothing but hiking boots and panties.

bit in the meadows. When the trail eventually descended, we reentered the forests, but with regret.

Backpacking brings out the aesthete. At home, I hardly notice flowers, but in the mountains, I am entranced by them: bright red Indian paintbrush, rich blue lupine, acres of white, gently waving mountain buckwheat heads, and sometimes in the wetter meadows, Jeffrey's shootingstars, which look just like small purple comets. Then there is my favorite, elephant-head pedicularis, with its vertical stalk surrounded by literally hundreds of tiny flowers, each one resembling a perfect little Dumbo: two big ears surrounding a gracefully curved trunk.

At home, I am nearly oblivious to views (although Seattle prides itself as a city with lots of them), but in the mountains, I'll walk several extra miles just to eat lunch while looking out over an unobstructed panorama. To be sure, some people go hiking in heavily wooded areas, but no one seriously disputes that throughout the world, mountains are the terrain of choice. They offer diversity, privacy, some of the largest remaining wildernesses, and—most of all, I suspect—views. We may never know why expansive views lead to expansive feelings, but I wouldn't be surprised if it springs at least partly from our evolutionary heritage, when as primitive savannah-dwellers, we recognized that a "good view" meant mastery of one's immediate environment and some confidence that no predators were about to leap.

In any event, there is a deep-seated and widely-shared joy that comes from looking out across miles of mountains, valleys, and lowlands, a curious mixture of reverence and ownership. There is also a well-justified feeling of one-upmanship. After all, we are told that even the King of Siam (no backpacker, so far as I know) insisted on keeping his head higher than anyone else.

There is a special delight in achieving a high point, whether the top of a mountain or of a ridge, and not only because of the mastery that is involved. It is also gratifying just to be able to see far and wide. Getting to a mountain pass is a favorite accomplishment as well, even though, by definition, a pass is a relative low point. This is because having reached the pass—almost any pass—a whole new world becomes visible. The bear went over the mountain, to see what he could see. And even though all that he could see was the other side of the mountain, hikers and backpackers know that this is enough.

Backpacking routes are often valued in proportion as they remain high and airy, "commanding" views that are both distant and sweeping. In this respect, our Pasayten trip was a remarkably domineering one, since out of the ten days, we were to spend about seven entirely above timberline—commanding our way along— and descending only rarely into the trees. Hiking in the Alps typically begins at tree level or above, since almost the entire European mountain range is a vast *massif* or elevated plateau. By contrast, Cascades trail walking takes more patience. Usually, there is an initial valley day, during which the backpacker proceeds through the forests, gradually gaining access to the sought-after "high country." In a sense, it is a respectful way to get started, assuring a due appreciation when the peak experiences are achieved.

Not everyone, however, is "into" views, even on a backpacking trip. Children, for example, seem utterly blind to them. For many backpackers, the best advice regarding the younger generation is to be found on aspirin bottles: "Keep Away From Children." But in fact, it is quite feasible to bring kids on lengthy overnight hikes, so long as the itinerary is tailored to their capacities, and they are given something to carry in their own packs, even if it is only a spoon and bowl, or a teddy bear. Whatever the anthropologists may say, however, children are a different species. No matter what their visual acuity, they are incapable of responding to anything more than two arms' length away. I have brought my daughters to some of the continent's most magnificent mountain places, surrounded by vistas that would make the most devout Philistine palpitate with poetry, that would bring a gasp from the most jaded and turn any sensate person into an apoplexy of aesthetic rapture . . . and they have eyes only for a stone by the trail or the shape of a leaf. I have pitched my tent with the little gremlins in the world's glimmering glaciers . . . only to find that their greatest delight was that a nearby log is just long enough, and wide enough, for cartwheels.

People get more farsighted as they age; perhaps this implies something more than changes in the physical structure of the human lens.

One respect in which backpacking adults and children generally agree, however, is in their attitude (generally positive) toward seeing wildlife. It isn't clear whether there are more animals at higher elevations, or if it just seems that way because the eye sees farther. Some animals—notably bears—inspire dread, although at least in the Cascades, black bears are shy and rarely encountered, and grizzlies are nearly extinct. There are deer, however, Columbian blacktails on their delicate black high-heels, and often, mountain goats as well. These white, billowy beasts, relatives of the African antelopes, are remarkably unafraid of people; I have encountered them on steep, narrow trails and elected to retreat rather than contest the passage like Robin Hood meeting Little John.

During their breeding season the large-hoofed mammals are in fact much more dangerous than the carnivores (grizzlies excepted). In October, Alaskan bull moose regularly collide with locomotives, and bison have treed many an excessively inquisitive photographer in Yellowstone and Grand Teton National Parks. Following a lonely trail in the Sierras,[4] I once came around a bend and encountered a cougar feeding on the carcass of a bull elk. The cat was gone in an instant and was probably even more startled than I. Certainly, it was more frightened. The biologist inside of me knew full well that there was not the slightest danger from *Felis concolor* and that the elk, were it alive, would have constituted a greater threat. Unthinkingly, however, I picked up a stout branch and carried it for the next few miles. But fortunately, I have carried something else much farther: a memory of tawny fur, moving effortlessly into the shadows, quiet as a shadow itself.

This time, in the distance, we spied a small herd of elk, feasting in the open meadows. Had it been September, we would have likely heard the bulls in rut, bugling their challenges to all comers; it is a peculiar sound (at least to the human ear), disconcertingly high pitched for so large and noble-looking a creature. More commonly encountered are pikas, also known as rock rabbits, but with ears that are adorably small and rounded. Pikas inhabit boulder slopes and make conspicuous hay piles during the late summer as

---

4. Yes, there are still a few lonely trails in the Sierras, although to keep them lonely, I won't divulge where.

provision for the long winter. Pikas are difficult to see, but easy to
hear, with their distinctive nasal "peent."

My own favorites, however, are the marmots, mountain dwellers
par excellence, who are the western relatives of the more parochial,
lowland, and lowly woodchuck. These hibernating rodents live in
distinct colonies, within which they experience a rich and elaborate social life. Unlike the hyperactive pikas, who remain busy beneath the snow, or the deer, goats, and elk, who migrate to lower
elevations, marmots have the good sense to hibernate from September to May. During their brief and intensive summertime existence, marmots dig elaborate burrow systems, cavort in the rocks
and meadows above timberline, and whistle their alarm at the approach of human, eagle, or coyote. They also have a curious habit
of standing on hind legs and boxing with each other, sometimes
straining against their fellows, as though each was trying to push
the other one on its back.[5]

Of course, there are birds as well: gray jays, also known as Camp
Robbers because of their fearless willingness to enter a backpack
or tent in search of food; olive-sided flycatchers who perch on the
highest trees to order, over and over, "hic, three beers"; and hen-
sized blue grouse, which either crash suddenly from the undergrowth near one's feet, startling the unwary hiker, or provide a
near-constant, deep, thumping drumbeat, sounding the way an elk
should. Also mountain bluebirds, bluer than the sky, and fussy little
gray-crowned rosy finches, living in large flocks and at such alti-
tudes that they ought to starve, but don't.

For us, though, the flower fields quickly became a memory as
we descended rapidly and ruefully two thousand feet down to
wade across (and wash in) the thigh-deep Ashnola River, then up
another two thousand feet to a glorious ten miles along the airy,
dry slopes of Sheep and Quartz Mountains and on to the trip's high
point, 7,100 foot Bunker Hill: lonely, austere and windswept,
graced with a knife-sharp beauty and full-sweep views of cold,
frosty mountains separated by warm, lush, dark-green valleys. It is
remarkable how many shades of green exist on this planet, most of
them visible in the retreating ranks of increasingly distant valleys;

5. Perhaps it is immodest, but anyone wanting more information about marmots
    could do worse than to consult my own *Marmots: social behavior and ecology*
    (Stanford University Press: Stanford, CA, 1989).

the closest, bright, clear, and kelly green, the most distant, a hazy, dusty gray. Bunker Hill was a high point indeed.

Climbs like the one up Bunker Hill can be called "grueling," but one person's gruel is another's meat. Actually, there is a two-part Zen of hiking, interpenetrating both physical actions and mental attitudes. First: rhythm. If you don't have it, get it. When swinging arms and legs are smoothly coordinated with rhythmic inhalations and exhalations, the walking is almost effortless. The biggest problem of an uneven trail, then, is not the unevenness *per se*, but rather, the fact that it disrupts that all-important rhythm. Similarly, even a steep and challenging uphill grunt can be "taken in stride" if it can be taken in stride. Consciousness contracts to the center of one's chest, or perhaps the calf muscles, and the miles fall easily away.

For another, the master Zen-hiker doesn't trouble him or herself about the goal. Indeed, more so than any other activity, there really is no goal, just the doing of the thing. As Cervantes puts in *Don Quixote, "La senda es mejor que la venda"* (the path is better than the inn). The backpacker carries this one step further: the path is everything; there is no *venda*. If we could get there some other way—like driving in a car—it probably wouldn't be worth going.

A journey of a hundred miles not only begins with a single step, but also consists of many thousands of them. However, such things are best kept secret. It can be crushing to burden each stride with constant awareness of how many more are left. ("One step. That means there are 3,000 more to go. Another. That makes 2,999.") So, rather than keeping the remaining effort constantly in mind, or even the destination, it helps to look no further than the next footfall, possibly the next snack spot, or, at most, the evening's campsite. On even the best planned backpacking trip, the end does not justify the means. Getting there—the means— is all there is. Unlike trophy hunting, or fishing, or even a photo expedition, at the conclusion of a backpacking trip, the hiker is typically left with nothing but sore muscles and memories.

Nonetheless, it is usually impossible to eliminate goals altogether, whether a lake or streamside camp, a pass or high point on a looming ridge, or the trip's end, back at a road. Unbidden, the destination seeps insidiously into one's thoughts. And regrettably, there is something about being ninety percent finished that makes the fatigued backpacker think that it should be one hundred percent. As a general rule, in fact, whenever I find myself wondering irritably "Shouldn't I be there by now?", I can safely assume that about one-tenth of the journey still lies ahead.

In a sense, longer trips, those lasting a week or more, provide the best opportunities to experience the kind of immersion that makes such memories truly memorable, experiences in themselves and not just brief games of tag, continuities rather than interruptions. Day hikes or ventures of even three or four days can easily become excessively goal-oriented and thus, limited, as the hiker strives to tag the particular meadow, lake, or summit that the trip is going "to," and then rush back to the car. By contrast, the longer the trip, the greater the immersion in the trip itself and the less the inclination to look beyond it. Off in the mountains for a good long stretch, it becomes possible to change plans and follow one's inclinations, thereby sculpting the experience as it develops rather than following a rigid, preordained schedule. The weather also becomes less worrisome, since—rain or shine—the trip will continue and so will you.

I well remember standing atop Devil's Dome (another beauty spot of the Casades, requiring a long two days' climb), with provisions for about another six days, and spreading out a series of maps in the flower-bedecked meadow, watching a storm pull itself together over one valley and unload on another, while I considered which drainage system looked the most inviting, taking into account the look of the high country and the likely weather pattern for the next week.

Back in our Pasayten journey, Bunker Hill was not only the high point, but also the midpoint of our trip, a place to take stock and congratulate ourselves that we were going to finish it more or less as originally conceived. After all, from the midpoint it is as long to return the way you came as to see the journey to its end. (Besides, we were feeling stronger than ever.) Midpoints also symbolize one of the conventional bits of moral wisdom that backpacking quickly impresses on its practitioners: an old-fashioned thing called personal responsibility. Once "in," there is no graceful way to back out, and thereby, get back out. Having gone the first five miles of a ten-mile trip, there is no alternative except going the other five; similarly, having gone up, you must come back down—even if you are getting tired and your knees would rather not. Sometimes I even indulge in the self-congratulatory thought that backpacking isn't so much about strength of back (or knees) as strength of character.

Bunker Hill was also a bit frustrating, however. A mass of dark clouds was approaching, and we distinctly heard thunder; thus, we were not only masters of what we surveyed, but also painfully vulnerable, up there at the rafters of the world. So, fearing lightning in our exposed condition, we had to hurry down to the valley's embrace.

The low point (not coincidentally, in spirits as well as elevation) was soon to follow: Almost two long days trudging by the banks of the often-heard but rarely seen Pasayten River. We joked about the ever-present flies. I thought of the time at Grand Park on Mount Rainier when I had swatted so many mosquitoes (the record was nine at a single one-handed smack) that I began to wonder if perhaps the human hand evolved for this purpose and not as conventional anthropologic wisdom would have it, for clutching branches or wielding tools. My hands actually had begun to *smell* different, oddly sweet and pungent. It is difficult, however, to take pleasure in an odor that you know to be essence of squashed mosquito guts, and, indeed, backpackers take no pleasure at all from mosquitoes or their fellow miscreants, biting flies. Insect repellents help some, but their oily odors are almost as bad as the bugs themselves.

The best solution is to keep moving. Some people—like myself—stubbornly insist on wearing shorts regardless of the insect population, and for such fools, flies and mosquitoes can be miserable indeed. There is one notoriously bad spot, the damp trail climbing to Hannegan Pass in the North Cascades, that is infested by uncountable swarms of a particularly obnoxious, soft-bodied biting fly. These creatures are also very slow moving and can be slaughtered by the hundreds during a few hours' trek up to the pass, but the carnage is scant consolation for the bloodletting they inflict.

Any resting is best done on exposed ridges or hilltops, where the wind keeps the flying annoyances in their places. Sometimes, however, the hiker is pursued, even while walking, as if by avenging furies, giving rise with remarkable regularity to the standard question: Whom do they eat when there aren't any people around?

(Answer: Nobody. Most species eat plant juices, using blood—human and animal—to nourish their eggs, not themselves.)

Trudging along, bugs or not, the mind often slips into a wordless mantra of sorts, frequently a conjunction of regular breathing and rhythmic footfalls, sometimes a snatch of tune that may dog one's steps for literally miles. On the other hand, sometimes the boredom and low-level discomfort leads to bouts of giddy foolishness, as in our case. As we walked, we found ourselves wistfully designing an all-purpose backpacker's tool: a combination flyswatter and pancake flipper. (Flies and blueberries are two of the Cascades' most abundant products, and sometimes I suspect that flies are merely blueberries that have taken wing.) Not too long ago, when looking at a new house that was within earshot of an interstate highway, we had complained about the traffic noise, whereupon the quick-talking realtor suggested, "Think of it as the surf." Our proposed motto, then, to counter any squeamishness about our Cascades swatter/flipper: Think of 'em as blueberries.

Mosquitoes excepted, the backpacker's mystique includes a predilection for items that are lightweight and small. You can always tell a devoted backpacker, it is said, by the sawed-off toothbrush. Items that can do double or tripe duty, like our swatter/flipper, are especially in demand. Witness the ubiquitous Swiss Army Knife, with it's multitude of attachments. (Most of these doodads are never used; it's the security that comes from having them—even more, the glee that comes from knowing how many different implements you would have to carry to give you the same options, even if, like a wood rasp or Phillips screwdriver, they won't ever be opened—that matters.) The next step, we decided, would be a new wonder liquid, simultaneously doing duty as sunscreen, bug repellant, stove fuel, boot sealer, soap concentrate, and seasoning for dehydrated chicken stew.

Hikers are understandably ambivalent regarding technology: On the one hand, technology is a large part of the "it" in getting away from "it" all. But on the other, there is much to be said for gadgets that increase comfort while reducing that old bugaboo, weight. One emporium in Seattle, Early Winters Inc., had a devoted clientele, based on its high-tech backpacking innovations, including a ridiculous contraption that stores water above the hiker's head, from which a tube provides a mouthful on demand.

The thirsty backpacker never misses a stride! In all fairness, Early Winters also made the best, sturdiest, lightest tent I have seen, plus a fine deluxe model, the aptly-named Omnipo-Tent. (Before they went out of business).

Along the Pasayten River, we noted a sign (tastefully carved on a wooden plaque, hence easy to overlook) that announced "Pasayten Airport 3 miles." Half expecting—fear mixed with irrational hope—a busy control tower with bustling terminals for international and domestic flights, we encountered nothing more than a big grassy meadow, large enough and maybe even flat enough to accommodate a jumbo jet, but somewhat lacking in amenities, not to mention commuter access. Maybe the "Pasayten Airport" occasionally serves for emergency Forest Service landings; better yet, perhaps it is a wilderness sign-carver's idea of irony tinged with whimsy.

But if the Pasayten River was boring, the worst was yet to come, an afternoon plodding painfully up the muggy, buggy, and viewless trickling headwaters of Chuchuwanteen Creek, sloppy of trail underfoot and—as far as were concerned at the time—devoid of any redeeming virtues. If by some odd chance you haven't heard of that ghastly place, here is a brief "Ode to the Mighty Chuchuwanteen" that we constructed that afternoon. Alternate title (with apologies to Robert Frost), "Glopping by Woods on a Hot, Sticky, Miserable Afternoon":

> Whose woods these are I do not care,
> For I have insects in my hair.
> I do not choose to stop right here,
> Amid these bugs, this heat, this glare.
> The woods are ugly, dank, and steep,
> And filled with biting flies that creep,
> And I have blisters on my feet
> And miles to go before I sleep.
>
> I give my shoulder straps a shake
> And ask if there is some mistake.
> The only other sound's the squeak
> Of sickly Chuhuwanteen Creek.
> The woods are ugly, dank, and steep,

But I have promises to keep,
And miles to go before I sleep.
And miles to go before I sleep.

* * *

But nothing is forever, not even the ascent along the churlish Chuchuwanteen. At last, we saw the rocky ridges of the Pacific Crest itself, running dutifully north and south, just as our map promised it would. After gaining the ridge, we were to run south, then stroll up and down about twenty miles along that precipitous divider between the eastern and western Cascades. But first we had to get there. For days our trail had led us reliably, and we had followed obediently; but now, it just seemed to evaporate in a wet meadow overlooking dainty, dark-blue Frosty Lake.

We weren't lost, just discommoded. Trails have an occasional habit of doing brief disappearing acts of this sort, after which they can almost always be picked up once more, on the other side of the apparent erasure. And this was no exception; we rejoined it after a few brief exploratory forays along several routes that eventually turned out to be elk and deer paths.

Unlike the Sierras or Rockies, cross-country travel is generally not recommended in the Cascades, largely because the abundant moisture makes for lots of undergrowth as well as steep valleys with fast-flowing, often impassable rivers. Not to mention glaciers. As a result, Cascades backpackers are more likely than most to stay on the various hikers' highways and not venture off those beaten paths. As to these paths, they vary. Usually, a trail is nothing more than a line of travel, perhaps two or at most three feet wide, from which the vegetation has either been scraped away or trodden down. Following it is as easy as following your nose.

The nicest trails are of compacted evergreen needles and forest duff, giving a spring to the step not unlike a gym mat. The worst thread their way over football-sized rocks, too small to provide a secure platform and too large to ignore. A trail through the snow quickly becomes a dirty little rut in the whiteness, and a trail over large rocks may be discernible by the moss or lichens that have been rubbed away. Trails may cross streams via slippery, unstable rocks, or—worse—treacherous, moss-covered logs that demand the soul of a tightrope walker. (Cowards like me traverse these on hands and knees, especially when unbalanced by a heavy back-

pack.) Through high alpine areas, trails may cross extensive regions of "scree," small flakes of rock and pebbles into which a boot
sinks deeply. Scree slopes give the impression of being soft, because they are so yielding, but they can be frustrating to climb
because the hiker sinks down almost as much as he or she climbs
up. Just below the summit of Mount Adams, for example, there is a
lengthy scree slope; to climb it—two steps forward, on step sliding
back down—is to feel empathy for the Northwest's migrating
salmon, trying to make headway in their journey upstream.

Sometimes, especially on little-traveled routes or those that
cross extensive areas of bare rock or snowfields, trails may consist
of nothing more than periodically placed "cairns," piles of rocks
too unlikely to be natural. In such cases, "following a trail" really
means navigating from one cairn to the next, a bit like children
doing a "dot-to-dot" puzzle. Demolishing a cairn in the mountains,
or building a false one, is equivalent to poisoning a well in the
desert. Usually, no more than one cairn can be seen at a time, so
following them is something of an act of faith. I have seen cairns six
feet high or just a few inches. Each one generates a little warm
glow of security, followed immediately by a doubt—usually short
lived—as to the next.

When cairns are used to mark a trail through rocky jumbles
known as "talus," they offer an interesting statement on the meaning of intelligence and of life itself. Thus, we know from the Second Law of Thermodynamics that things tend toward disorder; a
talus slope is a harsh demonstration of this fact, with its disordered
jumble of moderately large rocks and boulders. There is no mind
discernible in such a scattering of rock upon rock. Within such
entropic slag, even the most rudimentary of towers—a piling up of
three rocks—is an unmistakable sign that human intelligence has
been at work. From the mountain cairn to the World Trade Center
is only a matter of degree.

Down among the trees—or as we say in the Northwest, the
"timber"—trails may be marked by "blazes," small spots of paint,
little insignias nailed onto the occasional tree trunk, or strips of
bright ribbon tied above the snow level. It is both the backpacker's
bane and delight that a trail, especially at low elevation, is almost
invisible unless you are on it. Therefore, especially in heavy forest
or dense undergrowth, a trail can be just a few feet away, but un-

seen; once contacted, however, it can continue its otherwise fragile way for hundreds of miles.

And this, of course, is precisely what the Cascade Crest Trail—which we soon joined—does. It is the northern end of the Pacific Crest, an interstate system of trails that runs continuously from the Canadian border through Washington, Oregon, and California, to Mexico. Every year, scores of people make the entire trip, sending caches of food ahead to ranger stations or other contact points spaced seventy to one hundred miles apart. It is recommended to begin at the south end in spring or early summer. "Our" section, at the extreme north end, is not only the most rugged stretch, but is usually snow-covered until July. Because of its steep slopes, it is also difficult and sometimes dangerous for heavily laden hikers the rest of the time as well.

Once we found the cairns, we followed them gratefully, leading back to our trail which zigzagged up to the Crest itself. Distinctive zigzags of this sort are known as "switchbacks," or just plain "switches" to the initiated. They are the most efficient way for a trail to gain elevation, much easier than going straight up (as is often the case for the no-nonsense, near-vertical routes favored by miners or that equally single-minded group, the pursuers of fish). Admittedly, an endless, repetitive series of switchbacks can become boring, but each angle in the linked chain of Zs serves as testimony to the elevation being gained . . . if the hiker's legs and chest haven't already conveyed that information.

There is much that I haven't mentioned, perhaps because it is ineffable: the extraordinary personal closeness that comes from experiences that are intensely shared, precisely because they are unrelieved, undiluted, and unknown to anyone or anything else; the gratifying complacency of striding turtlelike through the world's most spectacular country, complete unto one's self and making the land one's own; a renewed appreciation of how brilliantly the stars shine, above the lowland smog and far from the competing city lights (there really is a Milky Way, and it's not just a candy bar!); and knowing, Gulliverlike, what it is to be very small, and yet also very big.

Traffic was heavier on the final leg of our journey. We must have met nearly a dozen people each day. By the time we finally reached our car, therefore, which we had parked at a trailside intersection on Slate Peak ten days before, we were getting ready to reenter society. Looking at us later that day, eating soup and sandwiches at the Mountain Song Restaurant in Marblemount, Washington ("Real Food" says the sign outside), someone might even have thought that we were just another pair of tourists, gawking at the mountains . . . which, of course, we were.

Mountain Climbing

Useless, Like Poetry, and Dangerous, Like Lovemaking

Right away, let me be clear: I am not a "serious" mountain climber. In fact, after injuring my left knee in an ice-climbing accident in 1976 and then tearing some of the muscles off my chest during a fall in 1988, I am hardly a climber at all. I have never been on a major expedition and never will be. I have never climbed El Capitan, or the Jungfrau, or Aconcagua. I have never experienced a life-or-death epic hanging perilously by my teeth, clawing desperately with rapidly ebbing strength at some inaccessible sky-cleaving pinnacle. I have not lost any body parts to frostbite, nor have I stalwartly carried a beloved, injured comrade, myself half-dead with exhaustion and hypothermia, down a treacherous avalanche slope. I have not pioneered any first ascents, of any peak worth noting, nor have I "put up" any new routes on crags already conquered by others more intrepid.

I have done just a bit of climbing, on rock, and ice, and over glaciers, just enough to fall in love with the doing of it, and also, to recognize my own limits. I like to lead easy "pitches," and as long as I have a good belay from above, I can psyche myself up to climb—or attempt—almost anything. I am not afraid of heights, just respectful of them and of those who measure themselves against such lofty standards. I am not particularly brave; I have looked down from cliffs and glaciers—neither high nor difficult by technical standards—and seen cars driving smoothly below, or the bright colors of spring flowers in bloom, and wondered why the hell I had gotten myself in such a fix.

I bow to no one in my admiration for those who mount expeditionary extravaganzas to the eight-thousand-meter peaks of the Himalayas or Karakoram, who push back the limits of the humanly possible in steep and slip-prone icy gullies, through endless, groaning mazes of near-vertical glacial confusion, or up and over stern, looming rock walls towering thousands of feet into the sky. But in all honesty, I have not done any of these things, so I shall write instead about what I know: climbing for the chickenhearted, out-of-shape, and short-of-breath.

Two of my friends have died in climbing accidents, and that, frankly, has diminished some of my enthusiasm for the endeavor: both of them—Al Givler and Dusan Jagersky—were far better climbers than I ever was, even in my prime and with knee and chest muscles intact, and (even more sobering) both were also far more careful than I had even been. Al was also my first climbing instructor. "Those that can, do," wrote George Bernard Shaw, "those that can't, teach." Al could teach and do. This chapter is dedicated to him.

"Mountains," according to Annie Dillard,

> are giant, restful, absorbent. You can heave your spirit into a mountain and the mountain will keep it, folded and not throw it back as some creeks will. The creeks are the world with all its stimulus and beauty; I live there. But the mountains are home.[1]

Maybe this is true of Virginia's Blue Ridge Mountains, about which Ms. Dillard was writing, and of the Appalachians generally, as well as the Adirondacks of New York, the Berkshires of Massachussetts, the Laurentians of Quebec—all of them elderly ranges, calm, thoughtful, friendly and downright homey, sandpapered flat and blunt by the winds and rains of time. And maybe this is true for those who sit back and admire mountains from a distance, or perhaps wander about on the lower slopes of the lower peaks. But

1. Annie Dillard, *Pilgrim at Tinker Creek.*

things are quite different among the brash, young, upthrust, up-start mountains of the West, like the Sierras, Rockies, or Cascades, or for that matter the Andes, the Alps or, the Himalayas. And for those who aspire to climb them, such mountains may be worthy adversaries, and occasionally, even beloved companions, but not comforting, and usually downright uncomfortable.

These places are too sharp, too steep, too icy and severe to keep anything of ours folded, close to their ever-loving bosom. More-over, they don't even have bosoms, but rather glaciers, cliffs, points and prongs, icefalls and lonely little tarns. Giant, yes; restful and absorbent? No way. They are destinations, challenges, places to explore, to cherish, to celebrate, and eventually—always—to de-part. They are many things, but home is not among them.

Many people think of mountains only as scenery, and distant scenery at that. (Many of these same folks also think of wilderness as the green stuff growing in the cracks of sidewalks.) I once heard a tourist from the Midwest complaining—only partly in jest, I sus-pect—that something should be done about the mountains around Banff because they blocked the view. In short, not everyone likes mountains. And that's just as well.

Yet mountains work powerfully on the human imagination. Even the names are magical: the Eigerwand, the Petit Grèpon, the Grandes Jorasses, the south face of Aconcagua, and (my favorite) the Rupal Face of Nanga Parbat. Perhaps even more than the re-grettable white-good/black-bad dichotomy, up has long been asso-ciated with good; low, with bad. The desirable is elevated; the de-spised, debased. We aspire to lofty heights of ecstasy, of accomplishment, of glory. And to fail is to fall, down, into the abyss. Heaven is above us, hell is below. God is the Most High. No mon-arch or deity has even been called "Your Lowness."

Religions around the world have found God on a mountaintop. Mount Olympus was the abode of the Greek gods. Moses received the laws of his god after ascending Mount Sinai. Zoroaster also descended from a lonely mountain, in Iran, to share his version of right and wrong. And the most significant sermon in Christian tra-dition was delivered on (what else?) a Mount. As for Mount Ever-est—highest of all—it is probably better called by its Sherpa name, Chomolungma, "Goddess Mother of the World."

Height typically implies dominance. (Most short people, male or female, would ruefully agree.) Mountains, by towering over the foothills, valleys, and plains, are clearly in charge.[2] From the top, the world can be seen, in its entirety, and thereby owned. At the same time, the summit straddler is also vulnerable: to lightning, to wind and cold, to intense sun, starvation, exhaustion. More than anyone else, the mountaineer is exposed, to the elements, to private fears, to personal inadequacies. And of course, excessive pride is quickly punished, as has long been the tradition, by a fall. Not surprisingly, then, coming down from the mountaintop is a return indeed, be it triumph or tragedy.

It hasn't always been so positive, however. Only since about the late eighteenth century have people looked with awe and reverence at mountains. Strange as it may seem to modern mountaphiles, lofty peaks were objects of horror and dread during medieval times, abodes of forces not only powerful but often malign as well. The ghost of Pontius Pilate was long thought to lurk near the Swiss Alps above Lucerne, and the crash of thunder, the devastating slide of rocks and snow and the menace of icy mists have long troubled the sleep of those living near the forbidding and—until recently—largely inaccessible peaks of the world.

But with the Enlightenment and the Age of Reason, mountains became sources of exploration, of conquest, and of wonder. According to Goethe's Faust, "Great powers the mountains boast, Where nature works omnipotently free," and scientists, adventurers and just plain people began to look to the hills for inspiration and recreation. In "Song of Myself," Whitman observed that "The white-topt mountains show in the distance, I fling out my fancies toward them." Many of us have gone farther yet, flinging not just our fancies toward the mountains, but also ourselves.

Mountaineering, in a sense, is the ultimate in putting our money where our mouth is: putting our bodies where our imagination dwells. Later, we shall look at the traditional—and unanswerable—question, "Why do people climb?" But before tackling "why" let us briefly consider "how."

There are many aspects of climbing, including planning the trip,

---

2. A wonderful T-shirt, advertising the recent American woman's expedition to Annapurna, proclaimed, "A Woman's Place Is on Top."

choosing one's companions, getting to the site, and talking or writing about it afterwards. But the crux of the thing is the actual climbing itself. And there are three major ways of doing it, depending on the nature of the terrain to be surmounted: rock climbing, ice climbing, and glacier travel.

Rock climbing is the most basic, requiring the least equipment. It is a union of primal elements: human skin, muscles, and bone on the hard fundament of rock. Even good rock climbers work terribly hard, often straining themselves virtually to their limits—at least during brief periods of intense effort—and yet, by some magical transmutation, they don't struggle. They don't flail. They don't thrash. They levitate themselves almost, it seems, by will power alone, or perhaps by spiritual purity, as much as by skill or strength.

Evelyn Waugh, normally among the most cynical and critical of observers, described a "little walk" he once took, ostensibly following his acquaintance, a Monsieur Leblanc:

> Mr. Leblanc led the way with light, springing steps. He went right up to the face of the cliff, gaily but purposefully, as Moses may have approached the rocks from which he was about to strike water. There was a little crack running like fork-lightning down the blank wall of stone. Mr. Leblanc stood below it, gave one little skip, and suddenly, with great rapidity and no apparent effort, proceeded to ascent the precipice. He did not climb; he rose. It was as if someone were hoisting him up above and he had merely to prevent himself from swinging out of the perpendicular, by keeping contact with rocks in a few light touches of foot and hand. In just the same way, one after another, the Leblanc party were whisked away out of sight.[3]

Needless to say, most of us have never climbed like that.

A good rock climber (who must climb rather than levitate) always keeps three points of secure suspension—two hands and a foot, or two feet and one hand—while moving the free limb to a new and higher hold. Like a daddy long legs or spindly marine crab, arms and legs move in a kind of rockbound tai chi, a pattern both fluid and deliberate, always relying more on balance, move-

3. Evelyn Waugh, *When the Going Was Good* (Boston: Little Brown, 1947).

ment, and rhythm than on sheer strength or any assist from clanking hardware. Mountains have poise, above all. And the climber must be no less posed than his or her quarry.

There is a quite a bit of cognition as well, a kind of body-thought in which the climber seeks to become one with the rock, calculating instantaneously and fluidly how best to use its cracks, bumps, and rugosities to ascend with a minimum of effort . . . not so much imposing one's will as using the natural features to surmount itself. On occasion, of course, complaining muscles must be overcome, along with the tendency of some rock to splinter, of cracks to shatter, or be too narrow, or too shallow for good purchase, of surfaces to be slimy with moss or dripping water, slick with frost and ice, or almost indomitably smooth and impregnable. And so, rock climbing is not really mind over matter, even if it looks that way to the admiring observer. It is more like mind *and* matter (the very personal matter of very fallible climbers) over and around and across and through and in spite of and—sometimes—because of the enormously diverse and unpredictable matter of this world.

The occasional, very rare climber, however, appears to transcend the limitations of the usual, even the possible, and is what might be called a "magical genius." I first encountered this phrase applied to the Indian mathematician Ramanujan, a prodigy who often worked out his extraordinary proofs in the sand, who died of malnutrition in his native India, and whose notebooks are only now being explicated by competent but distinctly nonmagical journeyman with tranditional Ph.Ds. Observing a regular, garden-variety type genius—whether mathematician or climber (or in fact, any genius)—one might conclude that with enough time, training, or incentive, it would be possible to do what he or she has done. But not a magical genius; there is simply no way that you or I could emulate the doings of magical genius. Among climbers, people like Gaston Rebuffat, Reinhold Messner, or the American John Roskelly would qualify.

For the rest of us, rock climbing still offers challenges aplenty. The first is to overcome some of the strictures, inhibitions, and fears that have been drilled into us since childhood, when a horrified parent caught us teetering on the top of the second-floor bannister. The rock climber must go farther back in time, several million years or so, and relearn what comes naturally, reversing our silly insistence on coming down from the trees to live in a two-dimensional world.[4]

First, you need good rock. Say it again and savor the sound of it, because there may be no more sonorously meaningful and beneficent combination of two words, in any language: "GOOD ROCK." Good rock means firm handholds, maybe some of them even well shaped like a cozy jughandle, to fit right into the palm of a grateful hand. It means flat, stable platforms for your feet, at least a few inches wide (no more are needed), so that your weight is not simply teetering from your toes until calf muscles cry out for relief. It means sharp, clean cracks, that will admit fingers but not cut like a razor, and that allow feet to work flat, body arched and suspended by combined and oddly reassuring tension, in what is known as a "layback." Good rock means the occasional "chimney," walls obligingly separated by perhaps twice the width of your shoulders, allowing for upward progress by a variety of upward maneuvers known as "stemming," in which pressure is applied on opposing walls, for example by pressing hands and feet against one wall of the chimney, shoulders and back against the other, or even right hand and foot on one, left hand and foot on the other, thereby ascending but with a lot of air around you, somewhat like a spider. It means just enough unevenness to allow you to "smear" a hand when needed—flat like a pancake—and then use the friction thereby gained (even if no protuberance can be seen) to push off to a new hold. Good rock means a wonderfully diverse surface, providing endless variations on the theme of hardness, but without tedious repetition as on the outside of a skyscraper, or unpleasant surprises, as when a ledge crumbles or a flake shatters. It means abundant grooves and undulations, notches and crevices, opportunities to insert a foot, knee, elbow or hand—that is, to "jam"—with confidence, if not serenity.[5] Good rock also means that if it proves necessary to hammer in a "piton" (often shortened to a "pin"), the

4. Unlike the squirrels, we regrettably do not have the ability to reverse the bones of our wrists and ankles, and thereby, to descend trees head first. We have to back down, instead, just as we climbed up, like a motion picture running in reverse, but with a whole lot more difficulty seeing hand- and footholds. That is how we presumably first descended from the trees to the floor of the African savannah, and it is tempting to conclude that we have been backing into our future ever since.
5. Twenty-seven different kinds of jam holds have been identified.

precious little metal spike will go in smoothly and securely, making a satisfying, high-pitched sound as it is inserted; and it will also come out quickly and cleanly.

And good rock also means an absence of bad: good rock does not crumble, flake, crack, or split like its opposite, "rotten rock." It means that the cracks positively yearn for the placement of a well-conceived "chock," a small piece of metal designed to hold without injuring the rock itself, and in good rock, every chock is held with a heart-warming firmness when you pull experimentally to seat the metal within the crack, never working free . . . except when directed to do so. To the climber, good rock is redolent with delight, cause for celebration, poetry in solid form.

Mountains, cliffs, walls seem so natural, so unstructured as to be almost homogenous in their featurelessness. It is difficult for non-climbers to appreciate that these tumbled rock piles grim and reckless, these heaven-ambitious peaks, what Walt Whitman called "these formless wild arrays," are actually crisscrossed by known routes, as real to the climber as boundaries between states or nations are to the geographer. There is a fine lead, we are told, up a granite wall just beyond where a thin stream cascades over the third gully, a nifty chimney to be found between the largest boulder and the southwest cliff face, a glorious overhang below the second belaying ledge, and so forth. Not only are such routes precisely known, evaluated, and pointed out, there are even specific instructions detailing how to follow these invisible pathways; hence, a guidebook might announce "toe jam on left, five feet above the 'open book' in center gully; then smear right and lay-back fifteen feet to a challenging overhang past the second red vein."

Good rock-climbing spots tend to be especially well known and increasingly popular. Prominent handholds may be spotted from a distance, coated wtih the chalk dust used to enhance friction (as in gymnastics) while convenient footholds are often rubbed shiny by the smooth-soled boots of specialized rock-climbing shoes. Often visible from the road, rock climbing differs from most forms of mountaineering in that it has become something of a spectator sport, with ascents often watched by nonclimbers in lawn chairs and Winnebagos.

Not surprisingly, there has come to be more than a little narcissism on rock, with bare-chested rock-jocks, each carrying his own personal bag of chalk dust, to be used before an especially difficult "move." Aficionados strut their stuff on three hundred foot cliffs at the Shawangunks near New Paltz, New York (affectionately known as the "Gunks"), or six hundred feet or so above El Dorado Canyon near Boulder, Colorado, or three thousand feet up, at the "big walls" in Yosemite, such as El Capitan. For many rock climbers, these cliffs and their well-worn and well-worked-out routes, their carefully designated problems, are virtually like outdoor gymnasia, serving not only for the practice and perfection of skills, but even as the goal of their endeavors. Just like the bodybuilder who never, never pulls a barge or lifts a bale, some rock climbers never seem to bother climbing mountains.

There is also a curious ethos among some rock climbers, one that may actually discourage conditioning, despising excessive healthiness, perhaps because doing it out-of-shape enhances the accomplishment. Some of the most revered feats have been those performed with a notable hangover, and many an imposing rock wall has been ascended by people fueled largely by cigarettes, pretzels, Pepsi, and some marijuana. (The latter isn't used for the climbing itself, but rather for enhancing the sunset, as witnessed from a cliffside hammock.)

It isn't feasible to brush up on crevasse-rescue skills whenever the mood beckons, or to get in a bit of ice climbing on your lunch hour. But all you need to practice rock climbing is some rock, and this can often be found without too much difficulty. One of the more popular pastimes, in fact, is "bouldering," clambering up and over the boulders that seem to abound wherever there are ountains nearby. Hanging around camp, waiting for the weather to clear, or after dinner and before dessert, ardent boulderers can be seen working out satisfying little problems, perfecting their confidence and technique.

It takes some learning (I never really mastered it, except occasionally on a medium-sized boulder with terra firma reassuringly close at hand) to trust your feet and stand directly over a foothold, leaving the hands free to grab if needed. The neophyte's error is to lean in toward the rock, thereby either occupying one or more hands or bumping the mountain with your nose. It also takes some learning (I never really mastered this either!) to avoid jerkiness or

desperate pawing at the rock, and to move like a carefully choreo-
graphed ballet dancer, climbing first with your eyes, using limbs
not to find or create a purchase but to take advantage of what is
already there, just waiting for you. But when it clicks, even if just
for a moment or two, the marvelous aroma of mastery lingers, a
whiff of wonderment at how a soft body can—if only momentar-
ily—work its way on the harsh, unyielding bones of this planet.

The climber puts in "protection" on the way up—pitons, or better yet (because it is less destructive of the rock), chocks—which
are then attached via metal clips known as carabiners ("beeners,"
to the initiated) to a rope and to the climber as well as to a partner,
who is somehow firmly anchored to the mountain, thereby "belaying" the leader.[6] Current etiquette calls for a minimum of pitons
and if at all possible, none whatever.

Rock is dead. (Not the music, the substance.) Therefore, few
people mourn its destruction. But because it is dead, it cannot
regrow the cracks that have been splintered or heal the scar made
by an unnecessary expansion bolt. As the crowds have swelled, so
has the pressure for "clean climbing."

"Learning the ropes" applied originally to seamanship, but it
aptly describes mountain training as well; to a large extent, climbing technique is proper rope handling. And the ropes themselves
receive rapt attention from mountaineers, and not only because
they are the thread from which lives may hang. They are nothing
less than wonderful: smooth, supple, just a wee bit elastic, and
patterned in beguilingly garish colors. An old and beloved rope,
moreover, is never thrown away, discarded, or junked; rather, it is
reverently "retired," perhaps to be used as a toprope for bouldering.

Hardware ranges from the incongruous, belchlike Rurp (for "re-
alized ultimate reality piton"), which is actually a small delicate-
looking blade, like a double-edged razor, to the grandly contoured
Bong, a six-inch piece of folded aluminum, with holes in it like a
thin slice of Swiss cheese, and which goes "bong" when pounded
into an obligingly large crack. Virtually all of my climbing on rock
has been "free climbing," using only natural features of the moun-

---

6. With experience, you also learn not to make too many zig-zags with your
    protection, or else the rope drag can become a serious handicap.

tain itself to help with the ascent; gizmos like pitons and chocks are employed—if at all—only to guard against falling, not to chin yourself upward. But the protection had better be good; a poor belay or a bad piton or chock is often worse than none at all, because of the false sense of security it may bestow.

Coming down is another story. If the descent is gentle, the nonchalant descender can face out, with back to the mountain; on steeper inclines, the opposite of ascending is to use one's derriere: ass-ending may be uncomfortable and relatively graceless, but generally safe. For yet steeper slopes, the (healthy) inclination is to face inward. But when the route approaches the vertical, then descending calls for artifice, notably the "rappel" down a firmly anchored rope. For some people, rappelling is repelling. After all, it is the second-fastest way of descending a mountain. Having reached this point, the down climber is tired, maybe elated and distracted by having gotten to the summit or disappointed by having to abort the attempt. Also hungry, thirsty, probably a little bit cranky. Furthermore, whereas climbing down is easier on the cardiovascular system than going the other way, it is a lot harder to do safely. Holds that were easily seen on the way up have a habit of disappearing, utterly, when climbing down.

While rappelling, the rope is doubled and typically run through a carabiner, so that after reaching a suitable ledge below, it can be pulled through and down, for the next rappel; the anchors, up above, are left behind. For nonclimbers, it may be the most spectacular part, although, in fact, it is probably the easiest (although not the safest) aspect of the whole enterprise. Roadside observers ooh and aah as helmeted climbers practice rappelling off a convenient cliff, perhaps with an extra bounce or two away from the vertical, just for effect. Meanwhile, the much more difficult maneuvers being accomplished on fifteen-foot boulder faces are generally ignored.

Rappelling, like much of climbing, requires a curious double standard of distrust and confidence. On the one hand, climbers are wise to trust no one, to check and double-check all protection, to insist on solid belays, not to assume that fixed ropes or rappelling anchors—just because they held, once, for someone else—are still in good shape. But on the other, the climber must make an acute suspension of distrust, putting his or her life in someone else's

hands (more on this later), in one's own skills, and in the adequacy
of the equipment. To rappel, for example, it is necessary not just to
wriggle down a rope, but to lean out from the cliff, boldly assuming
something close to ninety degrees against the perpendicular—
against what Shelley, in "Prometheus Unbound," called "this wall
of eagle-baffling mountain"—trusting in the rope, among other
things. One's first rappel is usually, at the very least, unnerving.

Climbing is done in a series of "pitches," each pitch being an
ascent that is no longer than the rope. With the belaying partner
secured to the rock via slings, chocks, pitons, or wraps around pro-
jections of rock or trunks of trees, the lead climber climbs, putting
in protection as he goes. If he or she falls, and if the rope holds (it
nearly always does), and if the protection holds (it usually does),
then the leader can still fall twice the distance to the nearest protection. If the leader falls while free climbing ten feet above a
chock, he or she will drop twenty feet before the tense rope, going
to the belayer, will arrest that fall. By contrast, once the leader has
completed the pitch, and located a secure belay spot, the person
below can climb with much more security, because with a solid
belay from above, and the rope kept reasonably taut, there isn't
much room for an unplanned descent.

There is a small triumph in every successful placement of reliable protection; a good piton, a solid chock, a stable belay anchor.
Although climbing is undoubtedly more dangerous than watching
television,[7] and to some extent, the *extremis* of the activity provides
the spice, the fact is that climbers do not go out of their way for
shaky pins, frayed ropes, or rotten rock. These things break the
unspoken contract: admittedly, the mountains present dangers to
those who would climb them, but these dangers are supposed to
be known and openly confronted. There are more than enough
unpredictables, like weird weather (sudden storms, including
lightning, fog with zero visibility, heavy winds that threaten to blow
you off your footing or to demolish your tent), snow bridges that
may collapse into yawning glacial crevasses, and (at high elevations) altitude sickness that can range from the uncomfortable,
such as nausea, to the deadly, such as pulmonary or cerebral

---

7.   Although in most cases, the most dangerous part of a climb is the drive to
     the mountain.

edema. So, having voluntarily entered a world of unknowns, climbers cling to the known, deriving great satisfaction from every accomplishment. Every ascent of a difficult pitch—especially if you led it—becomes an internal celebration.

More than that: every successful transition from foot to hand to foot to elbow to foot and so forth becomes a kind of joyous communion. Broken down into its smallest quantum parts, rock climbing is a series of linked "moves," each move being the process whereby a new hold is attained, the body suspended in a particular manner, or raised to a higher level. There are difficult moves, free moves, graceful and fluid moves, bold moves, conservative moves, desperate moves. There are also "problems" posed by the rock itself, and in the curiously understated language of rock climbing (probably attributable to the strong influence of the British on rock-climbing lore), an "interesting problem" may lead to a "novel" or "unanticipated move." Terrifying routes with sheer drops have "exposure," or some "air." Climbing Nun Kun Peak in the Ladakh Range of China, Ralph James glanced over a nearby ridge "which fell five thousand feet to the Faribad Glacier," and remarked casually that "the route to Camp III would be a bit airy."[8]

After such a route, or an especially difficult pitch, one might be tempted to say that the "worst is over." But in climbing, where challenges are sought, the distinction between "worst" and "best" is not easily made. The "best" part of a climb is never the easiest; sometimes, it is the most difficult that is most fondly remembered. Almost always, it is the reason for the climb.

One of the pleasures of climbing—especially if you are not following a known route—is the process of route finding, selecting the best way to proceed. But this is necessarily done at a distance; close up, things take on a different look. What had previously been a broad canvas ("We'll make for that ridge, then contour below the icefall, come across the rock face to the far ridge") becomes a matter of engrossing detail. Will this pitch "go"? Is that crack solid? Where is the next foothold? With vision often limited to just a few feet at a time, the world shrinks, quickly, powerfully, and intensely,

8.   quoted in F. C. Lane, *The Story of Mountains* (New York: Doubleday, 1951).

to the next toe jam or the prospects of "mantling"[9] up and over the ledge just in front of you.

When it all comes together, something as mundane as climbing a big piece of rock can be no less than sublime, a magical dance in which there is a dissolution of the boundary between the doer and the thing done. "I have stretched cords from steeple to steeple," wrote Rimbaud, "garlands from window to window, chains of gold from star to star, and I dance." He could have written that he climbed.

Kurt Diemberger did:

> Then followed the dream of a rock-climb, vertical, overhanging, pi-tonless, with innumerable small holes and wrinkles—perfect free climbing on a sheer wall, with an infinity of air around us. At such moments you are gloriously conscious of your fingers, your muscles; of the toes of your boots winning a hold on the rough Brenta rock, of the wall, close to your face, shining black, brown, and bright ochre amid the grey—like flower patterns in a carpet—and all of it high above the comb down there at the foot of the climb. You are en-meshed in a bright web of thoughts, on which you climb ever higher, pulling yourself upwards from hand-hold to hand-hold, foot-hold to foot-hold, towards an ever-increasing freedom, while every-thing below you falls away as you exalt yourself at the time.
>
> Down there at the bottom, you see the shadows of the towers lengthen, and feel that you belong to your mountain with every fibre of your being and yet, at the same time, here, high above the abyss, utterly free of mind and spirit, you are acutely aware that you have arms and legs—and a body to waft you upwards, because you have learned to overcome fear.[10]

It has been said, by those who—unlike Diemberger—have not overcome fear, that climbing involves lengthy periods of boredom punctuated by occasional moments of sheer terror. I have not ex-perienced very much of the latter, but lots of the former. Waiting for a break in an interminable high-altitude storm is the classic in mountaineering boredom, readily appreciated by nonclimber alike. Less widely known, however, is the interminable waiting

9. Imagine hoisting yourself onto your living-room mantelpiece using arms alone, or getting out of a swimming pool without using the ladder.
10. Kurt Diemberger, *Summits and Secrets* (London: Allen & Union, 1971).

while actually climbing: belaying a partner (either below you or above), who pokes along, probably much faster than you want, but nonetheless much too slowly when you have nothing to do but hold the rope, and who, somehow, can't even keep up an interesting conversation while poised perilously a thousand feet above a glacier, with the wind whistling all around. Added to the boredom of the belayer is the belated discovery—always when it is too late—that the sharp lump of rock that seemed so trival a few minutes ago has grown in size and discomfort, and moreover, that no amount of stalwart sitting upon it will cause it to soften. Or hatch.

While the ancients identified these four primal elements: earth, air, fire, and water—to which I added a fifth, wood—climbers recognize three: rock, snow, and ice. Although some of the techniques are similar on all three (such as belaying, use of ropes, and protection), there are notable differences, and differences in equipment as well. Whereas the rock climber uses bare hands and lightweight, flexible climbing shoes, the snow and ice climber typically wears much more clothing. Heavy, inflexible mountaineering boots are supposed to keep feet warm and dry, and to provide a secure platform for attaching metal spikes known as crampons, which enable secure walking on steep, hard snow or ice. The rock climber will typically carry a bandolier of assorted chocks, pitons, and carabiners, but with hands free; by contrast, the snow or ice climber will carry, at minimum, an ice axe.

Although occasionally useful as a walking stick, the real purpose of the ice axe is to provide a crucial third leg on steep slopes, to chop steps in hard snow or ice (if crampons have been lost, left behind, or are simply unavailing) and—most important—to contribute an emergency "self-arrest" if the climber or anyone else on the ropes should suddenly fall. There have been wondrous true tales of great feats performed by an ice axe, skillfully wielded, like the time during an early American attempt on K-2 (the world's second highest mountain) when Pete Schoening held literally five falling climbers, all of their lives dangling from his one axe, firmly implanted in the high Himalayan snows.

Use of the ice axe is not intuitive. It takes practice. Incorrect use, on an otherwise trivial slip, can even injure the climber: a sharpened metal instrument, flailing out of control, can inflict serious wounds.[11] But with a bit of training, the ice axe is the key to confidence on snow or ice.

In those airy reaches where more snow falls than melts, the compacted white stuff of earlier years becomes pressed into ice. And large rivers of ice, usually overlain with freshly fallen snow, flow slowly down from the heights and become known as glaciers. Often, they can be heard creaking and groaning as they inch along, suffering the stresses and strains of downward motion and unimaginable weight. Moreover, the uneven pressure brought upon them frequently causes glaciers to develop cracks or crevasses, openings into their interior that may be just a few feet deep, or several hundred feet, and that may be narrow enough to step across, or else a daunting prospect even for an engineering batallion equipped with suspension bridges.

It is always a strange sensation to step from solid rock to the white ocean of a living glacier, knowing that the snow and ice may be hundreds, even thousands of feet thick. (Later, it will be stranger yet to return to dry ground, and to contemplate that this is the stuff on which you normally live.)

To walk on a glacier, where no one lives, is to "rope up," so that if someone falls in, the others on the rope (generally two others) will be able to drop—instantly, if not sooner—into an arrest position, and keep everyone else from going in, also. Since a body plummeting into a crevasse will cause the rope to pull against the lip of the crevasse itself, the actual weight to be borne by the would-be rescuers is not as great as one might imagine . . . unless, of course, everyone in the rope winds up in the same crevasse in which case, as the French put it, "c'est la vie," or rather, "la mort." (Fortunately, this is very rare, especially since glacier travelers spread out on a rope, and morever, traffic tends to be linear and at right angles to the generally parallel lines of most crevasses.)

Glacier walking can be a long slog, with the normal exhaustion of uphill effort multiplied several-fold by the reduced oxygen to be found at higher elevation. Incredible as it may seem to people accustomed to lowland activity, just walking upwards at fourteen thousand feet can be a major exertion. Plodding along, the so-

11. Despite their menacing appearance, ice axes have only rarely been used as
      weapons. The most notable exception was the murder of Leon Trotsky...who
      to my knowledge never climbed a mountain.

called "rest step" goes like this: left foot forward, breathe in, breathe out, right foot forward, breathe in, breathe out . . . repeat as needed, but no more rapidly than one step every four seconds or so.

But such climbs have always been worth it, and then some. I mean the doing of it, not just getting to the top or reminiscing about it afterward. There is a fierce, undescribable joy in the continued, almost trancelike effort, going upward, and then more upward still, picking the way around crevasses, bypassing huge pinnacles of fluted and gleaming ice,[12] watching as the immense mounds of glacial snow recede below your feet, revealing yet more expanse and yet more wonders of white, silver,and blue, further up and then further up again, into the sky and yet with feet still somehow on something, even if it is not quite solid and not quite ground. In the cold air, razor sharp with the thin edge of altitude, every breath is the gasp of a hoarse, rattling bellows, and existence constricts to one step at a time and two labored breaths—infinitely precious—for each step. Some Zen masters claim that we should be especially aware of our breathing, deeply attuned to its wonder and grateful for each inspiration and expiration, for the flow of life in which we partake; perhaps this kind of satori remains elusive for most Westerners, but the high-alttude glacier traveler gets at least an inkling of what it may be all about.

Climbing Mount Rainier one time, I didn't achieve true enlightenment, but at least got a memento of my wholehearted breathing: a sunburned tongue and throat. The sun's ultraviolet rays—especially strong at high altitude—had reflected off the bright glacal snow and onto the roof of my panting mouth.

Crampons—although a whole lot better than regular boot soles—can be as much trouble as the hyperintense sunlight. For walking on ice, crampons are essential; likewise for very hard, steep snow. But often, snow has an unpleasant habit of balling up between the prongs, leaving the hapless cramponner standing atop what feels like a pair of thick, rounded stilts. The time-tested technique is to knock the crampons periodically with the side of your ice axe, and/or—in mixed snow and ice—to agonize about whether to put the darn things on at all.

12. "Seracs" in the mountaineering vocabulary.

Another important glacier technique (often useful on rock, as well) involves climbing up a rope, if, for example, you have fallen into a crevasse. Slings are tied to the rope using an ingenious knot known as a prusik (after its originator). The special quality of a prusik is that it slides freely when no weight is applied, but grabs securely under pressure. So, you can "prusik"up a rope by putting all your weight on your left foot, for example, whose prusik will bite onto the rope, then using right hand to move the other, un-weighted sling, which slides up freely. Then you step onto it, which holds, and after transferring all weight onto this side, you repeat the process on the other.

Mechanical devices are also available for those (like myself) who distrust knots or are just lousy at tying them. The best known of these is made by Jumar, and its success has made the trade name virtually generic, as fixed in the mountaineer's lexicon as Kleenex or Scotch tape. Jumaring up a rope, holding a mechanical ascender in each hand, the climber must override his natural tendencies: the gizmo grabs the rope only when you let go; if you grip tightly (the natural inclination, especially when falling!), it slides freely. When I was first learning to ride horses, I was astride my wife's thoroughbred (a retired and modestly successful racehorse). She got excited about something and started to run away with me; fearful and trying to stay in the saddle, I gripped her more tightly with my legs, which she interpreted as a signal to go faster yet. And so we went, accelerating in a positive feedback loop.[13] Something similar happened early in my Jumaring career: starting to slide down the rope, I instinctively clutched the ascender tightly, which caused it to slip yet more. Fortunately, *Homo sapiens* is also a creature of cognition, not just instinct.

Whereas crevices, in rock, are things to get into—hands, fingers, elbows, a Balszo Snell's delight or nightmare—crevasses are to stay out of, the *vagina dentata* of the mountain world. They are not black holes, however, but rather iridescent blue-green toward the top, richer, darker blue as you get deeper, with

13. This might be termed the Chinese finger-puzzle phenomenon, in which mindless, reflexive effort to get out of a situation only makes it worse. It applies in other contexts, as well, such as efforts to find security via the accumulation of nuclear weapons, but that particular tune is more a dirge than a lovesong.

glimmerings of turquoise and amethyst along the way. They positively gleam, these great icy cracks, with either delight or deceptive malevolence, depending on the climber's mood. And they groan and they yawn, simultaneously in friendly greeting and open-mouthed menace. They are cold, wet, small, huge, unpredictable, scary, and altogether fascinating.

It is also worth noting that crevasses are typically crossed by snow bridges, and that sometimes, these bridges collapse. Once, on a climb of Mount Baker in the North Cascades, my climbing partners and I followed the tracks of a previous group (who, presumably, were following yet an earlier party). The footprints led to a crevasse no less than twelve feet wide, and then continued, nonchalantly, on the far side. A snow bridge, which the earlier climbers had trod across, had evidently given way some time after they had crossed; there was absolutely no sign of it now.

When they are narrow enough, up to four or five feet, crevasses can be jumped with some safety. But a heavily laden climber, carrying ice axe and wearing heavy clothing, crampons afoot, and dragging one hundred feet of one-half inch rope, is not exactly a gazelle. (Some of us aren't very gazelle-like under the best of circumstances.) I shall long remember the time I took a running start, prepared to leap gracefully across a chasm barely three feet wide, only to sink up to my chest when the lip of the crevasse gave way a step before what had seemed to be the edge. Luckily, I don't embarrass easily.

Once, however, I was, when I paid the price of carelessness—indeed, carelessness twice repeated—in the mountains. I got off easily, suffering merely a cold, long night; it could have been death. (Part of the charm, and the horror, of mountain climbing is that it exerts so high a penalty for a single misstep, a momentary carelessness. Almost any error carries the potential for instant finality, something rarely found in other human endeavors.) I was climbing Mount Rainier, with John Edwards of the University of Washington's Zoology Department. John is a climber of some repute, having accomplished several first ascents in his native New Zealand. Hoping to get some privacy, we had camped a few hundred feet above Camp Muir, the standard base camp for ascents of the mountain. Instead, we got one of the banes of mountain travel: wind. Not just the puffy, blowing, cool-you-off kind of wind that lowlanders know and sailors enjoy, but the constant roar of an angry, icy, high-up-in-the-stratosphere hurricane, unrelenting, indomitable, easily able to collapse a tent and maybe even send it, occupants and all, pinwheeling down the nearest slope.

We could tell when we weren't wanted, so we collapsed the tent ourselves and prepared to beat a hasty retreat, down to the relative calm of forty mph winds at Muir. In the harried midnight departure, however, I evidently failed to lash my sleeping bag securely to my pack frame, because during our descent it came loose and rolled down the glacier, lodging perhaps fifteen feet in a crevasse. We set up a secure "boot-axe belay," constructed by inserting two ice axes full length into the snow, then wrapping the rope deftly around them and a firmly planted boot. The sleeping bag was duly retrieved: fortunately, the moon was full, yielding enough light. Then, as we resumed our interrupted retreat, the incredible happened: my renegade sleeping bag once again slipped off its moorings, this time finding refuge in a crevasse that may have been truly bottomless. It is probably still there. (John has never gone climbing with me again, and I don't blame him.)

All sorts of things can go wrong and most of them usually do: fixed ropes prove to be ice covered and unusable, a crampon breaks, someone loses a glove, you run out of water and have to spend hours using precious fuel to melt snow, a sunglass lens falls out, raising the specter of snow blindness. Then, a bird soars easily nearby, not so much lifting your spirits as mocking your awkward, landborne efforts.

And when it comes to mixed blessings, don't forget the emergency bivouac. Spending an unanticipated night fifteen hundred feet above my tent, on a woefully exposed and exceptionally cold ridge, I thought of these lines by Chinese poet Li Tai Po:

> As I sit alone with the Ching Ting Peak towering beyond,
> We never grow tired of each other, the mountain and I.

The stars, moreover, were memorably bright that night; I had time to count every one. And my "dinner," crumbled taco chips, a handful of M&Ms, one-quarter of a soggy tuna-fish sandwich, tasted a whole lot better than it sounds. But I confess, at any time during that very long night, I would gladly have sacrificed it, Buddhistic unity, celestial intensity, gustatory novelty and all, for a hot shower, a good meal, and a warm, safe bed.

Some things are mute portents of disaster: a child's pony coming back home riderless; a swamped canoe, floating capsized down a river; a crampon, if not a sleeping bag, careening down a snowy slope. On a subsequent climb, I watched, horrified, as an ice axe skidded from somewhere above, bounced into the air, then planted itself just a few feet below me. I never found its owner, although I was able to use it myself. I'd like to think that someone—maybe someone cold—eventually found my sleeping bag and appreciated it.

The usual routine for climbing most mountains that poke their heads above extensive mazes of jumbled glaciers is for the final summit push to begin in the very early morning, say 1:00 or 2:00 A.M. That way, even on a relatively warm summer day it is generally possible to get to the top by nine or ten in the morning, then return to high camp by mid-afternoon, when the warmest part of the day softens the upper snow bridges and might make crevasse crossing especially hazardous.

Snow is not immutable. It can be a firm, marvelous pathway early in the morning, heavy cement by noon, a bottomless pit of quicksand by 4:00 P.M., glazed and skiddy ice after dusk. The south slopes may be all slush, the north, hard and harsh. On spring ascents, these differences are accentuated; by mid- to late summer (when I have done most of my climbing, hoping to get good weather), the snow tends to have consolidated, minimizing the effect of daily temperature variations. Nonetheless, the condition of the snow is always on the climber's mind.

It is not easy going to sleep, knowing that you're going to wake up in just a few hours and start walking, in the dark, over glaciers and across hidden crevasses to the top of a mighty mountain. Even if you're bone tired from the climb to high camp, excitement makes the air vibrate, and telling yourself to hurry up and go to sleep, not surprisingly, doesn't help. Neither do the sharp rocks and hard ground of high camp. On the popular east side of Mount Rainier, the "standard route" calls for spending the night (or rather, a few midnight hours) at Camp Schurman, where the accommodations consist of piled rocks—to keep out the wind—

within which climbers are invited to sleep; these are shaped, disconcertingly, like coffins. At Camp Muir, there are some drafty stone cabins, used by the professional guide service; most of us prefer our own tents, on the stony ground.

And usually, in fact, sleep comes at last, just when you have despaired of it altogether, and generally just a split second before someone has begun stirring once again. Sure enough, now that your sleeping bag has finally warmed up, it is time to get out, into air so cold it might shatter if you spoke loudly . . . which no one does. If you've planned things well, however, the moon is full, and the glacial snow above is aglimmer with diamonds. And maybe you can see the lights of another world, far below. In any event, small head lamps, not unlike those worn by miners, will light the way for the first few hours before dawn.

The rudest shock, however, is your petrified boots, stiffened not with fear but with cold. Under the pitiless twinkle of a million frigid stars, they have become like a porcelainized cast of a child's first shoes, half-unlaced just as you left them, rumpled and rime-coated, frozen solid with yesterday's perspiration, and preserving—perhaps for eternity—every dimension of your tired feet. Why, then, don't they fit now, when you really need them? Did your feet change size or shape during the night? Roping up and heading out from Camp Muir, you can see the faint lights of yet earlier risers, tiny points of firefly light streaming up toward the summit.

The biggest danger isn't soft snow bridges ready to collapse, or hard, bottomless crevasses waiting to gulp you down, but rather avalanches. On that K-2 climb made famous by Schoening's heroic ice-axe belay, team member Art Gilkey was swept over the route of their descent by an avalanche, and the group had to climb down over a path smeared with their friend's blood and ragged patches of his clothing and flesh.

By following a ridge instead of crossing a glacier, you can gain relative safety from avalanches, but at some costs. For one thing, ridges offer exposure to bad weather—especially wind—and high on a mountain, where there is nothing to intercept winds that have gone screaming above the Earth for hundreds, maybe thousands of miles, wind is a formidable foe. For another, ridges are made of jumbled, uneven rock, much more difficult to ascend than the comparatively smooth glacier-highways that fill the space between the ridgelines; moreover, crampons don't "go well" on rock . . . and I have never been on high ridge route that didn't require crampons as well.[14]

For the standard routes up the great Northwest snow cones—Rainier, Baker, Glacier Peak, Adams, Olympus, Hood, St. Helens (before it erupted)—no rock or ice climbing is required, just the ability to walk up and down on glaciers. The same applies to many of the more straightforward snow climbs in the Alps, such as Mont Blanc or Monte Rosa. A more specialized technique, on the other hand, is ice climbing, the most extreme form of which involves using crampons with two forward prongs, coming almost straight out from the toes. The ice climber uses these to "front point," kicking each foot directly into an ice wall, thereby walking straight up. Typically, one hand carries an ice axe, the other, a shorter, specialized "ice hammer." With practice, strength, and some daring, the ice climber can ascend vertical walls of ice, alternately kicking in with the front points of one foot, implanting the business end of a hammer, then the other foot, then the axe or another hammer. Protection is also used, as in rock climbing; ice screws of different sorts can be inserted, not unlike pitons, but more likely to be twisted than pounded into place.

When lower legs ache from too much front pointing, it may be time to cut steps for a while, although that too can be exhausting. There is extra gratification, however, in listening to the swish of ice flakes sliding down the grooved furrow of your progress and in watching the neat progression of steps where previously there had been none.

While climbing—on rock, snow, and, especially, ice—each step upward is a debate between what we are and what we might be. It is a contest, or at least an interplay, between our spirits and our bodies, and between ourselves and our surroundings. High-angle rock climbing, or almost any sort of ice climbing, provides lots of opportunities for such interplay.

14. Some of us don't enjoy the rigamarole of attaching and removing crampons, especially not in a howling gale when it is well below freezing, and you can't do it wearing gloves or mittens, but can't rely on your fingers if you try it bare-handed. But most climbers enjoy steep, hard snow or ice, without crampons, even less.

Good ice climbing may often be found on a large "serac," a picturesque pinnacle of ice, carved by wind and gleaming like an ice sculpture, or the "bergschrund" or large break that typically occurs between a glacier and the rocky substance of its mountain. The classic ice-climb, however, is a frozen waterfall. (There is something counter-intuitive about the notion of a frozen waterfall; I, at least, have never been able to see a waterfall freeze and can't quite imagine how it happens. There is something even more counter-intuitive, however, about climbing one.) It's not easy, but not as hard as it looks. The "ice," moreover, is only rarely clear and ice-cubey, so called "verglas." Rather, it tends to be more of a solidified slurry containing lots of dissolved air, making it closer to hard-frozen snow.

There is something seductive about the macho appearance and style of the ice climber: metal spikes on feet, no-nonsense hammers in each hand, helmeted and gloved, a Rambo of the frozen outdoors—but, at least among the ice climbers I have known, none have exhibited any of that character's repellent murderousness or lowbrow, inarticulate, red-neck chauvinism. In fact, ice climbers—and mountain climbers in general—tend to be well-educated, environmentally sensitive, and surprisingly well-to-do. On the East Coast, you'll find them particularly during the winter at Huntington's Ravine, on New Hampshire's Mount Washington, and in the Northwest, on the headwalls and "schrunds" of various glaciers. Easy to recognize: they're the ones with the perpetually sore calf muscles.

More than any other lovesongs, mountain climbing is sung together: rock and ice climbing is generally done with two persons on a rope, glacier travel with three. Solos are discouraged. Of course, some climbers go it alone, as for example, Reinhold Messner's solitary ascent of Mount Everest, without oxygen yet, in 1978—perhaps the greatest mountaineering feat of all time. But even Messner is best known for his remarkable ascents in partnership with Peter Habeler. Whether composed of men or women, these climbing partnerships tend to be masculine in the worst sense: operational more than personal, designed to accomplish something. Climbing autobiographies, therefore, tend to have a kind of distance about them, what one mountaineer called "the coldness of competence."[14] In most cases, we are presented only the image of skilled, strong partners, hard men who would nonetheless risk death to help a buddy. Yet these partnerships can also be beautiful and touching in their intimacy, in the flow of their sharing, although they are more to be experienced, it seems, than written about.

Climbing is an intense union, with two or more people joined, umbilically, literally as well as figuratively, by their rope. Roping up together is an act of deepest trust. In fact, no human connection is more intimate—or at least, more crucial—than a belay on high-angle rock. If someone falls, the others are supposed to arrest that fall; on the other hand, as in Edward Whymper's tragic first ascent of the Matterhorn, a fall can drag others to disaster. So you want someone reliable on your rope in case you fall, and beyond that, you don't want a turkey; that is, you don't want someone who is likely to initiate a fall. (Better yet is someone ready to lead the pitches that you find too challenging.) Just as intimate partners are expected to work constantly on their relationship, climbing partners are always exhorting each other to take up the slack, keep that rope taut. But outside of Indian suttee, few other interpersonal relationships duplicate the urging of the leader ascending a knife ridge that offers no belay points, "If I slip, jump off on the other side."

Most of the time, however, climbing partnerships are less than matters of life or death, although they are generally more than simple teamwork.[15] They involve a kind of mutual self-reliance and testing, since someone has to lead, and everyone has to follow the same route, typically roped together. On a football field, by contrast, each member of the team goes a different way, spreading out in two dimensions, each doing his own thing. Likewise on a tennis court: although success or failure in a game of doubles, for example, may hinge on everyone's contribution, each participant gets a somewhat different experience. Your partner's backhand shot, for

15. French-speaking professional mountain guides typically address their clients with the formal *vous*. It is interesting to note, however, that when the climbing party reaches sufficient height, they switch to the more intimate *tu*. Presumably, having achieved a certain level of mutual dependence—and also, perhaps, in the face of a great mountain's immensity—the climbers have become close.

example, is different from the one that will come your way. But on a climb, although the effort is directed toward a third dimension, in fact the progression is actually one dimensional: a line, angled and twisting, but with everyone going the same route, one after the other, linear in time as well as space. It soon becomes clear who is the stronger, or faster, or sloppier.

Moreover, given the special importance of leading, a climbing team must be compatible, both in physical abilities and in willingness to share burdens and submerge egos when necessary. During lousy weather at high camp, you might also wind up spending hours, even days, with your fellow climbers under profoundly confining circumstances. The way someone eats, or smiles, or doesn't smile, or yawns, or snores, or farts can become an unparalleled irritation, a kind of Chinese drip-torture as sensibilities rub raw against one another's more private and trivial characteristics. Before going climbing with anyone, ask yourself whether you would be willing to spend a night (or two) rubbing his or her feet, to ward off frostbite.

Sometimes, the relevant characteristics are fundamental: willingness to cooperate, to sacrifice for another, to submerge an ego and a personal goal for a greater goal, as in expedition climbing in which huge numbers of people and material may be mustered, pyramidlike, transporting supplies and pushing base camps higher and higher up a mountain. Perhaps two people will make the summit, supported by the effort of dozens, maybe more. Most climbers will never participate in siege tactics of this sort, but those who do—especially in recent years—generally have stories to tell, stories in which the mountains are often backdrops rather than central characters, stories in which the personal strengths and painful foibles of fellow climbers take central place.

To some extent, the mortal reliance on others is not unique to climbing, and thus, shouldn't strike nonclimbers as being so strange. After all, we regularly entrust our lives to the skill, temperament, and equipment of others . . . every time we get into an airplane, or a bus, or an automobile, whether we are driving or merely passengers.

For all the mutual involvement, all the endless hours spent together, talking while walking, talking while eating, talking in the tent, it is ironic that during the intense periods of actual, serious climbing, very little is said, beyond the formulaic "Belay on?" (Are you prepared to hold me if I fall?), "On belay." (Yes, I am.), "Climbing" (Here I go.), and "Climb" (OK.), often bellowed against a heavy wind. Some manuals suggest that when the occasion warrants, you should also call out "Falling" (self-explanatory), whereupon I have wondered if the correct response is a cheery "Fall."

Once I heard a giggling voice from a hammock suspended precariously from the sheer, east face of Long's Peak, in Colorado: "Peeing," it declared, followed by an affirmative "Pee" from a neighboring cocoon. And while struggling to insert an ice screw in the Coleman headwall, on the lower slopes of Mount Baker, I announced, "Screwing," and was answered with an enthusiastic, "Screw." Clearly, it is the depth of the communication that makes climbing worthwhile.

Now we come to the traditional question: Why do people climb mountains? To someone asking the cost of a Rolls Royce, or a hundred-foot yacht, an appropriate answer is: If you have to ask, then you can't afford it. Similarly, if you have to ask why people climb mountains, then you probably won't understand the answer. Most climbers are remarkably inarticulate about why they climb, although many will refer to the views or the challenge, and some will even pronounce upon climbing as no less than a full allegory of the human condition, an open-ended endeavor in which the immensity of the universe is pitted against the outermost capacities of human ambition and spirit.

The classic answer, however, was by Englishman George Leigh Mallory, when asked why he wanted to climb Mount Everest: "Because it is there." In fact, Mallory died during this third attempt on the mountain; he was last seen, shortly below the summit, heading upwards . . . after which he was lost, forever, in the cold, swirling mist. Some keepers of climbing lore believe that he and his companion actually reached the top (many years ahead of Edmund Hillary) before perishing during the descent.

Even when they have been climbed—and even when they are less lordly and remote than Everest—most mountains have a habit of remaining "above it all." About that famous tree falling in the forest, with no one to hear, I cannot say. But as to the awesome spectacle of dun and black, glittering white and icy-blue, mile after mile, there can be no doubt: the great mountains exist, whether or not we are there to witness and whether we climb them or no. (Let's go back, however, for just a moment, to that theoretically toppling tree. And ask: what if *I* should fall—not some imaginary, mindless vegetable of a tree, but this warm, soft, sentient, vulnerable body that I call myself—from some hard and angley cliff? Then would there be a sound? And would the mountains hear? Would the rumor of my descent, my last desperate cry of fear and rage, the sickening thump of my ending make any difference to them?)

Oh well, if the mountains are short on empathy, at least they offer a chance for healthy outdoor exercise. John Ruskin even complained that for some especially boorish climbers, mountains were nothing but greased poles to ascend and then slide down. The exigencies of their sport made the "noble hills" little more than outdoor gymnasia. But I have never met a climber who does not know, and know intimately, the mountain he or she has climbed. There is simply no comparison between what a tourist sees, looking up at the Breithorn, and what the climber sees: perhaps mountains can never truly be known, but the mountaineer comes awfully close. It is a kind of knowing that must be earned, however, by looking into its crevasses, scrambling over its ridges, calculating the merits of one route versus another, the probability of avalanche, the intensity of its wind, the firmness and reliability of its rock.

Mountains are climbed for many reasons. For some people, the exercise is indeed important, just as for others, it probably is the views, or the personal challenge, the intimacy gained, or the existential quest. Mountains have been climbed as a means of venerating and adoring the work of God or of nature. (Pope Pius XI was an accomplished climber.) But I believe that more than anything mountains are climbed because they are ways of finding out about one's self. Several times I have met groups of climbers in the Alps, and once in the Andes, there to "size up the mountains," for forthcoming climbs. Fair enough, and true enough, undoubtedly. Once on the mountain, however, the scrutiny goes the other way: the mountain sizes up the climber. There is "something about the sport," wrote David Roberts, "some intricacy of deed that takes hold of the spirit and asks it fundamental questions."[16] Usually, but not always, the climber likes the answers.

Reaching the summit most assuredly conveys a feeling of grand-ness, of accomplishment, of enhanced self-esteem. Some of the majesty, the elevation of the peak rubs off on the climber who surmounts it. But most often, the feeling is not so much exaltation as diminution, an intensified awareness of one's smallness, a tiny, impertinent creature in a great vastness. Jim Whittaker, the first American to climb Everest (in 1963), noted upon reaching the summit that he felt "not expansive, not sublime. I felt" he said, "like a frail human being."

Moreover, often the moment of triumph is just that, a moment. Too tired to savor the success, or too cold, huddling in the wind and worried about the descent, climbers frequently hurry from their peak experience to a painful and anticlimactic return trip.

It is rare that a major mountain succumbs without reminding its "conquerors" who is really the boss: sure, a few people may make it, eventually, to the summit, but they don't stay very long. Quickly, often gratefully, they retreat, going home exhausted, filled with wild and vivid memories, back to calmer places and easier ways. The mountain remains, unconquered, no matter who climbed up to where.

Why, then, the urge to summitry? It must be more than just a yearning for an ironic kind of abasement . . . revealing our extraor-dinary strengths by highlighting our pitiful weaknesses. To some degree, the appeal is idiosyncratic; some people feel it, other's don't. My wife, for instance, doesn't. She loves to ride horses and to hike, but feels no particular yearning to stand atop mountains. She can easily turn around, a hundred feet below a summit, if the weather changes, or if she simply feels so tired that the payoff doesn't seem worth the effort. If isn't that she lacks competence or determination, either: she went through medical school as a single parent and has never failed at anything significant that she has attempted. (And she has attempted quite a bit.) Maybe that's the answer: she doesn't need summits because she has already proven herself, to herself.

For some of us, by contrast, turning back is terribly difficult.

16. Roberts, *Moments.*

And yet, the prudent climber often has to do just this, if equipment
fails, or the weather changes, or the route just turns out to be more
difficult than the skills of the climbing party can safely surmount.
By why do I (and many others) feel it so painfully? In part, it may
be what has been called the Concorde Effect: even when it was
demonstrated to be an economic failure, the British and French
governments persevered in developing the Concorde supersonic
transport plane because it would have been intolerable to accept
the loss of hundreds of millions of dollars with nothing to show for
it. So good money was thrown after bad, to diminish the pain of a
dumb investment. During the Vietnam War, Americans spoke similarly about the need to persevere in Southeast Asia, so that tens of
thousands of Americans will not have died in vain. Logical or not,
people resist cutting their losses; they would rather lose even
more, in the hope of redeeming wasted money, or lives. The climbing of a mountain involves a similar expenditure, this time of effort;
it is painful indeed to acknowledge that all the sweat, the blisters,
the freezing bivouacs on icy ledges, the crawl through a tortuous
frozen gully . . . all will have gone for naught if you turn around
with the summit unattained.

With age, on the other hand, has come modulation, an appreciation of process, and less susceptibility to the Concorde Effect. I
have finally come to recognize that it is OK to leave some peaks
unclimbed, that even if I was a real hot shot, there would still be
major mountains upon which I would never sit, if not in the Northwest, then in Alaska, the Sierras, Rockies, Alps, Andes, the Himalayas. An early flicker of maturation was the acceptance—at first,
grudging, by now, enthusiastic—that I would never drink all the
world's beer, make love to all the world's beautiful women, see all
the birds, ride all the horses, explore all the beaches.

Some "peak-baggers," out to climb as many summits as possible,
are really trophy hunters, seeking notches on their belt, scalps to
hang on their lance, stuffed heads for their wall.[17] Others—generally those who think about climbing, but don't do it—have suggested that climbing is a kind of phallic worship, redolent with
transmuted homoerotic gratification. And often, in fact, climbing is

17.   I have never seen a peak—even an oft-climbed one—placed inside anyone's
       "bag."

described in sexual terms, typically emphasizing a male sexual conquest: the mountain's defenses are overcome, through persistence, strength, technique. The clouds may part, revealing the summit, ripe for the plucking. And then, later, the alpine Don Juan looks for other mountains, preferably virgins.

Attaining the summit can, in fact, be a kind of orgasm. Physically strenuous, time consuming, demanding cooperation and all your attention, it is intense, it may or may not be worth the trouble, and yet it demands repetition. Perhaps this explains why some of us find it so compelling, and also so difficult to turn back short of completion. Maybe it also explains why one is not enough, why the satisfaction, although intense, is so transient. No one ascent quite suffices, at least not for long. In Goethe's great poem, the culminating moment is reached when the damned Faust, having experienced all manner of triumphs and satisfactions, finally exclaims that he has achieved the perfect moment, that the current instant deserves to last forever. What climb, what summit, has ever been *it*, deserving to stand for all summits, to last forever? What mountain is so perfect that after climbing it, nothing more remains to be done?

One might as well ask for a single breath—no matter how deep or sweet—or a single meal, no matter how gourmet, to meet your needs for a lifetime.[18]

This conundrum, the insatiability of the mountaineer, leads to a final reason for climbing mountains, and perhaps the most cogent one. Maybe mountains are climbed because they offer the opportunity for adult play: to be sure, play spiced with adventure and even occasional danger, but fundamentally, play nonetheless. Maybe some people climb mountains for the same reason children blow soap bubbles from a pipe, or play ring-around-the-rosie, or fart in the bathtub. Maybe mountain climbing offers—beyond the beauty, the sexual imagery, the self-glorification—the simple opportunity to grapple, gleefully, with the stuff of existence, to feel the slippery hardness of ice, the puff and crunch of snow, the primordial pleasure of granite, warm and rough, like a cat's tongue under your palm.

18.   I have a frustrating feeling that somewhere in the vast literature of mountaineering, I have encountered a similar metaphor, but try as I might, I cannot remember or locate it.

More than anything, mountain climbing is a quiet, joyous con-
spiracy, a revolt against what Max Weber called the "rationaliza-
tion" of modern life, in which everything is expected to be calculated, logical, sensible, reasonable and prudent, always staying
within the bounds of good sense, maximizing the difference between benefit and cost. To be sure, climbing has many rules: Don't
run ropes across carabiner gates, never let go of the brake hand
while belaying, do not deny a belay to anyone requesting one,
don't climb above your ability, thereby necessitating unsightly and
unnecessary protection on otherwise unspoiled rock, and at all
times, keep your clumsy boots off the rope. But ironically, despite
these and many other constraints of safety and tradition, climbing
offers freedom, the doing of something purely for its own sake,
chosen and embraced for no external reason, something sought out
freely and belonging entirely to the whim of the doer. Unlike the
workaday life, for example, which is typically justified by its extrin-
sic returns (e.g., income), the pleasures of mountaineering are entirely intrinsic. Climbing is its own justification. Furthermore, in
the course of such play, the climber may sometimes experience
part of the wonderful, free-flowing spontaneity of childhood, a delicious sense of selflessness borne of unity between the doer and
the thing done.

And of course, there is the pure, affirming, unmixed happiness
of shared success in spectacular surroundings. "Nowhere else on
earth," writes David Roberts, "not even in the harbors of reciprocal love, have I felt pure happiness take hold of me and shake me
like a puppy, compelling me, and the conspirators I had arrived
there with, to stand on some perch of rock or snow, the uncertain
struggle below us, and bawl our pagan vaunts to the very sky."[19]

So, with everything said and done, what good are mountains?
Well, they provide havens for certain fur-bearing animals. They
make the weather interesting. They yield scenic backdrops for
photographs. They give water a push to the sea. (Without them,
presumably, rivers would just be stagnant canals, moping around.)
And what good is the climbing of mountains? None whatsoever. If
utility and safety were paramount virtues, climbing would probably be banished altogether, as Queen Victoria once attempted after

19. Roberts, *Moments.*

the Matterhorn accident. Let's agree, then: climbing is "useless, like poetry, and dangerous, like lovemaking."[20] Maybe that's why people keep doing it.

20. Showell Styles, *On the Top of the World* (New York: MacMillan, 1967).